Willard Forester Warner

Banking

Ancient and Modern

Willard Forester Warner

Banking
Ancient and Modern

ISBN/EAN: 9783337111830

Printed in Europe, USA, Canada, Australia, Japan

Cover: Foto ©ninafisch / pixelio.de

More available books at **www.hansebooks.com**

BANKING

ANCIENT · AND · MODERN

Profusely Illustrated

with

Portraits of Men Prominent in Banking

AND ENGRAVINGS OF SOME OF THE PRINCIPAL
BANKING INSTITUTIONS OF AMERICA,

INTERIOR AND EXTERIOR VIEWS OF U. S. TREASURY BUILDING,

TOGETHER WITH FULL INSTRUCTIONS AS TO THE BUSINESS
METHODS OF THE TREASURY DEPARTMENT
AT WASHINGTON, D. C.

1895

WILLARD FORESTER WARNER
TREASURY DEPARTMENT, WASHINGTON, D. C.

JOHN G. CARLISLE,
Secretary of the Treasury of the United States, Washington, D. C.

JOHN J. VALENTINE.
President Wells Fargo & Co.'s Bank, San Francisco, Cal.
President Wells Fargo & Co.'s Express, San Francisco, Cal.

BANKING.

ANCIENT AND MODERN.

CHAPTER I.

ANCIENT BANKING.

BANKING is an outgrowth of commerce. In its most primitive form—money changing—it assumed the first function of banking demanded by the times, and as commerce increased between man and men and between country and countries, other functions developed as necessity required, until to-day the business of banking occupies a proud position among the institutions which have contributed to the development of the world.

The modern word bank seems to have been derived from the German word "banck," which was introduced into Italy by the dominant Germans in the twelfth century, and became Italianized into the word "banco," which was used interchangeably with the word "monte," to mean a collection of credit or money.

The late George Smith, during his researches among the ruins of Babylon, found tablets which are the commercial instruments or checks and notes of a Babylonian banking firm, trading under the name of the founder, Egibi. The firm appears to have been practically, a national bank of Babylonia, and its

LYMAN J. GAGE.
President First National Bank, Chicago.

transactions were of the most extensive character. Mr. W. St. C. Boscawen has studied these tablets closely and publishes the following information concerning them:

"Sula, son of Zirukin, son of Egibi appears as contracting party in the third year of Nebuchadnezzar, and continues to be at the head of the firm until the twenty-third year of that monarch. In the fifteenth year of this reign, his son Nabuakhi-idin, is taken into the firm and appears in company with his father as contracting party.

"The tablets give us a complete succession of annual transactions from the first of Nebuchadnezzar to the thirty-fifth of Darius. There is one tablet dated in the fourth year of Nabupaluzar (Nabopalassar); tablets dated in the reign of this monarch are very rare. By means of a lunar eclipse mentioned by Claudius Ptolemaeus as taking place in the fifth year of Nabopalassar, we are enabled to fix the date of this year to B. C. 621; this gives B. C. 625 as the first year of this monarch. From this date, for more than a century, this bank appears to have carried on its business regularly, but in the month Abb [the eleventh month, or July of the Jews.—ED.] B. C. 516, the revolt of Aracus, against Darius took place, the firm of Egibi was unable to transact any business owing to the revolt at Babylon, and the history of this remarkable bank cannot be traced any further."

J. J. P. ODELL,
President Union National Bank, Chicago.

In Greece, money-changers formed a distinct class of business men as early as the fourth century before Christ. It was their custom to receive money from depositors and to loan it to others at rates of interest varying from ten to thirty-six per cent. A portion of their income was derived from premiums received for exchanging coins which floated to

Greece from other countries. From Plutarch it is learned that discount was known to the Athenians, and the rate of discount was often made so excessive as to bring some money-changers into disrepute. This was possible under the Attic law which permitted every lender to charge as much interest as he chose.

Money-changers as a rule maintained a high credit and were so implicitly trusted that transactions with them were often carried out without witnesses. Of the best known of these primitive bankers was Pasion, whose profit from his exchange bank was one hundred minas annually, equivalent to $1,710. When Pasion died the bank was assumed by Phormio, who paid an annual rental of $2,730 for the office and business.

Of forms of business more nearly approaching the state banks of later times we are not without examples in Greece. At New Ilion a bank seems to have transacted the financial business of the state in the third or second century before Christ, paying ten per cent interest on money for public use.

There are also evidences that the authorities in charge of the temple of Delos, and that at Delphi, loaned money belonging to them, but there is no evidence that this money was that deposited for safe-keeping. In Byzantium a precedent for giving one organization the entire control of the banking business may be found, where, in a time of financial embarrassment, the money-changing business was farmed out to a single bank, and a penalty was inflicted for buying or selling money elsewhere, the penalty being no less severe than the forfeiture of the sums bought or sold.

In Rome the Decemvirate made stringent laws against usury in the year 449 B. C., and fixed the maximum rate of interest at ten per cent. It is evident that such a law was called forth by the existence of the occupation of money-lending. In 346 B. C., the rate of interest was lowered to five per cent, and in 341 B. C., the taking of interest was altogether forbidden, but the law being inoperative, interest was about this period established at one per cent per month.

The commerce which Rome had with the eastern and other countries, naturally created an influx of foreign coin, necessitating, as in Greece, the class known as money-changers, whose stone stalls were located along both sides of the Forum—the Exchange of Rome. While the Romans seemed to have adopted the simple methods of moneyed speculation from the Greeks, it is quite generally conceded that they enlarged and perfected the system until it became something more similar to modern banking than any system the Greeks had known. Indeed, Macleod goes so far as to state that banking, as a technical business, was invented by the Romans. In our judgement this is a wrong use of the term, as such businesses as banking are but simple developments made necessary by the increasing volume of financial transactions, and while the Romans may have produced some business forms which were novel, it is not correct to say that they "invented" banking.

No branch of Roman commerce was more vigorously prosecuted, according to Mommsen, than that of the money-lender and money-dealer or banker, the practice of placing large sums of money with a banking agent, who received and made payments, invested and borrowed, and conducted financial business at home and abroad, being fully developed in the time of Cato—209-149 B. C. With the activity of commerce which Rome enjoyed, bankers spread rapidly throughout the provinces and dependent states.

To the literature of Rome we are indebted for contemporaneous references which informs us of the uses of banking terms still in use, such as "checque," "drafts," etc.

In Italy the money-changers were established at a very early period of the middle ages, and the city of Florence became a recognized monetary center. As early as as the first quarter of the eleventh century, Florentine citizens loaned money to soverign princes. In 1265 the money-changers of that city formed themselves into a guild. It is probable that the business of the money-changers even at that early day was approaching the characteristic feature of banking —the dealing in credit, as in 1300 the Mozzi and the Spini families are mentioned as being the bankers of Popes, and the last named as having a branch at Rome under the management of Nero Cambi. By 1378 banking operations in Italy had attained great importance, due to the necessary transmission of money from distant parts of Europe to the Popes' court at Rome and Avignon, and most of the banking business was in the hands of Florentine citizens. The Strozzi were in later years, 1513 to 1534, bankers to Leo X and Clement VII, accumulating wealth by their sagacity which is still enjoyed by their descendants. about the middle of the fourteenth century the famous banking house of the Alberti had counters in Avignon, Bruges, Brussells, Paris, Siena, Perugia, Rome, Naples, Barletta and Venice. Still greater than the Alberti were the Peruzzi and their associates, the Bardi. In 1346 the failure of Edward III, of England, to pay 1,365,000 golden florins, borrowed of the Florentine bankers, caused a bankruptcy which seriously disturbed the entire commercial system of Europe. Later the Strozzi suffered serious losses by the king of France and the popes, but in spite

E. S. LACEY.
President Bankers' National Bank, Chicago.

of these losses the Florentine bankers regained their wealth through their lucrative business. From 1414 to 1423 times were prosperous in Florence, and at that period seventy-two banks could be counted in the streets surrounding the Mercato Nuovo. From 1430 to 1433, seventy-six bankers lent the State 4,865,000 gold florins, but, although there were said to be eighty bankers in Florence at one time, there was no public bank.

Mr. Henry Mann attributes the invention of bank notes to the republic of Carthage, but his testimony is not conclusive enough, being based on this statement of Æschines, the Socratic philosopher; "In a small piece of leather is wrapped a substance of the size of a piece of four drachms, but what this substance is no one knows except the maker. After this it is sealed and issued for circulation; and he who possesses the most of this is regarded as having the most money and as being the wealthiest man." Jevons shows that leather was one of the earliest of circulating mediums, and was used without regard to any system of banking.

HERMAN KOUNTZE.
President First National Bank, Omaha, Nebraska.

As early as 807, A. D., the Chinese are credited with the invention of the bank note. In that year the emperor exchanged all the money deposited in the public treasury by merchants and rich persons for notes, termed "flying money." It remained in circulation but three years in the capital, and became current only in the provinces.

In 960, A. D., an emperor revived the practice of giving notes for money deposited by merchants, and so great was the convenience of the notes that their circulation increased rapidly. In 997. A. D., there had been 1,700,000 ounces of silver exchanged for paper, while in 1021 the paper in circulation had increased to the value of 2,830,000 ounces. A company of sixteen rich merchants was then formed which was allowed to issue notes, payable in three years. The company was bankrupt upon the expiration of that time, and much suffering was caused by its failure to pay. The emperor then abolished the notes of this company and prevented the formation of other joint-stock companies. After that the government only possessed the power to issue notes, which were made of the value of one ounce of silver. In 1032 these notes were circulating to the value of 5,256,340 ounces. Banks of this nature were subsequently established in every province, but the notes did not have inter-provincial circulation. To these notes, exchangeable for, and convertible into money, is given the credit for being the first on record.

CHAPTER II.

EARLY BANKING.

In 1401 the "Tabla de Cambi" (Table of Exchange), was established at Barcelona, Spain. The city funds were its guarantee, and it was established by the city authorities as an aid to commerce. Foreign bills of exchange were negotiated in it, and a loan business was carried on. It seems to have been the result of the assumption by the city of banking privileges which had been granted the cloth merchants in 1360.

In 1781 the bank of San Carlos was established at Madrid, as a national bank on a plan advanced by the minister of finance. Its capital consisted of 300,000,000 reals, divided into 150,000 shares. Profitable contracts with the government were secured and enjoyed until 1785, when they were taken away.

Bills of exchange followed what were termed "assignments." Authorities differ as to the date of their first use. By some they are ascribed to Lyons, France. Weber states that they were in use in 1171. Among the earliest ones preserved to the present time, are those issued from Milan on Lucca in 1325, from Bruges on Barcelona in 1404, and from Bologna on Venice in 1381. To the Italians we are indebted for many of the technical terms used in banking, such as drafts, remittances, currency, sight, usance and discount.

The first public bank in Italy was that established at Naples in 1565. There had been sixty great bankers in Naples, but, notwithstanding they were obliged to deposit 40,000 ducats with the government as security, they frequently failed and caused great distress. On this account the government decided to establish a public bank to be known as the *Banco di A. G. P. et di Pieta*. Following this, several joint-banks were established—as the *Banco del Popolo*, in 1589; the *Banco dello Santo Spirito*, in 1591; the *Banco di S. Eligio*, in 1596; the *Banco di S. Giacomo*, in 1597; the *Banco delle Povere*, in 1600, and the *Banco de' SS. Salvatore*, in 1604. The private bankers were not able to withstand competition with the joint-stock companies and none survived after the last named date.

Following closely after the establishment and growth of banking in Florence, the Bank of Venice was established. Nearly all writers place the date of the organization of this famous institution at 1171, but Macleod has pointed out that it was not organized until 1587. The confusion has arisen because of the fact that in 1171, the Venetian republic, to meet financial necessities, levied a forced loan, bearing four per cent interest, with transferable stock, and managed by commissioners appointed in 1173. The loan was called the *monte vecchio*, and two similar ones following it, were termed *monte nuovo* and *monte nuovissimo*. The word *monte* has been translated bank, and thus these public debts have been termed banks, while, as a matter of fact, the public debt commissioners exercised no functions resembling banking.

The first bankers in Venice were two Jews who established themselves in 1400. Their success attracted other persons (particularly members of the nobility,) into the business, but the usual failures followed until in 1587 the senate prohibited the nobility from entering the business, and established the Bank of Venice.

Merchants were invited to deposit their money in an office managed be the commissioners of public debt, for which they received credit on the bank's books. This credit was transferable and payable in bullion on demand. An act was passed requiring all bills on Venice to be paid in bank money, which gave it a premium of about nine per cent. The bank transacted no business on its own account, but the money in its vaults was taken on various pretexts by the State, and in 1678, in 1691, and again from 1717 to 1739, it suspended payments. An attempt was made to raise a loan by creating credits on the bank's books, but the credits fell to a discount of twenty per cent as compared with specie, and the Government mortgaged a part of its revenue to collect a fund of "real current specie" with which to purchase these transfer credits, by which means their par value was restored.

The bank of St. George, in Genoa, occupied a most prominent position among the early influences which aided commercial development. As in the case of the Bank of Venice, however, most historians ascribe its establishment to a much early date.

It was in 1148 that the Genoese Government incurred its first formal debt. The creditors chose from their number a council to watch over the debt due them and to secure its collection, the Government having conceded certain customs duties for a term of years in payment of the debt. Each one hundred francs of the debt was a share, and each creditor a share-holder. In this manner were numerous loans made by the Government, each loan being termed a "compera" and all the loans collectively being known as the "Compere of St. George." In 1252 these loans became so numerous as to require consolidation under one head, with a chancellor in charge. In 1302, so great had become the national debt, stringent regulations were enacted by which no future loan could be effected without the consent of the representatives of the existing creditors. In 1339 a popular revolution occurred at which all the old books of the "compere" were burned, and a new regulation commission was appointed. This has been mentioned as that of the origin of the bank, but it was simply a step further in consolidating the national debt.

In 1371 is recorded, in connection with the Bank of Genoa, the first known instance of the compounding of interest. Francesco Vivaldi gave his shares in the Compere of St. George to the compere, the interest on them to be annually applied to the purchase of other shares, until a sum should be collected in addition to the principal, which should be sufficient to pay off one of the specific loans. This done, the process should be repeated. Others followed in Vivaldi's steps, and the credit of the compere grew apace.

In 1407 wars had so pressed the State into seeking money advances that an entire reorganization was decided upon. Nine men drew up a plan on which all the shares were reunited, and the interest for all was made seven per cent. New officers were selected and the organization renamed the Bank of St. George. It possessed peculiar powers of self-government entirely independent of the State, and in this year a new constitution was given it, under the provisions of which eight "protectors" were elected, each of whom was required to have an interest in the bank of not less than one thousand florins. These directors were given the offices of President, Treasurer-General, Superintender of the sale of shares, three Judges and two Secretaries, each of whom remained in office one year. Over these was the General Council of four hundred and eighty, and to this every holder of ten or more shares, and over eighteen years of age, was eligible. In return for money advanced by the bank to the Government, various colonies and provinces were made over to the bank as pledges for repayment.

In 1675 the directors of the bank saw the necessity of adopting some more convenient methods of doing business. The old title of "compere" then disappeared, and the institution became known strictly as a bank. It is from this year that Macleod ascribes the establishment of the Bank of St. George, because it first adopted functions of modern banking, such as the negotiation of loans and the deposit and withdrawing of money, but no history of banking would be complete which failed to give an outline of the fiscal measures from which modern banking grew.

P. M. CASADY,
President Des Moines Savings Bank, Des Moines, Iowa.

In 1675 four branches were established in different parts of the city. Later the invading Austrian army, in 1746, carried away most of the gold belonging to the bank, seriously crippling it, but in a "monte of preservation," established by the bank in 1750, a record of all suspended payments was kept and they were paid after the Austrians left. After a time the people came to see that the complex arrangement by which the public taxes were collected and retained by the directors of the bank, was a species of tyranny, and the bank was obliged to surrender its privileges. As these were its sole source of income, the bank notes were found valueless, and the bank was ignominiously closed about 1798. Efforts to re-establish it were made in 1804 and 1814, but they were entirely unsuccessful.

In 1609 the Bank of Amsterdam was established under a guarantee given by the city. The causes which led the creation of this bank were far different from those which caused the establishment of the banks at Venice and Genoa; which had their origin in forced loans by the Governments. The prominent position occupied by Amsterdam in international commerce, drew to its merchants the coinage of all countries, much of it worn and clipped. So marked was this influx of coin that the currency of Amsterdam was reduced about nine per cent below the value of newly-coined money, and, although money might be plenty in the city, merchants were frequently at a loss to secure enough of par value to pay their bills of exchange, the value of which, therefore, became uncertain.

The bank accepted all coin at its standard value; deducting a small amount for expenses of coinage and management, and gave a credit on its books for the amount. This credit was naturally termed bank-money. It possessed a constant value and was worth more than money in actual circulation.

ROBERT M. NIXON.
President Fifth National Bank, Cincinnati, Ohio.

When the bank was created, it was ordained that bills drawn on Amsterdam, or bills negotiated in Amsterdam, of the value of six hundred guilders or more, should be paid in bank-money. This gave a uniform value to bills of exchange, and obliged every merchant to keep an account with the bank, in order to pay his foreign bills of exchange.

Other conveniences of bank-money brought it to a premium; the safety of it seemed to be assured; the city guaranteed its payment on demand; payments made in it were in the most convenient form, and the premium on it was lost if the deposit was withdrawn. The natural result was that immense sums of money found their way into the bank vaults, where they were popularly supposed to remain.

Adam Smith published a statement made to him by Hope, the Amsterdam merchant, to the effect that the deposits of coin formed but a small part of its capital, as the bank had been in the practice, for many years, of giving credit for depositors of gold and silver bullion. For bullion the bank gave a receipt, which permitted its removal at any time within six months, on retransferring to the bank a sum of bank-money equal to the credit given for the bullion. For the care of gold bullion one-half per cent was charged, and for silver one-fourth per cent. If the bullion was not removed on the expiration of six months, it reverted to the bank at the price for which credit had been given on its deposit. The effect of this was to stimulate trade in bullion.

There was no cause for distrusting the statement that the entire deposits made to the bank were kept intact until 1672, when the French invasion as far as Utrecht occurred. A rush was made by depositors for coin to the amount of their credits, and, in accordance with the principle on which the bank was founded, the deposits were found to be complete, and the bank met every demand. This run, and its successful weathering by the bank, increased popular confidence in the institution and greatly raised its credit.

For one hundred and eighteen years after this the bank performed its functions with great efficiency, and solemn oaths were recorded with regularity that the treasures were intact. No public investigation of the bank was made in all this time, and the fact that the bank, contrary to the statements of its officers, had been advancing money to the unfortunate East India Company and to different provinces, was not publicly known until in December, 1790.

When Mr. Hope wrote Adam Smith (about 1775), he stated that there were about two thousand depositors, and that the bank possessed £3,000,000. In 1790 it was discovered that most of the deposits in the bank had disappeared fifty years before, and that there was then but a small sum left. The bank, to save itself, suddenly announced that in the future it would pay out silver only at a discount of ten per cent, and that no deposits would be paid of less than 2,500 florins. This practical confession of bankruptcy caused its receipts to fall from 105 to 50, and created a run. The order was rescinded, after a short time, and credit was re-established with the people, who had no knowledge of the bank's real condition.

In 1794 the French entered Amsterdam, and an examination of the bank's affairs showed that eleven millions of florins had been advanced by the bank to the East India Company and to the provinces of Holland and West Friesland. The disclosure of this breach of trust, and the inability to recover the money, brought its credits down to sixteen per cent below current coin, and the bank assigned its claims against the company and the States to its depositors.

In 1619 the present bank of Hamburg was established—ten years after the Bank of Amsterdam, and to remedy the same evils in Hamburg as prevailed at Amsterdam—to receive debased coins of uncertain value, and circulate in their stead bank-credits of a positive value. "In a city of the highest rank for commercial activity," says Palgrave, "but greatly circumscribed in territory, continually receiving payments for merchandise in the coin of other countries, a common standard of value was a matter of primary necessity."

The bank received at first only the rix dollars of the German Empire, a silver coin having a fixed standard. The German Government soon coined a rix-dollar of light weight, and large numbers found their way into the bank before the fraud was discovered. The confusion was so great as to cause the closure of the bank for a short time.

A basis of value was adopted, midway between the standard and debased coins, on which settlements were effected in 1770. This basis of value was termed a "mark banco," and from that time the "mark banco" was the unit of the money of account in the bank. Deposits were received by weight (whether of coin or bullion), and credits were made on the basis of "mark banco" for every $59\frac{1}{3}$ parts of a metrical pound of silver of the fineness of $\frac{882}{1000}$ or over. For its services the bank charged one-eighth per cent to the seller of the silver. This system required the assaying of each quantity of silver received. The bank-money on this basis was quite as permanent as any, Colwell saying of it in 1859 that it had commanded a premium above the currency of coins in general circulation of from twenty to twenty-five per cent for a long period.

Payments made were merely transfers from one person's account at the bank to that of another, and payers were obliged to appear personally, or by attorneys, with checks with printed signatures. Only merchants in Hamburg are allowed to keep accounts. In connection with the bank there is a loan office, in which advances equal to three-fourths their value, are made on pledges of gold, silver or jewels.

The credit of the bank has been uniformly well sustained. In 1770, as we have mentioned, the bank was affected by a depreciation of the German rix-dollar. Again it overextended its loans on pledges, and Napoleon's army once took its money, but it was repaid, and the bank resumed operations.

In 1853 it was found that the distinctive and altogether peculiar system of conducting the bank's business, based, as it was, on bar silver, lacked convenience for modern business methods, as no facilities were given for credits or discounts. On February 15, 1873, the German Government required all banking to be on a gold standard. The ancient Bank of Hamburg was obliged to abolish its bar-silver standard and its "mark banco," and use a monetary system, which is rix money in marks, 150 marks being equal to 100 marks banco. The bank is governed by five directors, two counsellors, two treasurers, and two of the principal city magistrates.

The first bank in Sweden was established by a Swede named Palmstruck, in 1656, and in 1668 it became the bank of Sweden. To Sweden is given the credit of introducing the use of the bank-note in Europe, the first one having been issued in 1658. To Sweden is also given the credit for great advances in methods of banking similar to our present methods. The circulating medium of Sweden was copper, and large payments were made with great inconvenience. To remedy this, the bank received the copper money and issued bank-notes against it, which passed current all over the country. Later on the bank did a loaning business, and nearly suffered disaster in 1752.

CHAPTER III.

EARLY ENGLISH BANKING, AND THE BANK OF ENGLAND.

In England banking as now understood had no existence previous to the sixteenth century. The first public institution of the nature of banking was the Exchequer, founded by William I., which is still in existence, modified in form from a repository of cash to an office of accounts. In the reign of Henry III., 1216-1272, we are informed that money-lending bankers, chiefly Jews, were settled at Oxford, where shameful practices were carried out in discounting for students, forty-five per cent being a common discount. On the expulsion of the Jews from England the business of private banking fell into the hands of the Lombards, sent to England by Pope Gregory IX, some fifty years previously. Their business was undoubtedly much the same as is at present carried on under the sign which they carried from Lombardy, the three golden balls. They gave way to the goldsmiths, who afterwards became bankers proper. Collins states that our "lumber" and "lumber-room" are from their name and method of storing pledges in what were called "Lombard Rooms." It is well known that Lombard Street, the banking center of London, took its name from the custom of Lombards and foreign merchants assembling there twice each day.

L. C. NELSON.
President St. Louis National Bank, St. Louis, Mo.

The custom of depositing money with goldsmiths, says a contemporaneous writer, grew out of the fact that servants could not be trusted as cashiers. In the hands of goldsmiths, persons accustomed to handling valuables, it was safe. The business of receiving and making payments, of collecting rents, and of loaning money at interest, was a natural one, and soon followed the first practice of acting simply as treasurers of deposits. Goldsmiths were well-respected members of the community, and record of their holding high offices in London are found in the reigns of Henry I., Richard I., and Edward I. In 1598 the houses in Goldsmith's Row were spoken of as being very beautiful. These were destroyed by the great fire of London, after which the goldsmiths settled in Lombard street. Their surplus money was placed for safety in the Royal Mint in the Tower of London, from which Charles I. took £200,000, ruining many bankers and forcing them all to consider it a loan. It was repaid in a few months, but the mint never recovered its credit.

H. W. CANNON.
President Chase National Bank, New York City

During the civil war which marked the reign of Charles I.; nearly all the surplus money of the country found its way into the hands of goldsmiths, many of whom, encouraged by their success in loaning money, subsequently confined themselves exclusively to banking operations. The first "run" on a bank is recorded as occurring in 1667, the "run" being on a banker named Backwell, and become general. The bankers adopted the expedient of requiring twenty days' notice, but suffered a shock to their credit, which was entirely destroyed in 1672.

The custom of depositing surplus money in the mint had given way after its robbery by Charles I., to that of its deposit in the Exchequer. Once a week they withdrew this money, with which to meet the demands of their customers. On Jan. 2, 1672, Charles II., needed money very badly, on the advice of Sir Thomas Clifford, stopped the payment of the money in the Exchequer belonging to the bankers. The suspension of this weekly payment (there being £1,328,526 on deposit) involved the bankers and customers in common ruin.

In an attempt to satisfy this debt Charles gave letters patent to the various robbed bankers, agreeing to pay the principal with interest at 6 per cent. A list of these creditors of the King shows that Sir Robert Vyner, Edward Backwell, Gilbert Whitehall, Joseph Horneby, Jeremiah Snow, Bernard Turner, and George Snell were the principal London bankers of the time. The interest was paid a few years and then suspended. The creditors were obliged to prosecute their claim to the court of last resort, and a judgement against the Crown was secured. In 1699 an act was passed which provided that 3 per cent per annum should be paid on the principal sum, but that the indebtedness might be cancelled by the payment of a moiety thereof, £664,264. This indebtedness is the first item of the present national debt of England, and interest is still paid at 3 per cent on the whole amount.

Of the old London bankers whose business is still carried on may be mentioned Edward Blackwell, who was succeeded by Sir Josiah Child, founder of the present house of Child & Co. In 1692 the business of Middleton & Campbell, goldsmiths, came into the hands of James Coutts, and the business still carried on by Coutts' bank was thus established. We are told that the use of pass-books by banks originated with Mr. Coggs, a goldsmith, in the Strand. Previous to their use it was customary for depositors to call regularly and check up their accounts.

Although no public bank was established in England until 1699, there had been proposals, petitions, and discussions looking to the establishment of a public bank, so that the organization of the Bank of England was but the result of a growth of public sentiment, and the increasing need that the public service should effect a large loan. Two schemes devised by William Paterson for the establishment of a national bank failed. In the third scheme, in which he was aided by Michael Godfrey, he was successful, and an act incorporating the Bank of England received the royal assent from William III., on April 25, 1694. The act provided that £100,000 should be annually appropriated to persons making a voluntary loan of £1,200,000 for the purpose of carrying on the war with France. Commissioners were appointed to receive the subscriptions before Aug. 1, 1694. The stock was transferable, and the stockholders were called collectively the Governor and Company of the Bank of England. The Government retained the power to pay the sum at twelve months' notice after Aug. 1, 1705, upon which payment the corporation should cease. The corporation was allowed to deal in bills of exchange, to buy and sell bullion, gold and silver, to lend money on security, and its bills of credit were made transferable. The corporation was forbidden to advance money to the Crown without permission of Parliament.

In ten days the whole sum of £1,200,000 was subscribed, and on July 10 and 11, officers of the company were elected. On January 1, 1695, the bank began active operations at Grocers' Hall, Poultry. Notes of £20 were issued, and the bank commenced discounting mercantile bills of exchange. The bank was authorized to advance money on pledges, but no very considerable business of this kind seems to have been done. At first the bank stood in high credit with all but usurers, with whose business it seriously interfered.

Its first trouble came May 5, 1696. Coin had been clipped, filed, and counterfeited to an enormous extent, so much so that gold guineas of full weight passed current at thirty shillings. It had been the bank's practice to receive degraded coin at its nominal value, and when the great issue of new coin began the bank was obliged to pay its notes in full-weighted coin, so that for every seven ounces it had received it was obliged to pay twelve ounces. Of course, this caused a "run", on the bank. Its enemies, the private bankers, improved this opportunity to the full extent, and on the day mentioned they suddenly presented £30,000 in notes and demanded payment. The bank suspended cash payments, but it got through the trouble by good management and Government assistance, but as a precautionary measure its capital stock was increased by vote of Parliament on Feb. 3, 1697, new subscriptions to be paid in exchequer tallies and bank notes. The life of the bank was prolonged until twelve months after notice given Aug. 1, 1710, and the bank was given a monopoly of the public banking business.

It should be noticed that a bank was chartered by the Government just before this, its advance to the Government to be £2,564,000, but it had been impossible to secure subscriptions.

The Bank of England was authorized to issue bank notes to the extent of its new capital, payable on demand and secured by the Government. The new subscriptions amounted to £1,001,171, 10s.

In 1707 the threat of invasion by Louis XIV. threw the country into a panic, and the enemies of the bank again attempted to cause its downfall, but it was reinforced by the queen and several nobles, and came through the trouble safely.

In 1709, the Government being greatly embarrassed, the bank was appealed to again, and an arrangement was made with it by which the interest which the Government was paying on its original stock of £1,200,000, was reduced from 8 to 6 per cent, with an annual allowance of £4,000 for managing the debt, the bank was to advance £400,000 more at 6 per cent interest; the capital stock of £2,201,171, 10s, was allowed to be doubled at a price of 115 for the new stock, upon which the bank agreed to circulate £2,500,000 in Exchequer-bills, and to receive an allowance of 6 per cent, one-half for interest and one-half for repayment of the principal, and that no more Exchequer-bills should be issued without the bank's consent. The life of the bank was further extended to August 1, 1732.

The subscriptions to this new stock were paid in four hours after the lists were opened.

Although the act of 1697 prevented the creation of another bank by Paraliament, private joint-stock banks were formed, and any corporation and company could perform a banking business. To cut off these adventurers an act was passed that during the life of the Bank of England no more than six persons could be united to do a banking business. The result was the prevention of the formation of any other joint-stock bank than the Bank of England.

In 1713, upon loan to the Government of £100,000, secured by Exchequer-bills, the life of the bank was prolonged to twelve months' notice to be given after August 1, 1742, and the payment of £1,600,000. In 1716 the life of the bank was prolonged indefinitely until three annuities of £88,751, £100,000, and £76,830, and other debts, upon which an annual interest of 5 per cent was paid, were extinguished. In 1717 the temporary victory and final collapse of the great South Sea company occurred, resulting in a "run" on the Bank of England which was artfully met and overcome. In 1722 the reserve fund known as the "rest" was created.

As 1742, the time when the life of the bank was to expire, drew nigh, the bank advanced £1,600,000 to the Government, and its capital (enlarged in 1720 to £8,959,995 14s. 8d. by the purchase of £4,000,000 in South Sea company's annuities) was increased to £9,800,000; its life was also prolonged until twelve months' notice to be given after August 1, 1764. An attempt was made to close up the loose ends of the act of 1709 by an amendment intended to make the bank's monopoly more exclusive.

In 1745 the rebellion in Scotland was the cause of a "run" on the bank, and its notes fell to a discount of ten per cent, but one thousand six hundred merchants pledged themselves to support the credit of the bank notes, and the "run" was stopped. In 1746 the bank's capital was advanced by further loans to the Government to £10,780,000. In 1759 notes for £15 and for £10 were first issued.

C. HOOD,
President Emporia National Bank, Emporia, Kansas.

The charter of the bank expired in 1764, and it was renewed upon the absolute gift of £110,000 to the nation, and a loan of £1,000,000 on Exchequer-bills for two years at 3 per cent, the renewal of the charter being until twelve months' notice after August 1, 1786. In 1781 the charter was again renewed upon the advance of £2,000,000 at 3 per cent for three years, until twelve months' after August 1, 1812, and the payment of the public debt. In 1782 the capital was increased to £11,642,400.

The London Clearing House was established in 1773, and occupied its building in Lombard street in 1775, but it was many years before the Bank of England joined it.

Up to this time the monopoly of the bank was nearly complete. Private bankers now began to give customers blank check-books, and the use of them in London became universal, entirely superseding the use of bank-notes and circumventing the monopoly of the Bank of England.

During the period of unusual industrial activity which followed the termination of the war of 1713, England felt for the first time the great need of reliable banks of issue other than the Bank of England. Its monopoly was complete, and to provide a currency small shopkeepers and irresponsible persons turned bankers and inundated the country with a miserable currency. In 1775 an act prohibited bankers issuing notes of less than 20 shillings. In 1777 the minimum value was made £5.

In 1782 the extension of foreign commerce consequent on the conclusion of the war with the American colonies, led to overtrading. The Bank of England made unwise issues. Banks which had sprung up like mushrooms all over the country, in almost every hamlet, issued currency freely, and, strange as it may appear, all was received without hesitation.

J. H. LINDENBERGER
President American National Bank, Louisville, Ky.

The actual money at the command of the bankers became ridiculously small for the magnitude of operations carried on. In the fall of 1792 the revulsion occurred, and bankruptcies were unusually frequent. The declaration of war with the Government of France under the Convention was the last blow to staggering credit, and the financial storm which swept over England carried down three hundred of the three hundred and fifty bankers doing business.

The Bank of England refused to support credit by meeting the demand for discounts. The Government came to the rescue, issued Exchequer-bills to the amount of £5,000,000, and freely loaned them to struggling institutions. Credit was immediately restored.

In 1797 a combination of untoward events had the effect of withdrawing large sums of specie from the bank. The danger of invasion by the French became the cause of numerous "runs" on country banks, which rapidly spread to London, and on February 26, 1797, the Bank of England was directed to suspend cash payments until the opinion of Parliament could be taken. The bank gave notice that its affairs were most prosperous and its notes perfectly secure. Parliament continued the suspension of cash payments until six months after a definitive treaty of peace should have been concluded. The result of this action practically made the bank-notes legal tender, and for the first three years after the passage of the restriction act they were on a par with gold or possessed a small premium. From 1800 to 1810 the history of the bank-notes was one of gradual depreciation, until in 1810 the attention of Parliament was called to the subject and a committee of inquiry was appointed which reported that the depreciation was due to over-issue, and recommended that the Bank of England resume specie payments within two years. The recommendation was not adopted, and the over-issue continued until in 1814 the maximum depreciation was 25 per cent.

In 1813 the number of country banks had increased to 900, but in the three years following 240 of them stopped payment, and, of course, their paper was withdrawn from circulation, causing the Bank of England's notes to rise nearly to par. The bank was directed to resume specie payments in 1823, but in fact it did resume on May 1, 1821. No legislation was had to prevent the unwise issue of notes by country banks however, and in 1823 such issues were greatly enlarged, and in 1825 the amount in circulation was estimated to have been 60 per cent greater than in 1823. Speculation became hazardous in the extreme, and when exchange began to fall in 1824 trouble began. London currency was contracted in September, 1825, and country banks began to fail the moment they could not secure accommodations in London. In less than six weeks more than seventy banks were carried down, and the demand for gold at the Bank of England was so great as to have drained it of about seven millions of bullion before the outflow could be stopped.

The crisis in London lasted one week, when the tide receded, and the safety of the bank was assured. The exchange turned to the favor of England, and gold began to flow towards the country. The Bank of England then issued notes with prodigal abundance, £5,000,000 being issued in three days. The next week uneasiness in the country was again apparent, but it was stayed by the bank's issue of £500,000 in £1-notes, and by the first of 1826 credit was entirely restored.

In 1826 the issue of less than £5-notes was prohibited in England. In 1833 the charter of the bank was extended for ten years, and joint-stock banks of issue defined and permitted. In 1839 the issue of the Bank of England again became redundant, and but for assistance from the Bank of France, the bank would have stopped payment.

In 1844 and 1845 Sir Robert Peel introduced measures into Parliament, the passage of which greatly improved England's banking system. The power to issue notes payable on demand was limited by making the amount of such notes in circulation vary with the amount of bullion possessed by the issuer. The issuing and banking departments of the Bank of England were entirely separated, and over the first department the Bank was given no control. The issue of the Bank was made £14,000,000 on securities, and it was allowed to issue two-thirds of the amount of notes which any country bank was authorized, but failed, to issue. Under this provision the issue had increased to £15,000,000 in 1875. Above this sum its notes can only be issued upon the receipt of an equal amount of coin or bullion. By this legislation its notes are made equal with gold.

The act of 1844 also provided that no new bank of issue should be established in the United Kingdom, and that the maximum issue of notes by the existing country English banks should be limited to the average amount which they had in circulation during the twelve weeks preceding April 27, 1844. No other bank than the Bank of England was allowed to issue notes in or within sixty-five miles of London. The charter of the bank was extended until twelve months' notice after August 1, 1855.

On three occasions, in 1847, 1857, and in 1866, it has been found necessary to authorize the Bank to issue notes beyond the limits of the act of 1844, in order to restore credit to the mercantile community.

Such, in brief, is the history of the Bank of England. With it is closely connected the history of banking in England. Branches of the Bank have been established at Manchester, Liverpool, Birmingham, Bristol, Leeds, Plymouth, Newcastle-on-Tyne, Hull, and Portsmouth. The capital stock of the Bank is £14,553,000. The "Rest" on October 26, 1887, was £3,100,053. The dividends for the year ending October 5, 1887, were at the rate of £9¾ per cent. The price of bank stock on October 26, 1887, was £304. On that day there were £24,210,255 in circulation, and of its unemployed notes there were £10,824,670. Of gold and silver coin and bullion there were £20,092,263.

CHAPTER IV.

MODERN EUROPEAN BANKING.

The history of banks in England other than the Bank of England can be sketched in a few words. The end of the war between France and England in 1815, was soon reflected in the brightening of commerce, but it was a long time before the people paid attention to banking laws or facilities. The Bank of England, together with private bankers, had been able to meet all demands. The crisis of 1825 showed the weakness of private banks, and the necessity of public banks. The legislation restricting the formation of joint-stock banks in order to protect the monopoly of the Bank of England, has already been mentioned. In 1826 six joint-stock banks were registered, and seven in 1828-9 and seven more in 1829-30. In 1833 legislation was had permitting joint-stock banks of deposit in London. In 1834 the prospectus of the London and Westminster Bank was promulgated by James William Gilbart. In 1836 the London Joint-Stock Bank was organized, and in 1839 the Union Bank of London was established. The act of 1833 did not permit the banks to sue or be sued in the name of their officers, but a later Act of Parliament corrected that defect. At present there are 173 joint-stock banks in the United Kingdom, the banker's license being £30 annually.

The restrictive legislation of 1708 against joint-stock banks in England did not extend to Scotland. The Bank of Scotland was organized in 1695, the year following the establishment of the Bank of England. Its original capital was £100,000, and it had a monopoly for twenty-five years. In 1774 its capital was increased to £200,000, and at several other times, until it now stands at £1,500,000, of which £1,000,000 is paid-up. It is the only Scotch bank, established by Parliament. In 1696 it began to establish branches, and began to issue notes as early as 1704. It was a bank of deposit at an early period—certainly before 1729—and interest on deposits was allowed. The Bank has branches in all important Scotch towns. Of other joint-stock banks in Scotland may be mentioned: The Royal Bank of Scotland; established in 1727, and now having a capital of £2,000,000, and numerous branches; the British Linen Company Bank, established in 1746, with a capital of £1,000,000; The Commercial Bank of Scotland, limited; The National Bank of Scotland, limited; The Union Bank of Scotland, limited; and the Caledonian Banking Company, limited. In Scotland the system of giving cash-credits in limited sums upon personal and other security, prevails. Failures in Scotch banks have been infrequent, those of the Western Bank and the City of Glasgow Bank, being notable instances.

E. ROTAN.
President First National Bank, Waco, Texas.

The Bank of Ireland dates from 1783. Previous to this a primitive system of private banking prevailed, goldsmith, tradesmen, and general dealers being the bankers. The earliest reference to the subject of Irish banking is an act of the Irish Parliament in 1709. The business at that time was entirely uncontrolled, and any person could issue bank notes, silver or copper coin. Upon the establishment of the Bank of Ireland, banking privileges were much curtailed. In 1797 the suspension of cash payment by the Bank of England was extended to Ireland, and the Bank of Ireland greatly increased its issue of bank-notes. Private banks sprung up all over the country, and they also swelled the currency until it became greatly depreciated. In 1804 there were fifty-seven banks in Ireland. In 1819 but nineteen remained, and in 1827 there were but ten banks in all Ireland. In 1821 a law was passed permitting joint-stock banks to be organized, but none were founded until additionnal legislation in 1824 made the restrictions less objectionable. Then the Northern Bank of Belfast was organized. In 1825 the Provincial Bank of Ireland was started with a capital of £2,000,000. In 1834 the Agricultural and Commercial Bank of Ireland was organized, but it went under in the crisis of 1836. In 1864 the Munster Bank at Cork was established. It has over forty branches, and pays 12 per cent dividends.

STEPHEN BULL,
President Manufacturers' National Bank, Racine, Wis.

On May 2 and 20, 1716 the French Government granted a concession to John Law, a Scotchman, for the establishment of a bank, of which he was to be director and the Regent its protector. In June, 1716, it began business with a capital of 6,000,000 francs, and was authorized to issue notes payable at sight and to bearer, to discount paper, to receive deposits, to make collections and payments, and do a general banking business. The success of the bank was assured until Law and his *Compagnie d' Occident* ruined it in one year. It was fifty years later before the country was ready for another credit establishment. In 1776 M. Besnard was authorized to establish in Paris a discount bank, and, although of value to the business world, the Convention suppressed it in 1793. So soon as the public quiet was restored, organizations were founded which in 1800 resulted in the Bank of France, with a capital of 45,000,000 francs, which was increased to 90,000,000 francs in 1806. It is a bank of deposit, discount, and circulation, and has the sole power to issue notes. Its government consists of a governor and two deputies, and a council-general of twenty members. Bills are discounted within three months of maturity, guaranteed by two, or generally three, approved signatures. The annual dividends are limited to 5 per cent. All other profits are invested in consolidated stock to be returned to the stockholders upon the expiration of the charter in 1897. In 1848 the joint-stock banks which had been started in several large cities were consolidated with the Bank of France as branches, and their issues of notes suspended. Since then branches have been established in each department. In 1848 the bank suspended cash payments, but resumed them in 1851. The Government is largely interested in the Bank of France and they are mutually helpful. In 1870 specie payment was stopped, but through all the troublesome times which followed, the management of the bank has been prudent, and its credit is restored.

A few other joint-stock banks exist in France, but do not possess the power to issue notes.

The Royal Bank of Prussia was established June 17, 1765, as an exchange and loan bank, with a capital of 400,000 thalers.

In several of the German States banks were founded under laws peculiar to each one, and with local circulations, but the union of these states into the Empire called for a national currency. On January 30, 1875, an act was passed which met this demand. The Royal Bank became an Imperial Bank, which was established with an "uncovered" or unsecured issue of 250,000,000 of marks, with a right to increase this issue if one-third the increase is represented by cash in hand and two-thirds by bills not having more than three months to run. Thirty-two other banks were permitted to have an "uncovered" issue to the extent of 135,000,000 of marks, and to exceed their authorized issues subject to the payment of 5 per cent interest on the excess above the authorized limit, plus the cash in hand. No note is issued less than 100 marks, and no new right of issue can be conceded except by a law of the Empire. The State itself has power to issue 120,000,000 of marks in state-notes of small denominations. There are but nineteen note-issuing banks in the Empire. The Empire shares in the profits and superintends the conduct of the Imperial Bank (Reichs Bank), and it is entitled to erect branch offices in any part of the Empire. Its capital is about $30,000,000.

The Bank of the Netherlands, at Amsterdam, was first chartered in 1814, with the Bank of England as a model, with a capital of 5,000,000 florins, which was increased to 10,000,000 in 1819, and to 15,000,000 in 1838. In 1863 it was re-chartered. It is a bank of deposit and issue.

In 1814 the National Bank of Copenhagen took the place, and all the debts, claims, rights and privileges of the Rigs Bank in Denmark, upon the cession of Norway to Sweden. The bank was obliged to maintain the notes of the Rigs Bank at their par value, and to do this it was required to collect and preserve silver coins, bars and banco money sufficient to redeem the notes when presented. The proportion of cash to outstanding notes has usually been from one-half to two-thirds. The bank also receives deposits and makes loans and discounts. It was required to hold silver for one-half its notes in circulation, one-half of which silver must be of the coinage of Denmark, the other half to be in silver bars or Hamburg banco. In 1848 the bank was permitted to substitute sterling money for one-quarter of the banco. In 1854 the bank increased its paper money from £2,222,000 to £2,660,000, the increase being secured by an equal amount of sterling money (one-quarter), silver bars, (one-half), and banco, (one-quarter). In 1855 it was allowed to increase its paper issue by the purchase of silver bars. From 1853 3 per cent interest was paid on money loaned to the bank, and from May 1, 1860, the State surplus has been left with the bank, which pays interest upon it. There are several private joint-stock banks in Copenhagen with no peculiar features.

In 1830 the "Enskilda" banks were first organized in Sweden. They are private banks with large numbers of partners, and issue notes payable in silver or in notes of the Riks Bank.

The notes issued are based on sound securities, the Government's banking law being a model of clearness and cautiousness. In 1884 the Post Office Savings Banks were established in Sweden, to receive money under guarantee of State, allow interest upon it, and by accumulating interest and capital, hold it at the disposal of depositors. The rate of interest is fixed by the King, and is added to the capital at the end of each year. The smallest amount received on deposit is one krona. All funds are invested in the Bank of Sweden.

The National Bank of Austria was established in Vienna, in 1860, with a view to restoring the credit of the Government. It has the exclusive privilege of issue, and in return loaned the State 80,000,000 florins without interest. It established numerous branches in different cities in the Empire. On December 24, 1867, the Government established a forced currency, and consolidated its debts to the National Bank into one loan of $40,000,000, and re-organized that institution into the Austro-Hungarian Bank, extending its charter to January 1, 1888, and giving it the exclusive right to issue notes. These notes are payable to bearer on demand, in coin of the realm at Vienna and Buda-Pesth, where are located the head offices of the bank. Should any of the notes be refused payment within twenty-four hours after presentation, further issues are prohibited and the bank's charter is forfeited. These notes are not issued for sums of less than $5, and issues over $100,000,000 must be secured by gold or silver coin or bullion. Notes issued on deposit accounts in excess of the amount of the reserve of the bank must be covered by banking securities—discounted bills and notes, loan on precious metals, convertible notes, redeemable obligations, or coupons of the Empire, or foreign bills of exchange. The bank's affairs are administered by a governor nominated by the Emperor, two deputy governors, and a board of twelve directors.

The Bank of Norway was established in 1816, its capital being a forced loan raised by levying a tax on all landed property. Each taxpayer became a shareholder in the bank to the extent of his payment, and their shares soon came to a premium. All its securities, like bills or notes, must be available at short notice. It loans its own notes on land, the loan being but two-thirds of the value of the security. The interest paid semi-annually by borrowers is 4 per cent per annum, and 5 per cent of the principal must be paid each year. The security is sold in case of non-payment. The bank has the exclusive privilege of issuing notes, which are legal tender and payable in gold on demand.

The oldest of the Belgium banks is the *Societe Generale*, founded August 28, 1822, with a capital of 50,000,000 florins. It did a discount business and manage the Government's finances until Belgium and Holland separated, when that branch of business was resigned to the Bank of Belgium of Brussels, which was chartered in 1835, with a capital of 20,-

000,000 francs. In 1838 the Bank of Belgium suspended payment, and again in 1839, the Government coming to its assistance each time. In 1841 its capital was increased to 30,000,000 francs. In 1850 the management of the Government's finances was relinquished to the National Bank of Belgium, of Brussels, organized May 5, 1830—a joint stock bank—with a capital of 25,000,000 francs, of which the *Societe Generale* took 10,000,000 and the Bank of Belgium 15,000,000, both ceasing to issue notes and agreeing to abandon their discount business. Its charter was renewed in 1872 and its capital stock increased to 50,000,000 francs. It pay 5 per cent dividends, and one-third of its profits above 6 per cent goes to form a sinking fund. Its has a governor, six directors and a council of censors, and the funds of the State are kept on deposit in its vaults.

LOGAN C. MURRAY.
Vice-President American National Bank, Louisville, Ky.

The Bank of Belgium now has a capital of 50,000,000 francs, and the Bank of Flanders, in Ghent, has a capital of 10,000,000 francs.

The earliest Swiss bank of issue is that of St. Gall, which dates from 1836. At the end of 1869 there were nineteen issuing banks in the Swiss Confederation. There are now thirty-three legalited banks of issue. In 1885 their average circulation of notes was $23,822,183. There are 325 savings banks, the deposits in 1882 being $47,547,-428.85. There are also 162 other banks of deposit, mostly of a private nature.

Although the oldest existing Italian bank dates from 1622—the Monte de Pashi, in Siena—the National Bank of Italy has a history dating only from 1850, it having been organized by consolidating the Bank of Genoa, founded in 1844, and the Bank of Turin, founded in 1847. At its organization a sum was to be paid for Government superintendence, and it agreed to advance to the State a sum of not over 18,000,000 lire, secured by a deposit of public stocks or treasury bonds bearing 3 per cent interest, or less if the market rate was lower than that. Three bank seats and four branch banks were established, and the capital, originally 40,000,000 lire, is now 200,000,000 lire. It has numerous branches, and its circulation is national. In April, 1874, the Government restricted the right of issuing bank-notes to six banks: The National Bank of Italy; the National Tuscan Bank, organized in 1857; the Roman Bank, 1850; the Tuscan Bank of Credit, 1860; the Bank of Naples, 1816, and the Bank of Sicily, 1843. This law authorized the Bank of Naples to increase its capital, by 1885, to 48,750,000 lire, and the Bank of Sicily to 12,000,000. The National Tuscan Bank had a capital of 30,000,000 lire; the Roman Bank, 15,000,000, and the Tuscan Bank of Credit, 10,000,000. By this law these six banks were organized into a union, which, if required, should furnish the Government 1,000,000,000 lire in bank-notes, but by a law passed April 7, 1881, this union was terminated.

T. J. GROCE,
President Galveston National Bank, Galveston, Texas.

There are also numbers of "People's Banks," credit societies, "Agrarian Banks," friendly societies, etc., the People's Banks increasing very rapidly.

The Imperial Bank of Russia was founded in 1860, to regulate the issues of currency and aid commerce. Its capital is subscribed by the Government, and it is managed by a committee of the treasury. Its charter was to run for twenty-eight years. When founded, its capital was $11,875,000, and one of its principal aims was to restore specie payments. In 1864 the circulation had a nominal value of $630,000,000, based on a specie reserve of but $43,330,000. In 1877-78 the currency was greatly expanded because of the Turkish war. The bank enjoys the sole privilege of issuing notes, and it has numerous branches. There are more than two hundred communal Russian banks.

Greece has two modern banks, the National of Athens, with a capital of $540,000, and the Ionian Bank, at Corfu.

Savings banks were known in Europe as early as 1765, at which date there was one at Brunswick. In 1778 one was established at Hamburg which still exists. In 1786 one was founded at Oldenburg, in 1790 one at Loire, in 1792 one at Basel, in 1794 one at Geneva, and in 1796 one at Kiel, in Holstein. In England they had a rapid growth. In 1799 Rev. Joseph Smith put into execution Jeremy Bentham's suggestion by the establshment at Wendover of a "frugality bank." In 1801 Mrs. Priscilla Wakefield established a savings bank in connection with a friendly society, and others followed rapidly. In 1817 so numerous had they become, Parliament passed a law for their control. Penny banks have lately been established in various cities of Great Britain. Savings Banks for the army were established in 1842, and for the navy in 1854. Several railway companies maintain savings banks for their employes. In Norway there were twenty-two savings banks in 1840, and 311 in 1880, of which 249 were rural. In Sweden the first savings bank was founded in 1813. In 1840 there were fifty-eight, and in 1880 the number had increased to 340, of which 252 were rural.

CHAPTER V.

EARLY AMERICAN BANKING.

The history of banking in the American colonies before the revolution is very obscure, and nearly every early mention of "banks" is apt to be misleading. The word "bank," as used by the colonists, meant simply a batch of paper money, issued by one of the provinces, or in rare instances, by a company or association of individuals more or less directly authorized by law. The modern commercial bank of deposit and discount, as we know it, did not exist, because there was no business to support it. There was no equivalent for the "moneyed-class" of to-day. The capitalist had not yet come. With few exceptions, men in easy circumstances were merchants or the large land owners then everywhere called "planters." Men of property derived their wealth from commerce or agriculture, and re-invested their gains in land or trade. The population was widely scattered, and the number of those within reach of any one business center, having cash to keep, was too few to make its custody and handling a profitable business for any one. Each merchant or planter kept his own cash in his own strong box at his own house. When a note or draft was presented he counted out the "broad Joes," or hard dollars, to pay it, if it were during one of the rare intervals at which specie payments were in vogue. Oftener the payment was made in depreciated paper at the fluctuating rate of discount, at which it just then happened to be current. This discount varied, with time and place, from a minimum of 8 to 10 per cent to a common rate of 2 to 10 for one. In extreme cases this depreciation reached 1,000 of the debased paper for one of specie.

This issue of a depreciated paper as an expedient for the relief of every real or supposed pecuniary distress, was a prominent feature of colonial politics, especially in New England and South Carolina. The exigencies of Indian wars and numerous futile expeditions for the conquest of Canada led to repeated issues of bills of credit by the Governments of the several provinces. The prompt action necessary to be taken in getting up these expeditions, made it impracticable to wait for the levy and collection of a tax, and the scarcety of capital made it difficult or impossible to borrow money through channels commonly resorted to in older and wealthier States. Bills of credit, made legal tender, operated as a forced loan without exciting the opposition and clamor which would have followed had the authorities adopted that plan without disguise, or had they openly "pressed" or "requisitioned" the needed stores and material in kind. Wasteful and extravagant, if not actually ruinous, as such measures always prove in the long run, the exigencies of the occasion seemed not only to justify, but imperatively to demand their adoption in these cases. We of this generation have seen measures, which we now perceive to be of at least equal folly, promoted and sanctioned by the most trusted statesmen of the day as a "military necessity." Even depreciation enhanced, in some respects, the popularity of these forced issues, as it afforded debtors, always a large class, especially in a new country, the "cheap money," which enables them to discharge their debts at a discount; and the rise in prices, in proportion to the depreciation of the currency, gave a fallacious appearance of general prosperity. The "scarcity of money," or appreciation of currency, which followed a redemption and withdrawal of a portion of the outstanding paper, was represented as a public calamity. This apprehension of countless imaginary ills attendant upon any "contractions of the circulation," led to loan schemes devised and sustained by that restless, unsettled class, numerous in every age in a growing community, which arrogates to itself a special claim to be called and esteemed "active business men," whose members, under the guise of public spirit, strive to make the capital of the rich and the labor of the poor alike subservient to their own selfish schemes for personal profit.

The earliest issue of paper money in North America was made by the French Governor-General of Canada, in 1685. At that time the Indian tribes of Central New York—the redoubtable Iroquois, or Five Nations—were the most dangerous foes of New France. The English colonies were not yet strong enough to attack their French neighbors. The Iroquois, however, had made repeated incursions into Canada, capturing and destroying Montreal, and threatening the French settlements with complete extinction. In 1685 the Marquis de Denonville, Governor-General of Canada, set on foot an expediton against the Senecas, the most westerly of the Five Nations, and to furnish funds for this enterprise issued "card money," which was made redeemable in bills upon France. In 1690 Massachusetts issued the first paper money emitted within the present limits of the United States, of which we have authentic record. In December of that year the expedition which Sir William Phipps had lead against Quebec—the first serious attempt by the English colonies at the conquest of Canada—returned to Boston, having made complete failure. There was no money in the treasury to pay the troops, as the authorities had relied upon the spoil which a successful expedition was expected to bring home, to meet all such charges. To provide for this emergency the General Court resolved: that, "Considering the present poverty of the country, and, through the scarcity of money, the want of an adequate measure of commerce," bills of credit in notes of 5 shillings to £5 should be issued "to be in value equal to money, and accepted in all public payments." The first issue was fixed at £7,000 subsequently increased to £40,000, equal, as Massachusetts money was then rated, to $133,333. Before this limit was reached, however, the bills sank to a discount of one-half. To raise their credit they were made full legal tender. In 1691 £10,000 of this paper then remaining in the treasury was ordered to be burned. In 1692 it was ordered that, in lieu of interest, the bills should be received by the treasury at a premium of 5 per cent over coin. These measures, coupled with a promise to redeem the entire issue in twelve months, sufficed to bing this paper to par and to maintain it in circulation at that point for twenty years.

J. S. CHICK.
President National Bank of Kansas City, Kansas City, Mo.

South Carolina was the first to follow the example of Massachusetts. In 1702, being then the most southerly of the English colonies, this province attempted to wrest Florida from the Spaniards. A disastrous siege of St. Augustine ended the invasion and left the province burdened with debt. Pleading the example "of great and rich countries," and confident that "funds of credit have fully answered the ends of money, and given the people a quick circulation of their trade and cash," the colony issued bills of credit to the amount of £6,000. This was to be paid off within three years by a tax on liquors and peltries. In 1707 Rhode Island and New Hampshire issued their first bills of credit to provide means for taking part with Massachusetts in the attempted conquest of Acadia, or Nova Scotia from the French. New York, Connecticut and New Jersey made issues of bills of credit for the first time in 1709 to equip their quotas of troops to assist in another futile attempt at the conquest of Canada, and in 1713 North Carolina "paid" with bills of credit, the expenses of the war against the Tuscaroras, which ended in the expulsion of that tribe from its old home, to wonder northward until it settled in western New York as the sixth nation of the Iroquois Confederacy. Virginia issued no paper until 1755, when bills were emitted to equip the battalion of provincial militia, commanded by Washington, which accompanied Braddock's disastrous expedition against the French on the Ohio. As will be related hereafter, Pennsylvania and Maryland first authorized banks—issued paper money, that is—to be loaned to their people as currency. There is no record of any considerable or authorized issue of paper in any form in Delaware or Georgia until a later date. Thus it will be seen that of the eleven colonies which resorted to the issue of paper money, before the revolution, in the case of nine of them it first appeared as an adjunct of military enterprise and of military defeat and disaster.

South Carolina had issued bills of credit in 1702 to meet urgent demands upon the treasury, in a desperate emergency. In 1712 this colony invented a modification of the original plan, which was quickly imitated by most of the other provinces. "To defray the expense of an expedition against the Tuscaroras and to advance and accommodate domestic trade," the Legislature established a "public bank," and issued £48,000 in bills of credit, called bank-bills, to be loaned out at interest, to individuals upon real estate and personal security. The loans ran for twelve years, to be repaid one-twelfth each year. In this case the military necessity was used only as a decent pretext, and when the next bank was authorized the cloak was laid aside. Although made a legal tender, these bank-bills were early discredited, and before the end of the year were current only at a discount of one-third of their nominal value. In 1716 a second "bank" of £30,000 was ordered to be loaned out on the same terms as the first. This was disallowed by the Lords' Proprietaries of the colony of England, in part because among the taxes provided for its redemption, a duty of £10 per head was imposed on all negroes imported. This was the first and

R. L. DURHAM,
Vice-President Commercial National Bank, Portland, Oregon.

principal cause of discontent with the Proprietary government which led to tumults and finally, in 1719, to an open insurrection which ended in the complete subversion of the Proprietary authorities. A revolutionary convention, chosen by the people, assumed the management of affairs, and appealed to the British home Government for relief. The English ministry instituted proceedings to revoke the Proprietary charter, proclaimed South Carolina a crown colony, and, in 1721, appointed a royal Governor. In 1722 a bill was introduced in the Assembly for adding £120,000 to the paper money of the colony. Twenty-eight of the principal merchants of Charlestown protested against it, and in their remonstrance alleged as the chief cause of the then excessive depreciation of paper money, "that every legislative engagement for recalling the various emissions of bills had been broken through by every Assembly." Provoked by this plain statement of unpalatable truth, the assembly pronounced the merchant's petition "a false and scandalous libel," and sent the petitioners to prison for a breach of privilege. The Governor not daring to interfere, they were released only on payment of large sum by way of fees. The bill for the new bank, though passed by the Assembly, was disallowed by the English Government, and the Governor "was strickly enjoined to consent to no new law for creating a further paper currency, neither to any act for diverting the sinking fund already established." At least a part of these disallowed "banks" seems to have been issued, however, in spite of the prohibition, for, in 1725, the Assembly resolved that, "Whereas, the circulating bank money is already reduced to £87,000, and is likely soon to be entirely paid off," there was grave occasion to apprehend a scarcity of money. To escape this imminent disaster the Assembly tacked a rider on the annual revenue and appropriation bill, stopping the redemption and withdrawal of the bank paper. The Governor and Council proposed to strike out this provision; but the Assembly denied their rights to amend money bills, and left them to choose between a breach of their instructions and a failure of supplies. Next year, 1726, this policy was followed up by a bill for the issue of another bank, which the Governor's Council again refused to pass. The planters then entered into a combination to pay no taxes, alleging their inability to do so unless aided by the issue of more bank bills. When, in 1727, a conspicuous member of this association was arrested and imprisoned, the Chief Justice denied him a writ of habeas corpus on the ground that his offense amounted to high treason, and was not bailable. After an acrimonious controversy in the Courts and in the Assembly, two hundred and fifty horsemen entered Charleston from the neighboring country and compelled his liberation. The Assembly impeached the Chief Justice, because involved in a violent quarrel with the Governor and his Counc'l, adjourned themselves of their own motion, and when again summoned, refused to attend. This disorder lasted until 1730, when a new Royal Governor came out, and a new council was appointed, from which were omitted all those who had been most strenuous for obeying the royal instructions forbidding further emissions of bills. The paper money party thus strengthened, the Assembly suspended the redemption of all outstanding bills, and voted another issue of £104,000, both of which measures seem to have obtained the Governor's assent. In 1736 still another bank of £100,000 was authorized, to be loaned out at 8 per cent like the previous issues. Before the time the bank-bills had steadily depreciated until they reached a discount of seven of paper for one of specie, at which the currency of South Carolina remained, almost without variation, until the eve of the revolution.* The case of South Carolina is perhaps the only instance in which the never-ending controversy between the advocates of expansion and those who favor a contraction of the currency led to a complete and radical change in the form of government.

As South Carolina was the first to follow the example of Massachusetts in issuing bills of credit to meet demands upon the public treasury, so Massachusetts was the first to adopt the plan devised in South Carolina of manufacturing paper money to be loaned out for the promotion of trade. As we have seen, the earliest issue of bills of credit was made by Massachusetts in 1690 to meet the cost of Phipps' futile attempt on Quebec. The next resort to the same device in this province was in 1711, when bills, amounting to £40,000, were issued and paid out directly by the Government to equip the New England troops attached to the even-more disastrous expedition led by the English Admiral, Sir Hovenden Walker, against the same fortaress. In 1714 a very general agreement had grown up in Massachusetts in favor of the loan system of issuing paper, but differences arose as to the precise method of carrying it out. The more adventurous and speculative element proposed a private bank, to be incorporated by the General Court, to issue bills on its own credit and responsibility. Others preferred the indorsement of the colony and proposed to issue colony bills, as heretofore, to be loaned on landed security for a term of years, the interest and one-twentieth of the principal to be paid annually. If this scheme was adhered to, the whole debt would be paid of and the entire issue of paper redeemed and retired in twenty years. In the meantime the interest would reduce, by so much, the amount necessary to be raised by taxation for the current expense of the colony. An inconsiderable party opposed all bills of credit, and argued in favor of a specie currency and a real bank of deposit and discount; but these were stigmatized as "capitalists" and "money princes," and, finding the drift of public sentiment almost wholly in favor of an issue of paper money of some sort, were soon compelled to come to the support of the provincial issue, called the "public bank," as the least objectionable of the two plans most in favor. According to Hutchinson, the party favoring the "private bank" was composed generally of persons in difficult or involved circumstances, or such as were possessed of land, but had no command of ready money, or men of no substance at all. They proposed to issue bills which all the members of the company promised to receive as "money," but at no fixed value as compared with gold or silver. The Assembly rather favored this plan owing to the support given it by the Boston members, but, after a long struggle, the party for the "public bank" prevailed in the General Court for a loan of £50,000 in bills of credit, which were put into the hands of five trustees, to be loaned for five years only, to the inhabitants of the several towns in the ratio of their taxes, in sums of £50 to £500, on real estate mortgage, at 5 per cent interest, one-fifth of the principal to be paid each year.†

Certainly no scheme for the emission of bills of credit ever was more carefully devised or more scrupulously guarded. But having thus, once for all, demonstrated their prudence and caution, the people and authorities of Massachusetts proceded to give full swing to their conviction that it was impossible, in a state of colonial dependence, to maintain a metallic currency, and that it was the duty of Government to provide a currency made and kept equal to the requirements of trade and commerce. New issues of bills of credit were made for the payment of ordinary, current expenses, and to supply deficiencies of inadequate tax levies. Provisions made for the payment of old issues were repealed or ignored and new issues made with no present purpose of redemption. The efforts of the Governor and Council to restrain these issues were unavailing, the Governor's consent, or connivance in disobedience of his instructions, being extorted by withholding his salary. In 1733 there was a general complaint throughout the four New England colonies of the unusual scarcity of money. There was as large a sum current in bills of credit as ever, but the bills having depreciated, they answered the purpose of money so much the less in proportion. Massachusetts and New Hampshire, restrained by the instructions of their Royal Governors, had not issued bills to so great an amount as Rhode Island. Connecticut, being an agricultural colony, with fewer traders, did not so much feel the want of money. The people of Massachusetts complained bitterly that Rhode Island bills should circulate among them to take away their substance to be employed in the trade of the sister colony, and many wished to see the bills of each colony forbidden to circulate outside the limits of that by which they were issued. In the midst of this discontent an act was passed in Rhode Island for a new issue of £100,000, to be loaned to its people for twenty years, who, it was argued, would thus have it in their power to add that sum to their wealth, by purchases of horses, sheep, lumber, fish, etc., from the people of Massachusetts. The merchants of Boston thereupon confederated and mutually promised and engaged not to receive any Rhode Island bills of this new emission. Then, to provide a currency to fill the void in the circulation,

M. W. FLOURNOY,
Vice-President First National Bank, Albuquerque, New Mexico.

which, it seemed to be universally agreed this action would occasion, a large number of Boston merchants formed themselves into a company, entered into covenants in co-partnership, etc., chose directors, and issued £110,000 in their own bills, redeemable in ten years in silver at nineteen shillings to the ounce, the then current rate, but being about three times the true or specie value, according to Massachusetts standard, or in gold in the same proportion, one-tenth part annually. About the same time the Massachusetts treasury, which had long been closed, was opened and the debts of several years were paid at one time in bills of credit. To this was added the ordinary emissions of bills from New Hampshire and Connecticut. Then some of the Boston merchants, tempted by the opportunity, broke their engagement and received the Rhode Island bills, an example which all the rest were speedily forced to follow. All these issues made a flood of paper money, before which silver—then standing nominally at nineteen shillings to the ounce—rose to twenty-seven shillings to the ounce, or, rather the paper which stood at about three to one for specie, sank to a discount of four and one-half of paper for one of specie. Every creditor was thus defrauded of nearly one-half of his just dues. As soon as silver rose to twenty-seven shillings the ounce, the notes issued by the Merchants' Association, payable at nineteen shillings to the ounce, were hoarded up as too valuable for every-day service, and no longer used for the purposes of money.

J. N. SIMPSON.
President National Exchange Bank, Dallas, Texas.

As early as 1732 the English Government began to instruct the Royal Governor of Massachusetts to consent to no further issue of bills of credit to remain current longer than the time fixed for the redemption of that already in circulation, the last of which would mature in 1741. It would have been easy to raise each year, by taxation, a sum sufficient to pay the current expenses, and to redeem all the paper maturing during that year. Instead of pursuing this course, the wisdom of which so plainly appears, the revenue from taxation was allowed to fall below the necessary and inevitable expenditure, so that not only were the bills maturing allowed to go unredeemed, but new paper, to fall due in 1741, was each year emitted. As the time for the payment of this great mass of paper drew near, and as hope grew fainter that the policy against new issues would be relaxed and the promised payment of the bills in some way evaded, a great clamor arose against the Governor, who, in spite of all attempts to starve him into compliance by witholding his salary, adhered resolutely to his instructions. In 1740 it became apparent that it was impossible to levy in one year a tax sufficient to discharge all these accumulations. A general dread of the further depreciation or entire withdrawal of the currency took possession of nearly the whole people. Hutchinson, the historian of Massachusetts, did, indeed, propose to the General Court to borrow in England a sum in silver equal to the bills then extant, and therewith to redeem those bills and thus furnish the colony with a sound currency; the repayment of the loan to be spread over several years so as to escape burdensome taxation in any one. But this plan was rejected in favor of what was called the land bank, or manufactory scheme. It being held that the royal instructions against bills of credit were no bar to private action, the projector and chief advocate of the "private bank" of 1714, hereinbefore mentioned, "put himself at the head of some seven or eight hundred persons, some few of rank and good estate, but generally of low condition, of small estate, and many of them insolvent. This notable company were to give credit to £150,000 lawful money, to be issued in bills, each person to mortgage land in proportion to the sum he subscribed and took out, or to give bond with two sureties, but personal security was not to be taken for more than £100 from any one person." Ten directors and a treasurer were to be chosen by the company. Every subscriber or partner was to pay 3 per cent interest on the sum taken out, and 5 per cent annually of the principal. He that did not pay his dues in provincial bills might pay in the produce and manufacture of the province, at such rates as the directors should fix from time to time, and as they should commonly pass for lawful money. It was claimed by its friends, that by thus providing a medium and currency for trade, not only would the people be better able to procure provincial bills to pay their taxes, but trade, both foreign and inland, would revive and flourish. The principal merchants refused to receive the bills, though they had a large currency among the smaller shop-keepers, mechanics and farmers. To lessen the temptation to receive these bills of the land bank, a number of leading merchants agreed to issue their own notes, or bills, payable in silver at the end of fifteen years, much like the private bank of 1733, and dubbed their scheme the "silver bank." The Governor issued a proclamation forbidding either of these companies to issue bills. But both did make large emissions in defiance of the prohibition. The Governor and Council then applied to the English Parliament, which, early in 1741, declared that the law commonly called the Bubble Act, passed twenty years before on the breaking of the South Sea bubble, which prohibited the formation of unincorporated joint-stock companies with more than six members, applied to all the American Colonies. This declaratory legislation, giving retroactive effect to an old statute, was at the same time cautiously cited as "an instance of the transcendent power of Parliament." It was, in substance if not in form, *ex post facto* legislation of a specially dangerous and provoking type, and became, in the end, one of the strongest inducements to the prohibition of such laws which, not many years later, was incorporated in express terms in every American Constitution. Both the banks, or companies, were dissolved. The members or partners were held individually liable for the entire mass of their notes, not at the depreciated rates at which they had been issued, but at par with accrued interest. The manufactory or land bank scheme especially, the affairs of which remained unsettled and in the utmost confusion for several years, proved extremely ruinous to all such persons concerned in it as had anything to lose. Earnest efforts on behalf of these unfortunate speculators, of whom his father was one, first introduced into politics Samuel Adams, afterward so celebrated, then a young man, a recent graduate of Harvard, designed for the ministry but compelled by his father's ruin and shortly ensuing death, to adopt a more active life. In 1741 a new royal Governor was appointed who construed his instructions as aimed only at preventing a further emission of depreciated currency or a further depreciation of that already afloat. Holding that it did not matter how large a sum in bills was current if only their value was secured, and that neither the spirit of his instructions required, nor the circumstances of the case permitted, the literal observance of that proportion of them which directed the redemption of all outstanding paper in that one year, a scheme was patched up which seemed to promise at least a brief postponement of the evil day. The General Court passed and the Governor, after obtaining at least the tacit approval of the English Ministry, assented to an act intended to establish an ideal measure of value in all trade and dealings, let the instrument of exchange be what it would. This declared that all contracts should be understood to be payable in silver at 6s. 8d. per ounce. The true value of silver at that time was about 5s. 2d. sterling per ounce, but the old Pine Tree coinage of Massachusetts had been light weight and 6s. 8d. of that currency had been coined from an ounce of silver, so the standard now fixed was that which had obtained before the first issue of paper and, to that extent, was an honest one. Bills of a new form were issued which bore on their face a promise to pay three ounces of silver for every twenty shillings of their nominal value. These were made a legal tender for all dues, public and private. It was also provided that in case they should depreciate in value an addition should be made in all debts equal to the depreciation of the currency from the time of contract to that of payment. How to ascertain the depreciation from time to time was the great difficulty in framing the act. To leave it to a common jury never would do, nor could the impartial integrity of the House of Representatives be trusted. At length it was agreed that the eldest member from each county, of the Council, a body answering in some measure to our present State Senates, should meet together once a year and ascertain and declare the depreciation. But the measure afforded no real relief. The counselors appointed to estimate the depreciation seldom had the firmness to make the full allowance as there was a popular outcry against every addition made to the fixed discount. No effectual steps were taken for the redemption and withdrawal of either the new issue or any of its predecessor's, save those made by the private companies. Things went from bad to worse. The confusion of the currency was such as seriously to cripple foreign and domestic trade. The depreciation increased and financial chaos seemed to be near at hand.

The authorities of Massachusetts seemed now to be possessed of a spirit near akin to desperation. For the operations which resulted in the capture of Louisberg and conquest of Cape Breton in 1745, and for the several attempts at the reduction of the other French Colonies made in 1746 and 1747, this province issued new bills of credit to the nominal value of more than £2,000,000. These were paid out by the treasury at an average discount of eleven or twelve of paper for one of specie. It becoming apparent that either redemption or repudiation must be faced in the near future, the General Court was, though with difficulty, persuaded to levy taxes sufficient to retire a considerable portion of the redundant paper. In 1747, on the application of the agent of the province, the English Government granted Massachusetts an allowance of £180,000 for the partial reimbursement of the expenses of the conquest of Cape Breton. This sum would become available, in specie, in 1749. Thomas Hutchinson, the historian, who was then speaker of the House of Representatives, who also was warmly supported by Governor Shirly, perceived in this a favorable opportunity for abolishing the bills-of-credit system and substitute a stable currency of silver and gold for the future. About £2,200,000 in bills would be outstanding in the year 1749. At eleven for one—although the current rate was twelve for one—£180,000 sterling would redeem £1,980,000, which would leave but £220,000 outstanding. It was therefore proposed that the sum thus granted by Parliament should be shipped to the province in Spanish milled dollars, and applied to the redemption of the bills, so far as it would serve, and that the remainder of the bills should be drawn in by a tax for the year 1749. This would dispose

JACOB FURTH.
President Puget Sound National Bank and Peoples Savings Bank,
Seattle, Washington.

of the bills. For the future, silver of sterling fineness at 6s. 8d. the ounce if paid in bullion, or in milled dollars at 6s. each, should be the lawful money of the colony, and no person within the province should receive or pay bills of credit of any of the other English Colonies. When it became known that a bill for an act on these lines had been introduced in the Provincial House of Representatives, a great clamor was raised against it. It was said that the greater part of the people were no sufferers from a depreciating currency, as the number of debtors was always greater than that of creditors. Even those who were for a stable currency were divided. Some argued that the paper might be so reduced volume as to be fixed and stable in value, and therefore were for redeeming only so many bills as should be agreed to be superfluous. Others, including many of good standing and good sense, were for finishing the bills, but in a gradual way, otherwise, they said, a fatal shock would be given to business. The bills, it was said, had sunk gradually to one-twelfth their original value, and as by this means creditors had been defrauded, it was but reasonable that they should rise gradually that justice might be done. To this it was answered that the creditors and the debtors would not be the same, so, that instead of righting one wrong, another injustice would be done; the injury being the same when one is obliged to pay more, as when he is forced to receive less, than is justly due. Others were for exchanging the bills for silver at a higher rate, the Boston representatives favoring a ratio of about five to one, which would have given an exorbitant profit upon that redeemed, and would have left more than half the volume outstanding. These were the objections urged by the most reasonable and most intelligent. The strongest opposition came from the ignorant and the interested who strove to impress the people with the contradictory ideas, first, that no redemption should be made because if there were no other money than

J. H. McGRAW.
President of First National Bank, Seattle, Washington,
Governor of the State of Washington.

silver it would be engrossed and hoarded by the rich, and that the poor would get no share of so precious a commodity; and second, that if the bills were redeemed at all it should be at their nominal and not at their actual value. After debating the bill for many weeks the Assembly reached a vote upon the proposition as a whole, and, after once rejecting the bill, finally passed it. After this favorable action the measure speedily received the sanction of the other branches of the General Court and became a law early in 1750.

The indemnity money having arrived in specie, the paper, amid much public gloom and doubt, was redeemed at a rate about one-fifth less than the current value; and for the next quarter of a century Massachusetts enjoyed the blessing of a sound currency. Resolved to drive the other New England colonies into the same measure she, in the redemption legislation of 1750, prohibited the circulation of their paper within her limits. Connecticut called in and retired her bills of credit, but Rhode Island, the most persistently given to inflation of any of the old colonies, refused to follow the lead of her more conservative neighbors. Forgetting former constitutional scruples as to the extent of parliamentary right to interfere with the domestic affairs of the colonies, Massachusetts, in 1751, applied for, and obtained an Act of Parliament prohibiting the New England Assemblies, except in case of war or invasion, to issue any bills of credit, for the redemption of which, within the year, provision was not made at the time of issue, and expressly forbidding that any such bills should, in any case, be made a legal tender.

The experience of the other colonies issuing paper money, was, on the whole, very like that of Massachusetts and South Carolina. In some of them matters came to a worse pass, in others the trouble never reached so grave a stage. The expansion and depreciation and attendant disorder were greatest in Rhode Island and least in Pennsylvania. We have already noted the circumstances under which Rhode Island, in 1707, first issued bills of credit. In 1715 this colony authorized its first "bank," on the plan of South Carolina and Massachusetts, for £30,000 to be loaned out for ten years. In 1728 the time for payment was extended to thirteen years, and then ten years more were allowed, without interest beyond the were issued for current public expenditures which should have been me first thirteen years. In 1721 a second bank of £40,000, was issued and loaned out for five years, which term in 1728 was also extended to thirteen years, and, at the same time the interest made payable in hemp or flax. In 1733 a new bank of £100,000 was struck off and loaned out. Bills of credit by taxation, and loan banks were authorized on any and every pretext. Those who took loans after the expiration of a portion of the period for which each bank was lent out, complained that they were compelled to pay back within a time shorter than that for which those who borrowed when the bank or loan was new were allowed to enjoy the use of the money. These and other applicants for loans clamored for new banks on the ground of "justice" and "equalty." All who had received loans were heartily in favor of new banks as the currency depreciated with each issue and they were thus the more easily able to pay back. But repayment of these loans was the exception rather than the rule. Titles to mortgaged estates were found to be in such confusion that little could be made from them. The legislature was composed too largely of men who were themselves borrowers to allow any effectual measures for collection to be taken. Foreclosures were rare and did not pay expenses of the proceedings. In 1750 the ninth loan bank was authorized to pay a bounty on manufactures of wool and on the cod and whale fisheries. The several issues were then at various stages of depreciation, "old tenor" standing at about eight or nine of paper for one of specie. The Act of Parliament of 1751, forbidding further issues of paper save under the restrictions noted in the account given above, of affairs in Massachusetts, stopped further issues for a time. But the quantity of paper in circulation was so large that the shrinkage continued, and when, in 1763, the courts fixed a scale of depreciation for the settlement of old debts, it put the Spanish milled dollar, worth 4s. 6d. sterling, at £7 in notes, a ratio of about thirty of paper for one of specie. Although some pretense at redemption was made, Rhode Island managed her financial affairs wildly and recklessly to the end of the colonial period. Her policy throughout was so far the reverse of business like, honest or honorable that her relations with her sister colonies were least amicable of the thirteen, and her bills of credit were so debased as to be little better than a pest to herself and her neighbors.

Pennsylvania, as we have said, suffered least of all the colonies which adopted the loan-bank system. In the rare instances in which this colony issued bills of credit to meet demands on the treasury, the sums were insignificant and the bills so emitted were promptly redeemed. The loan banks were also small in proportion to the wealth and population of the province and were strictly managed. The first issue was made in 1722, of £15,000, to be loaned on the security of real estate mortgages or upon gold or silver plate deposited in the loan office. The loan was to run for eight years at five per cent, the interest and one-eighth the principal to be paid annually. Loan offices were established in each county. The smallest loan made was £10 10s. and the largest £100, unless bills lay in the office six months without borrowers, in which case £200 might be lent one person. The bills were a legal tender and the penalty for refusing to receive them was confiscation of the debt or forfeiture of the commodity. A proportionate penalty was imposed on any one who bargained or sold any article for a less sum if paid in specie than for paper. In 1723 £30,000 more in bills were issued to be lent upon the same terms. In 1730, when the time arrived for the redemption of these issues, an Act was passed increasing the amount to £75,000, and providing for reissues sufficient to keep that sum in constant circulation. This was consented to by the English proprietaries only on condition that they should receive an equivalent for any loss on their quit rents by the depreciation of this paper, and that their Governors should be strictly instructed to consent to no further issue on any terms. Benjamin Franklin wrote an essay, published in 1729, advocating this measure, in which, from a just and clear view of the utility and effects of banks of deposit, he deduces an argument in favor of the radically dissimilar loan bank then in vogue; overlooking the fundamental truth that the value of a paper promise to pay depends fully as much on the certainty and reasonable nearness of the time at which it is to be paid, as upon the sum named or the credit of the promisor. The quantity of paper issued being thus rigorously limited, the Pennsylvania bills kept their value so well that they were commonly used as bills of exchange between the other colonies. This prudent reserve, imitated in Maryland and enforced by royal instructions in New Jersey and New York, saved the paper currency of the middle colonies from that excessive depreciation by which New England and the Carolinas was impoverished and disgraced. But the average discount on the bills of even these provinces was from twenty to thirty-three per cent. There was not a single colony in which paper money stood at par.

Virginia appears to have issued no loan bank, nor is there any record of the use of bills of credit until 1755, and then for a comparatively moderate sum only. Maryland's first and only loan bank was issued in 1733. Connecticut first authorized the issue of paper to be loaned in the same year, and in 1751 followed the example of Massachusetts in retiring its paper. New York suffered but little from the loan-bank craze, but its government made repeated and scandalous issues of bills of credit for the payment of trumped-up and fictitious claims upon the treasury. New Jersey, in 1721, created a loan bank of £40,000 to be lent out in small sums. Another was authorized for £20,000, in 1728. These, with a few emissions of bills of credit to meet temporary deficiencies, and for the equipment of troops to take part in the wars with the French in Canada, seemed to have been the limit of the issues of paper in this province, and the common rate of depreciation was about two of bills for one of specie.

D. H. MOFFAT,
President First National Bank, Denver, Colorado.

CHAPTER VI.

THE REVOLUTIONARY PERIOD.

Banking, in any sense in which the word is now understood, had its birth in America during the revolutionary period lasting from 1775 to the adoption of the Federal Constitution in 1788. Yet the financial policy of the Confederation, while directed by the Continental Congress, as well as that of nearly every one of the thirteen states during the same time, was so far a repetition of the worst sins of the colonial period as to make legitimate private banking impossible for the greater part of this term and difficult or unprofitable for the remainder. Until the constitutional prohibition of bills of credit and of legal-tender paper came into force there was no room for the modern bank.

It was estimated that just before the war of the revolution broke out, the whole "circulating cash" of the thirteen colonies was equal in value to about $12,000,000, or perhaps not more than $10,000,000, in hard money, and that the proportion of paper included in this total was from one-half to three-fifths of the whole. So the total of specie may have been anywhere from $4,000,000 to $6,000,000. Great as was the nominal expense of that war it is altogether probable that this sum in specie, together with what would have come from abroad, or even with what actually did flow in from French and Dutch loans and from sums paid out in the country for the support of the British and French armies, would have been ample for every occasion. The people of the thirteen colonies were then, in proportion to their numbers more opulent than those of France, and, had they possessed the inclination and the means of organizing their resources, easily could have paid the price of their independence without resorting to a disastrous and demoralizing issue of paper.

JOSHUA S. RAYNOLDS,
President First National Bank, El Paso.
President First National Bank, Albuquerque, New Mexico.

The most pressing necessity which confronted the second Continental Congress when it convened May 10, 1775, was that of providing money to carry on the war, which, with the battle of Lexington, fought the month before, was now flagrant. Having no authority to levy taxes directly, and unwilling to await the slow process of a call upon the states for money, on June 23, in conformity with the suggestion of the New York Provincial Congress, it was voted to issue $2,000,000 in continental bills of credit. The new paper did not get into circulation until the next August. Other issues followed rapidly. For about one year, and until the paper in circulation exceeded $9,000,000, the bills were freely received at their nominal value, no distinction being made in ordinary transactions between continental money and gold. The liability for the bills was distributed among the colonies, subject to future revision in the ratio of the supposed "number of their inhabitants, of all ages, including negroes and mulattoes;" and were to be redeemed in four annual installments, to commence at the end of four years. With successive issues the time for the commencement of redemption was extended, first to eight years and finally to eighteen years for the latest issues. In February, 1776, the first issue of continental notes of less denomination than one dollar was authorized. In 1777, when continental bills had sunk to one-half their nominal value, Congress denounced every person who would not receive them at par as a public enemy, liable to forfeit whatever he offered for sale; and requested the States to declare the notes a lawful tender. Massachusetts had already made them legal tender and this example was at once followed throughout the Union. The several States were at the same time invited to cancel their respective quotas of continental bills. They all had irredeemable currencies of their own, and, as they possessed nearly all the real powers of government, under the Confederation, their bills were less insecure than the continental currency. Congress, therefore, urgently needed the exclusive right to issue paper money, if by bills of credit the war was to be prosecuted, and to that end recommended the States to call in their bills and to issue no more. This request was often renewed but never heeded; so the notes of each one of the thirteen states continued to compete for circulation with those of the Continental Congress. The value of the continental currency was further impaired in 1776 by the ignoble stratagem of the British Government, under whose authority Lord Dunmore and others put into circulation in Virginia and other States a large number of counterfeit bills manufactured for that purpose in England. In 1779 this counterfeit money had become so largely circulated by the agents making purchases for the British army, who were regularly supplied with it, that Congress was compelled to recall, for other paper, two entire emissions of $5,000,000 each. The excessive issue was, however, the principal and all-sufficient occasion of its depreciation. As we have seen about $9,000,000 of it circulated at par with gold. No very marked sign of depreciation appeared until $20,000,000 had been issued, or until about January, 1777. The ratio of depreciation was then one and one-fourth of paper for one of specie. Before the end of that year it became four for one. At the end of 1778 it reached ten for one. When, in September, 1779, the ratio had fallen to twenty for one, Congress determined that the total issue should not exceed $200,000,000, renewed the declaration that this currency should be redeemed in full, and went into a lengthy argument to prove that the States had the ability to do so, but did not stick to its resolution to restrict the issue. In March, 1780, these issues had so depreciated that their value as compared with specie was as forty to one. Congress now required the whole to be brought in for redemption at its market value in coin, and authorized the emission of new notes bearing interest at five per cent, and payable in six years from date in silver and gold. These were to be exchanged in proportion of one dollar of the new for twenty of the old. During 1780 the bills sank to one hundred for one. By May 31, 1781, they had fallen to five hundred for one, or two-tenths of a cent on the dollar, after which they ceased to circulate as money. They continued to be bought on speculation at ratios varying from four hundred for one to one thousand for one of specie. Massachusetts, Rhode Island and New Hampshire redeemed their quotas of continental currency by receiving it for taxes at the rate of forty for one. Connecticut, Delaware, the Carolinas and Georgia took up none. The other states redeemed parts of the quotas assigned to them at the same rate as Massachusetts. The estimates of the total issues of continental currency vary astonishingly, as authorities of seemingly equal credit reach amounts as widely apart as $200,000,000 and $350,000,000. The last figure seems to be nearest the truth, although it is probable that no more than $200,000,000 of it was in circulation at any one time.

Besides the continental paper issued by Congress, all of the States put out bills of their own. In some States, as Massachusetts and Pennsylvannia, these bills were ultimately called in and funded at their nominal value. In others, especially at the South, they were partially redeemed by the issue of land warrants. The remainder shared the fate of the continental currency, being either repudiated outright or funded at an immense depreciation. No State made such profuse issues as Virginia, and such of her bills as were not paid in for land warrants—and enough of these bills could be bought for five dollars in specie to purchase a warrant for seven hundred acres of land—were finally funded at the rate of one thousand for one. The total issue of these State bills of credit from 1774 to 1783 was upward of $210,000,000. The benefits which the Continental and State governments derived from all these issues were in no way commensurate with the burdens which they entailed upon the people. According to the estimate of Mr. Woodbury, secretary of the treasury from 1834 to 1841, the depreciation and subsequent repudiation of the continental currency entailed upon the country an aggregate loss of $196,000,000, most of which fell upon the friends of the revolutionary cause, as the Tories either declined to receive that paper or parted with it as soon as possible. Pelatiah Webster, writing in 1780, declared that the country suffered more from this depreciated currrncy than from every other cause of calamity; that it killed more men, did more to corrupt our choisest interests, and worked greater injustice than all the armies and artifices of our enemies.

"Shay's Rebellion" which broke out in New England in 1785 and 1786 was an insurection of debtors who were suffering from the collapse of the currency and return to specie values. They were clamorous for paper money. Although no concessions were made to the rioters in that particular, Massachusetts did pass a law delaying the collection of debts. In Rhode Island this movement was not riotus, but took the form of a new political party. The payer-money party carried the elections in 1786, and then began a new period of this mania. Bills amounting to £100,000 (there was yet no federal monetary system or coinage) were issued, by the vote of the rural towns against the cities, and loaned on mortgage of land for fourteen years. They were made a legal tender and depreciated at once. Merchants refused to receive them and closed their shops. The farmer retaliated by refusing to bring food into the cities, and a ridiculous struggle followed which brought business to a stand-still. The paper-money party met and petitioned the authorities to enforce the penal laws against those refusing to receive the bills. By these laws cases involving a legal tender took precedence of all others and must be tried within three days after complaint made, without a jury, and without a right of appeal. The fine for a first offence was from £6 to £30, and greater for a second. In a case brought against a butcher for refusing bank paper, five judges agreed the act was unconstitutional. A special session of the Assembly was called and the judges were summoned to assign the reasons and grounds of their decision, and subsequently, four of them were removed. A law was proposed which disfranchised any one who refused to receive the paper on an equality with specie, but this failed to receive the sanction of the towns. Land rents were paid in produce. The State debt, incurred during the revolution, was paid off in the depreciated currency. The question of the ratification of the new federal constitution coming up at this time, the paper-money party was strong enough to procure its rejection and keep Rhode Island out of the Union for three years. When, in 1787, numerous suits were brought in the courts for the redemption of estates from mortgages, "the suitors came prepared with paper money in handkerchiefs and pillow cases to redeem their lands." The money continued to depreciate until 1789, when the legal tender laws were suspended and the depreciation fixed by law at eighteen for one. The people of Rhode Island were, at that time, thoroughly imbued with the belief that money is something which derives its value from the authority of government. They gave to fiat paper money all the countenance and support which public opinion, public favor and the most stringent laws in its aid could afford. The result was wide-spread pecuniary disaster and financial

JEFFERSON RAYNOLDS,
President of First National Bank, Las Vegas, New Mexico.

and moral disgrace to the people, while the State came dangerously near to extinction through partition and annexation to Massachusetts and Connecticut.

In May, 1780, Robert Morris, George Clymer and other leading citizens of Philadelphia associated themselves under the name of the Bank of Pennsylvania, and having subscribed a small capital in hard money, commenced the issue, as a joint-stock bank, of promissory notes, which were employed without profit to themselves in the purchase of supplies for the army. Congress deposited with the bank a considerable sum in bills of exchange drawn upon John Jay, then negotiating a loan in Spain, as a support to their credit and indemnity in case of loss. This bank was of very considerable service in procuring and forwarding supplies. It continued in existence until after the end of the war, finally closing its affairs towards the end of the year 1784.

JOHN W. ZOLLARS.
President Sierra County Bank, Hillsborough, New Mexico.
Vice-President First National Bank, Las Vegas, New Mexico.

On May 17, 1781, a plan for a national bank was submitted to Congress by Robert Morris, the principal provisions of which were as follows: The capital was to be $400,000 in shares of $400 each; each share to have one vote for directors; the directors to be twelve in number, chosen from the stockholders, who at their first meeting were to choose a president from themselves; the directors to meet quarterly; the board to be empowered from time to time to open new subscriptions for the increase of the capital stock; regular statements of its condition to be made to the continental superintendent of finance, and it to be at all times subject to his examination; the notes of the bank to be payable on demand over its counter and to be made by law receivable for taxes and duties in every State, and from the several States by the treasury of the United States. On May 26 Congress adopted a resolution approving this plan, promising to promote and support the same by such ways and means, from time to time, as should appear necessary for the institution and consistent with the public good; and providing "that the subscribers to said bank shall be incorporated agreeably to the principles and terms of the plan, under the name of 'The President, Directors and Company of the Bank of North America,' so soon as the subscription shall be filled, the directors and president chosen, and application for that purpose made to Congress by the president and directors elected." On December 31, following, Congress passed "an ordinance to incorporate the subscribers to the Bank of North America." The first president was Thomas Willing. The bank opened for business at Philadelphia on January 7, 1782. Its success was immediate and complete. Its issues which at first circulated in the eastern States only, at a discount of ten to fifteen per cent, speedily rose to par and were sustained at that point without further difficulty. It was of great and timely service to both the Federal and State Governments. Of its original capital of $400,000 which it might increase to $10,000,000, the Federal Government subscribed $254,000. In April, 1782, Pennsylvania granted its first State charter, an example followed by several other States. In 1783 and 1784 it declared dividends averaging fourteen per cent. In this last year the directors were warmly urged to increase the capital stock in order to allow new subscribers to share in the business, and on their refusal an application was made to the Legislature of that State to charter a rival concern to be called the Bank of Pennsylvania. The Assembly was "plagued with long arguments on both sides" and endless evils were prophesied in case two banks attempted to do business in opposition to each other. But "all at once the thing was hushed up and accommodated." The directors consented to increase the capital to $2,000,000 and to allow the projectors of the new enterprise to become stockholders in the old. In 1785 a new party arose in Pennsylvania which demanded the issue of more paper money by the State on the plan of the colonial land-loan schemes. The credit of that State being manifestly too bad to float such a currency, it was demanded of the bank that it should give its credit to the proposed issue. As the directors were both unable and unwilling to do this, and as it had prudently limited its own issues of notes, the bank was regarded as the opponent of the paper-money scheme, the friends of which were powerful enough to obtain by way of revenge, a repeal of its Pennsylvania charter in September, 1785. Although this action did in some measure shake the confidence of the public in the bank, the stock of which fell to a discount of five per cent, it continued to do business under its continental charter and charters granted it by other States. It was even proposed to remove the bank to Wilmington or to New Castle, in Delaware, by which State one of its charters was granted. In 1787, after several efforts to procure from Pennsylvania a renewal of its charter, the Legislature of that State granted a new one, though quite unlike the first. In 1789, when the present Federal Government went into operation, its charter from the congress of the confederation was held to have lapsed, and, though the bank was invited to take a national charter, it preferred to remain a State institution under the laws of Pennsylvania. Passing through many vicissitudes, it was rechartered from time to time by that State until, on March 3, 1864, it was converted into a national bank. It is still doing business under the national banking system, with a capital of $1,000,000 and a surplus in excess of its capital.

The success of the Bank of North America induced the organization of the Bank of Massachusetts, in Boston. This bank received its charter from the State of Massachusetts on February 7, 1784. Its original capital was $300,000, and the charter "allowed three dollars of currency for one dollar of metallic deposit." The restrictions placed upon its officers did not permit the lending of more than "$3,000 to any individual at one time, and but $5,000 in the aggregate to any one borrower." Loans could be granted for no more than sixty days upon the pledge of merchandise, bullion, or other securities as collateral, and for thirty days only on personal obligations with two sufficient sureties, "without the privilege of renewal on any terms." It continued as a State bank until 1864, when it reorganized under the national banking law, and is now doing business as the Massachusetts National Bank of Boston, with a capital of $800,000.

The merchants of New York were but a few days behind those of Boston in following the lead of their competitors in Philadelphia. The success of the Bank of North America stirred up the speculative element in New York, and, on February 12, 1784, a proposal was advertised in the *Packet* newspaper for the establishment of an institution to be called the Bank of the State of New York, with a capital of $750,000, in shares of $1,000 each. The management was to be in the hands of a governor and six directors, who were to serve without pay until the first dividend was declared. Two of the directors and the governor were to attend constantly at the bank, and no money was to be paid out without their consent. The subscribers were to pay one-third their subscriptions in "cash," and for the other two-thirds "landed security" was to be given by mortgage or deed of trust. No lands outside New York and New Jersey were to be accepted, and all lands were to be appraised at not more than two-thirds their value. The directors could borrow "to the extent of one-third of the value of the lands" in case they found it necessary to increase the cash resources of the bank, but no further. The folly and danger of this scheme, which was nothing but the old land bank with little more than a semblance of disguise, was quickly perceived; but it served to hasten the action of those who desired a really sound banking institution in that city.

After several meetings had been held, a number of leading business men, on February 26, 1784, agreed upon a plan for creating a bank, to be called the Bank of New York, under which an organization was speedily effected. This provided for a capital stock of $500,000 in silver or gold, to be divided into one thousand shares of $500 each; that as soon as five hundred shares should be subscribed a meeting of the subscribers should be held to elect a president and twelve directors; that at all meetings of subscribers or share-holders every subscriber or stockholder should have one vote for each share of stock held by him to the number of four; the holder of six shares to have five votes, for eight shares six votes, and for ten shares seven votes; but no stockholder should have more than seven votes, be the number of his shares ever so great. This last provision was afterward amended to allow one vote for every five shares in excess of ten. A dividend was to be made at the end of the first year, and semi-annually thereafter. To encourage trade, the proprietors of the bank fixed the rate of discount at six per cent. Sufficient stock having been subscribed, officers were elected March 15, 1784. Alexander Hamilton was among those chosen on the first board of directors; and the "constitution" under which it commenced operations was written by him. As none of the newly-selected officers, nor any other trustworthy person in New York, was familiar with the methods of banking business, the cashier, Mr. Seaton, was dispatched to Philadelphia with a letter of introduction from Hamilton, to procure the desired information from the Bank of North America and to purchase such material as could not be had in New York. On May 22 "the president and directors qualified before His Worship the Mayor as required by the the constitution" of the bank. On June 7, the subscriptions having been paid in, and some deposits having been made, notice was given that the bank would formally commence business on Wednesday, June 9, 1784; and that applications for discounts would be received on the succeeding Wednesday. The following rules, to be observed in transacting business with the bank, were also published.

L. H. HERSHFIELD.
President of Merchants National Bank, Helena, Montana.

"The bank will be open every day in the year except Sundays, Christmas-day, New-year's-day, Good Friday, the Fourth of July, and general holidays appointed by legal authority.

"The hours of business will be from ten to one o'clock in the forenoon, and from three to five o'clock in the afternoon.

"Discounts will be done on Thursday in every week, and bills and notes brought for discount must be left at the bank on Wednesday morning, under a seal cover, directed to William Seaton, Cashier. The rate of discount is at present fixed at six per cent per annum; but no discounts will be made for longer than thirty days, nor will any note or bill be discounted to pay a former one. Payments must be made in bank notes or specie. Three days of grace being allowed upon all bills, the discount will be taken for the same.

"Money lodged at the bank may be redrawn at pleasure, free of expense, but no draft will be paid beyond the balance of the account.

" Bills or notes left with the bank will be presented for acceptance, and the money collected free of expense; in case of non-payment and protest, the charge of protest must be borne by the party lodging the bill.

" Payments made at the bank must be examined at the time, as no deficiency suggested afterward will be admitted.

" Gold coin is received and paid at the Bank of New York at the following rates:

A Johannes	Weigh'g 18 dwt.			$16.00
A half Johannes	"	9 "		8.00
A Spanish doubloon	"	17 "		15.00
A double Spanish Pistole	"	8 "	12 gr.	7.48
A Spanish Pistole	"	4 "	6 "	3.72
A British Guinea	"	5 "	6 "	4.64
A British half Guinea	"	2 "	15 "	2.32
A French Guinea	"	5 "	4 "	4.52
A Moidore	"	6 "	18 "	6.00
A Caroline	"	6 "	8 "	4.72
A Chequin	"	2 "	4 "	1.78

" An allowance is made on all gold exceeding the above standard at the rate of three pence per grain; on all gold short of the above weight four pence per grain is deducted.

" By Order of the Board of Directors.

" ALEX. McDOUGALL, Pres't."

GEORGE F. COPE.
Cashier First National Bank, Helena, Montana.

Both the Johannes and the Moidore were gold coins of Portugal; the Johannes being so called from the figure of King John which it bore. The Caroline was a German coin, and the Pistole was of the same value as the Louis d'or. The Chequin, also written zecchin, zechin, and sequin, was a gold coin deriving its name from La Zeche, that quarter in the city of Venice where the mint was situated. The clipping and the sweating of the gold coin in cirlation had long been practiced in the colonies. In 1770 the New York Chamber of

Commerce stigmatized it as "an evil and scandalous practice," and passed a resolution to take no light coin except at a discount of four pence for each grain it fell short of just weight. The bank experienced much trouble from this source. The practice was to weigh it in quantities on receiving and paying out gold, a course attended with many difficulties where the variety of coins were so numerous, but for which, in the absence of a national coinage, it was not easy to find a substitute. The paper currency of Pennsylvania and New Jersey, which circulated largely in New York, was a cause of endless trouble and vexation to the bank and to its customers.

Application had been made to the Legislature of New York for a charter incorporating the bank before it began business; but this was delayed and operations were begun without it. As in Pennsylvania, a paper-money party existed in New York which persistently opposed the efforts of the bank to obtain a charter. The direst evils were predicted from the establishment of the bank, and it was maintained that the only remedy for existing and threatened evils was to be found in an emission of legal-tender paper by the State. The directors were popularly charged with working in the interest of British capitalists and traders, and with refusing discounts a few days before the sailing of the European packet that they, personally, might profit by the distress thus occasioned. The bank, it was contended, had destroyed private credit as well as that confidence, forbearance and compassion formerly shown by creditors to their debtors. The enforcing the payment of notes at maturity by lodging them at the bank was especially disliked.

A strong pressure was now brought upon the Legislature in favor of an emission by the State of paper money, to be made a legal tender. The merchants of New York, as a body, opposed the scheme, and the Chamber of Commerce forwarded a memorial remonstrating against the passage of any bill to that effect, and setting forth the evils which would result from such an issue. But outside the city there was a general belief that financial relief and permanent prosperity would only come with an abundance of paper money. The experience of the past had not deterred people from this conviction, and several of the States had recently issued bills of credit. The Legislature passed a bill in 1786, authorizing the emission of $200,000, to be loaned out at five per cent, "for the purpose of increasing the currency," and to be a legal tender of all dues, public and private. This was the last issue of bills of credit by New York. In June, 1787, the paper money issued by the State having then obtained a considerable circulation and being largely depreciated, the Bank of New York decided to open accounts and make discounts and payments in this currency, distinct from those in specie or the bills of the bank. This was continued for several years, discounts in paper being done on Tuesdays and in specie on Thursdays. The 1791 the bank obtained its first charter from the State, and on May 2, of that year the directors named in the Act of the incorporation formally accepted the charter, assumed all the existing liabilities of the former company, and re-elected the former officers. Its paid-up capital was then $318,250, with deposits amounting to $773,-709, and discounts $845,940. The circulating notes outstanding were $181,254. The business flourished and semi-annual dividends were regularly declared; that for the first half year under the charter being seven per cent. During the same six months, May to November 1791, the discounts were $10,558,669, and the total cash received was $42,661,664. These figures will illustrate the extent of mercantile transactions in the City of New York at that time.

The Bank of New York enjoyed a substantial monopoly of the banking business in that city for fifteen years. From 1784 to 1799 it had no competitor nor rival, save the branch of the Bank of the United States which during this time did but little business. It had obtained its charter with great difficulty and those interested in its prosperity could scarcely be expected to look with complacency on any attempt to establish an institution to compete with it. "Neither," says its historian, "did the public desire any additional banking facilities." Had any open attempt been made to obtain a State charter for a rival concern, the older bank undoubtedly would have opposed it to the bitter end. But suddenly and without premonition a formidable corporation made its appearance as a bank of deposit, discount and issue in New York. This was the result of the craft and sagacity of Aaron Burr. In the spring of 1799 a petition was presented to the Legislature asking for a charter for a company with a capital of $2,000,000 for the purpose of introducing a supply of pure water into the City of New York. The prevalence of yellow fever during the summer before had been largely ascribed to the use of contaminated water, and had created an alarm which made the passage of any bill to improve the sanitary condition of that city an easy matter. Toward the end of the session the bill incorporating the Manhattan Company was accordingly passed by the Legislature, without a suspicion on the part of the great majority of those who voted for it that it contained a grant of banking privileges or indeed anything else but a franchise for the distribution of pure water. But the real purpose of the scheme was soon made manifest. While the bill had been on passage throug the committee stage it had been suggested that the whole of the new corporation's $2,000,000 capital might not be needed at once in constructing waterworks, and a clause was added providing that the surplus capital might be "employed in the purchase of public or other stocks, or in any other moneyed transactions or operations not inconsistent with the laws and constitution of the State of New York." No sooner had the bill become a law and the stock fully subscribed, than the persons interested proceeded to carry out their plans by giving notice that the new corporation would begin banking operations in September with a capital of $500,000. The discovery that so broad a franchise had been so incautiously granted occasioned no little excitement and indignation. It was charged that the Legislature had been cheated and tricked in order to allow Burr and his friends to obtain control of a majority of stock of the company and power to use its capital for their own purposes. But it was too late. The Manhattan Company continues to this day to be the leading state bank of New York, as distinguished from the national banks, and, under the same broad clause of its charter has organized life and fire insurance companies and conducted a great variety of other enterprises.

On July 6, 1865, the Bank of New York re-organized under the national banking act, taking the title of "The Bank of New York National Banking Association," which it still retains, with a capital of $2,000,000. During the first hundred years of its existence it paid to its stockholders dividends amounting, in the aggregate, to 910½ per cent, and never passed a dividend except in 1837 when it was compelled by law to do so.

CHAPTER VII.

THE FIRST AND SECOND BANKS OF THE UNITED STATES.

On the organization of the government of the United States under present Constitution, Alexander Hamilton, Secretary of the Treasury, in his masterly report on the finances of the country, made to Congress December 13, 1790, recommended the establisment of a bank of the United States and opposed the issue of paper money by the Government. At that time there were in existence in the country only the three banks —the Bank of North America, the Bank of Massachusetts and the Bank of New York, with an aggregate capital of $2,000,000 —of whose organization sketches have been given. There was no provision for the reception and paying out of the bills of these banks bp the Government and the supply of gold and silver was meagre. The Government daily suffered for the want of small sums in ready money. So long as specie only could be used, and there was no national bank, the delay and expense incurred in transferring money from place to place were burdensome and vexatious. Therefore, it was argued, a national bank was imperatively required, which would only serve these purposes but many others as well, by making temporary loans to the Government. The bill for the bank was debated chiefly on two grounds—its constitutionality and its expediency. It passed the Senate with little opposition but was

M. D. THATCHER.
President First National Bank, Pueblo, Colorado.
First National Bank, Trinidad, Colorado.
First National Bank, Silverton, Colorado.

vigorously resisted in the House of Representatives. On February 8, 1791, the House passed it by a vote of thirty-nine to twenty. Before signing it President Washington required each of its cabinet officers to submit a written opinion on its constitutionality. The cabinet was equally equally divided. Hamilton, Secretary of the Treasury, and Gen. Knox, Secretary of War, affirming its constituality, and Jefferson, Secretary of State, and Edmund Randolph, Attorney General, denied it. But the bill became a law by the President's approval, on February 25, 1791, and the bank at once went into operation. The capital was fixed at $10,000,000, divided into 25,000 shares of $400 each; one-fifth of which might be subscribed by the United States, but no other subscriber might take more than 1,000 shares. The subscriptions, except that of the United States, were to be payable one-fourth in specie and three-fourths in certain six per cent stocks of the United States or in other three per cent stocks at half their nominal value. The institution was incorporated under the style of "The President, Directors and Company of the Bank of the United States," to continue twenty years, expiring March 4, 1811. The bank was authorized to hold property of all kinds, not exceeding, exclusive of its capital, $15,000,000. Twenty-five directors were to be elected, by a plurality of votes, on the first Monday of January in every year, for one year only, who were to choose a president from their own number. It also provided "That no other bank shall be established by any future law of the United States during the continuance of the corporation hereby created, for which the faith of the United States is hereby pledged." The bank was authorized to established offices of discount and deposit in the several States, and to issue notes which were to be received in payments of all dues to the Government. It was authorized to sell the Government stocks received for subscriptions, but was forbidden to become the pur-

H. M. JORALMON,
Joralmon & Co.
Bankers, Financial Agents and Attorneys, Denver, Colorado.

cha-er at such sales. Of the capital, $6,700,000 was reserved for the chief bank, which was established at Philadelphia, and the residue of $4,300,000 was to be divided among the eight branches to be established in the principal cities of the Union. The entire capital was subscribed and applications made for 4,000 shares in excess of the whole stock, within two hours from the time the books for subscription were opened. The enterprise was immediately successful. The dividends averaged eight to ten per cent per annum, being much below those of the Bank of North America in previous years; which, in the words of a distinguished writer, "now gradually declined as other banks sprang into existence." The payment of the Government shares was to be in ten annual installements, but the treasury department found it very difficult to comply with this requirement as to the entire payments, the urgent demand for money to meet other pressing occasions being continious for several years. Neither bank nor Government had been long in operation when the need arose for a temporary loan from the bank. Congress authorized the treasury to procure loans to pay the appropriations of the year, and to pledge the duties on imports and the tonnage tax for their repayment. The revenue came in so slowly that its anticipaton in this manner could not be avoided if Government expenditures were to be paid as they became due. This policy was condemned by Albert Gallatin, but was generally defended on the ground that it was a well-known practice with older governments, and that there was no other way of getting the money imperatively required.

These loans obtained from time to time, were of three kinds: First, those made in anticipation of taxes to meet current expenditures; the last of which was made in 1795. Second, the sinking commissionners were authorized to borrow money, not exceeding $1,000,000 annually, in anticipation of the revenues, to pay interest. Each loan of this kind was to be reimbursed within one year after it was made. Third, loans were also founded on a pledge of the revenue to meet the exigencies of a specific case rather than for a general purpose. The first loan of this kind was to cover the expense of an Indian war. Of other subsequent loans, one was to provide money to ramson American sailors held in slavery by the Algerines. One still later was to equip and maintain the ships which carried on the war which the United States, first of all civilized powers, waged against the Barbary States for the protection of its commerce and citizens rather than pay tribute.

Between the years 1796 and 1802 the United States disposed of its stock in the bank at a net profit of $1,137,152.29, equal to fifty-seven per cent on the original investment. In August, 1791, we are told, United States Bank scrip sold for 195, in consequence of the mania for speculation. In September of the same year, it fell to 110, but rallied, almost at once, to 145. The last sales of its stock on Government account, in 1802, were made at 145. It was a successful and prosperous enterprise from first to last.

But, unfortunately for the bank, during the entire term of its existence it was looked upon and dealt with by a large majority of business men, and by men in public life with scarcely an exception, as a political rather than a business undertaking. Its projector, Hamilton, in 1791 urged its creation "as a powerful political engine." Political opposition continued from the beginning to the end of its career. When Jefferson became

President he desired Albert Gallatin, then Secretary of the Treasury, to make a judicious distribution of his favors among all the banks, since the Stock of the United States Bank was held largely by foreigners, and, "were the Bank of the United States to swallow up all the others, and monopolize the whole banking business of the United States—which the demands we furnish them will tend shortly to favor—we might, on a misunderstanding with a foreign power, be immensely embarrassed by any disaffection in the bank." When the territory of Louisiana was purchased in 1803, Gallatin was desirous of establishing a branch bank at New Orleans. He considered the step of the highest importance. But the President vehemently opposed every extension of the bank. He wrote to Gallatin: "This institution is one of the most deadly hostility existing against the principles and form of our Constitution. What an obstrution could not this Bank of the United States, with all its branch banks, be in time of war!" But Gallatin, being brought into more intimate relations with the bank, did not share the fears which Mr. Jefferson expressed, and the branch was established at New Orleans. While the bank existed the funds of the Government were deposited with it to the credit of the United States Treasury. They were considered in the Treasury from the time of depositing them, and were subject to the Treasurer's control. The Government ceased to be a stockholder in 1802, and only once applied for a loan after 1803. The revenues of the Government had grown more ample, its wants were not so pressing, and loans were unnecessary. With the great majority in Congress the bank was endured only as a convenience for obtaining such loans. Yet the other advantages derived by the Government from the bank were neither few nor unimportant. As stated by Gallatin in a communication to Congress recommanding a renewal of the charter, these advantages were, first, with respect to keeping the public money ; another concerned its transmission from point to point, both at home and abroad ; a third, and the greatest, related to the collection of the revenue. The punctuality of payments introduced by the banking system, and the facilities which it afforded importers indebted for revenue bonds, had enabled the Government to collect with greater facility and fewer losses the revenues from the imports than it could have done had no such bank existed. One chief complaint was that the bank and its branches, and particularly the branch in New York, were more inclined to grant loans to the members of one political party than to others. Whether this charge contained any truth or not the complaint ceased to be heard after the creation of the Manhattan Company in 1799.

The bank was required to make weekly reports to the Secretary of the Treasury, but the following, for Jannuary 24, 1811, is one of the only two balanced statements found on record:

RESOURCES.

Loans and discounts,	$14,578,294
United States six per cent stock,	2,750,000
Other United States indebtedness,	57,046
Due from other banks,	894,145
Real estate,	500,653
Notes of other banks on hand,	393,341
Specie,	5,009,567
Total,	$24,183,046

LIABILITIES.

Capital stock,	$10,000,000
Undivided surplus,	509,678
Circulating notes outstanding,	5,037,125
Individual deposits,	5,904,423
United States deposits,	1,929,999
Due to other banks,	634,348
Unpaid draft outstanding,	171,743
Total,	$24,183,046

In 1808 the bank petitioned for a renewal of its charter which would expire three years later. This application was favored by Gallatin, Secretary of the Treasery, and by Crawford and Pickering in the Senate, and opposed by Mr. Clay. The trouble with France and England then impending made war probable in the early future with one or both of these powers. The State banks expected to profit from the disturbances which would accompany open war and contributed largely to prevent any consideration of the bank's application until 1810, when a decision could no longer be delayed. The necessity of the bank was warmly urged by the Treasury department. The debate in both branch of Congress was long, able and bitter. The old question of its constitutionality was discussed at great length, and its opponents denied that the institutionn was at all necessary to aid the Government in discharging its functions, insisting that it was evident, from the rapid muliplying of State banks, that there was a redundancy of capital. It was asserted that in case the bank should not be rechartered that the quantity of specie in the country would

MEDFORD E. WILSON.
President Capital National National Bank, Indianapolis, Indiana.

be reduced by the exportation of the large amount of its capital which belonged to foreigners. The bill was defeated in the Senate by the casting vote of the Vice-President, George Clinton, on February 20, 1811, and subsequently failed in the House by a minority of one vote. The bank was now obliged to wind up its affairs, which was done with very little disturbance to the business interest of the country. Within eighteen months from March 4, 1811, the stockholders had received 88 per cent upon their stock. On finally closing its business, the assets yielded to the stockholders an excess of 8½ per cent above the par value of the stock. Before going into liquidation, the bank made an unsuccessful application to the Legislature of Pennsylvania for a charter for a State bank with a capital of $5,000,000.

JOHN K. OTTLEY.
Cashier American Trust and Banking Co., Atlanta, Georgia.

During the war of 1812-15 the National Government, which was embarrassed by the want of means, had received very considerable loans and other timely service from the State banks. Owing largely to such advances, the State banks, with the exception of those of New England, were, in August and September, 1814, driven to a suspension of specie payments. Toward the end of 1814 the finances of the Government were again in seemingly inextricable confusion. Alexander J. Dallas became Secretary of the Treasury on October 6, 1814, and, within a fortnight thereafter, made to Congress a report of extraordinary ability and lucidity upon the condition of affairs. In this communication he strongly recommended the re-establishment of a national bank, as the remedy required to bring the finances once more into order. The State banks again were opposed to its creation. With them were the speculators in exchange, whose influence was very considerable, and all whose interest were served by a continuation of the suspension of specie payments. Various plans were brought forward in Congress which resulted in nothing, until, on January 20, 1815, a bill was passed. This was vetoed by President Madison, not for lack of constitutionality, as he considered that point already settled by the courts, but on the ground that it would not accomplish the objects rendered necessary by the state of the revenue and the condition of the country. On April 3, 1816, however, a bill for a Bank of the United States, which had previously passed the House of Representatives, was adopted by the Senate, and, receiving the signature of the President, became a law on April 10, 1816.

The charter was limited to twenty years and the capital to $35,000,000, composed of 350,000 shares of $100 each, $7,000,000 was to be subscribed by the Government, payable in coin or in United States five per cent stocks at the option of the Government. Other subscriptions were payable one-fourth in coin and the remainder in coin or United States stocks. Five of its twenty-five directors were to be appointed by the President of the United States. The bank was to be made a public depository and was to aid the Government, free of charge therefor, in negotiating its loans. It was empowered to establish branches and to issue circulating notes which were to be receivable in all payments to the United States. No other bank, outside of the District of Columbia, was to be established by Congress during the continuance of this charter, and, in consideration of the grants therein, the bank was to pay to the United States $1,500,000 in three installments. It was authorized to organize and commence business as soon as $8,400,000, exclusive of the subscription of the United States, was paid in. It was prohibited from lending on the account of the United States more than $500,000, or to any State more than $50,000, or to any foreign prince or power any sum whatever, without the sanction of law being previously obtained. It went into operation January 7, 1817, and it was through its agency that the other banks throughout the country were enabled and induced to resume specie payments. At that time bank-notes at Washington and Baltimore were twenty-two per cent below par; at Philadelphia from seventeen to eighteen per cent; and at New York and Charleston they were from seven to ten per cent. In the interior the depreciation was much greater. This was nearly the worst stage of the monetary trouble resulting from the late war, and at the verge of that financial crisis which culminated in 1819-20. As soon as the bank opened the Secretary of the Treasury directed importers to lodge their bonds with it, the bank agreeing, greatly to the relief of the Treasury, to discount the notes given for duties, to secure which these bonds were deposited. Congress resolved on April 30, 1816, that all duties, taxes and debts payable to the United States after February 20, 1817, should be paid in the "legal currency" of the Government, or Treasury notes, or in notes of the Bank of the United States, or of other banks which paid their notes on demand "in the legal currency of the United States." The State banks agreed to resume specie payments in July, 1817, but neither Mr. Crawford, Secretary of the Treasury, nor the United States Bank, had much faith that they would fulfill their agreement. Both the Government and the bank were desirous of hastening the return of specie payments, and the latter began negotiation to that end. One consideration moving the bank to do so was that, if it succeeded, the obligation which it had incurred of discounting all the notes of importers would be very much diminished, for if the State banks paid in specie their notes would be readily taken by the Government. On the other hand, if the State banks refused to make any arrangement for resuming specie payment, a large amount of valuable paper for discount purposes would go immediately to the National bank, and the State banks would thus lose many of their best customers. As the result of this community of interests a plan was devised for resuming on February 20, 1817. On that day the balances due to the Government in the several banks, which ever since the closing of the first Bank of the United States had kept its deposits with the State banks, were to be transferred to the Bank of the United States, retained by it until July 1, when they were to be paid, with the interest thereon. In liquidating the balances which might be due, The United States Bank agreed to credit the banks respectively with the amount of their checks on all banks which were party to the agreement. The payment of the balances which might accumulate against the banks, subsequently to the transfer of the balances previously mentioned, from the payment to them of Government dues in return for money previously borrowed, was not to be demanded by the Bank of the United States until it and its branches had discounted for individuals, other than those having duties to pay, certain specified sums in the several principal cities of the country, provided the money should be called for within sixty days, by borrowers offering good securities. If the whole amount so to be loaned should not be taken by individual customers then the residue was to be lent to the banks signing the agreement. This plan for restoring specie payments was wholly successful. They were resumed and maintained while the charter of the bank continued in force.

When the bank began business eighteen branches were established in different States. The notes of the bank, whether issued by the parent bank or by any of the branches, where everywhere received in payment of duties and taxes, and were redeemable in specie at any office of the bank. Another very important function which it performed was in equalizing the rates of domestic exchange. Through its agency funds could be transmitted from one part of the Union to another at an expense not exceeding one-half, and frequently less than one-fourth that commonly charged by private dealers, not exposed to the competition of the bank.

From 1820 to 1835 the country was prosperous, the bank recovered from its embarrassments, and its stock rose steadily in value. Long before 1828 the bank had lived down all respectable opposition; and it was therefore a surprise to all parties when President Jackson, in his first message, in December, 1829, took ground against a renewal of its charter when it should expire in 1836. The agitation thus awakened grew in intensity, until it culminated on July 16, 1832, in the veto by President Jackson of a bill re-chartering the bank.

The interval of about six years between the commencement of Jackson's warfare upon the bank and the expiration of its charter is memorable for the violence and acrimony of the dispute between the administration and its supporters on one hand, and the bank and its friends on the other, both in and out of Congress. The famous order for the removal of the Government deposits was issued in 1833 by Mr. Taney, who was made Secretary of the Treasury for this purpose, his predecessor, Mr. Duane, having declined to issue such an order. When Congress re-assembled in December, 1833, resolutions were adopted in both Houses; those of the Senate censuring the President and Secretary of the Treasury for usurpation of powers, while in the House it was declared that the bank ought not to be re-chartered, that the public deposits ought not to be restored to it, that the State banks should be continued as depositories, and that Congress should further regulate the subject by law. Among the early results which followed the removal of the deposits was the expansion of their issues by the State depositories, and the wild and general inflation of the currency by the multitude of other banks, old and new. The aggregate of circulating notes, exclusive of those of the Bank of the United States, increased from $61,000,000, in 1830, to $149,000,000 in 1837. In 1830 the currency of the country had been characterized by the finance committee of the Senate as being more sound and uniform than that possessed by any other country; and yet within seven years after this all the banks then in operation, including the great Bank of the United States, which had been re-chartered by the State of Pennsylvania, went into suspension. The bank, when denied a renewal of its charter by Congress, did not close up its affairs, but applied for, and obtained, a charter from the State of Pennsylvania, February 18, 1836, thirteen days before the expiration of its charter from the National Government. This was substantially a renewal for thirty years of the old charter and under the old corporate name, but with a change as to the

C. H. SILLIMAN.
American Manager Land Mortgage Bank of Texas (Limited),
Fort Worth, Texas

amount and terms of the bonus to be paid the State for such charter. Colonel Benton, a sincere if not unprejudiced opponent of the Bank of the United States, characterized the Pennsylvania charter as indicating, by every circumstance of its enactment, corruption and bribery in the members who passed it, and an attempt to bribe the whole people of that State through the bonus to be distributed among them. This bonus, had the bank remained solvent and in existence long enough, would not have fallen short of $5,000,000.

The history of the bank subsequent to the crisis of 1837 was a disastrous one. It suspended payments as frequently as other State banks, and finally succumbed to difficulties which prudent management would have enabled it to overcome. It made three several assignments in 1841, to secure various liabilities, the last and final assignment being on September 4, 1841. The $7,000,000 of stock held by the United States previous to the time at which the institution became a State bank, was paid back in full, and the Government realized a very handsome profit upon its investment, as will appear from the following statement, taken from the report of the Comptroller of the Currency for 1876:

Bonus paid by the Bank of the United States,	$1,500,000.00
Dividends received from the bank, ...	7,118,416.29
Proceeds of Stock sold and moneys received from the bank, ...	9,424,750.78
Total, . .	$18,043,167.07

Subscription of capital stock paid in United States five per cent bonds, ...	$7,000,000.00	
Interest paid by United States on same, . .	4,950,000.00	
		11,950,000.00
Profit on Investment, . . .		$6,093,167.07

Nicholas Biddle was president of the bank from January, 1823, to March, 1839. At the time of his resignation the shares were selling at 111, having in 1837 sold at 137; but in 1843, after the failure of the bank, the shares were quoted at one and seven-eighths per cent. The circulating notes of the bank, together with the deposits, were paid in full, principal and interest; but the whole capital of $28,000,000 were lost to the share-holders.

CHAPTER VIII.

STATE BANKS UNTIL 1816.

We have seen that at the time of the establishment of the first United States Bank three State banks existed: The Bank of North America, the Bank of Massachusetts, and the Bank of New York. The course of business to the beginning of the present century is sufficiently indicated in the accounts given of these institutions. They served quite as much to steady the business of the country as to extend it. They inculcated a promptness of payment and regularity in conducting all business affairs, to which merchants had generally theretofore been strangers. As business expanded merchants gradually adopted the habit of selling their goods on credit, and, requiring Spanish milled dollars for shipment to India and China and doubloons for the purchase of West Indian produce for Europe, they became more dependent on the banks for accommodations and facilities, and the number of these institutions multiplied with the growth of trade. The bank obtained specie from various sources, but while war lasted between Spain and Great Britain our countrymen were the carriers and commercial agents of Spain, and as nearly all the silver product of Mexico and South America passed through this channel, the banks of this country early accumulated a substantial and abundant fund of specie. From the peace of Amiens in 1801 the influx of silver abated, although still considerable. Gouge says: "The specie constantly *in transitu* from South America through the United States to other parts of the world was so great in amount that a retention of the quarterly or semi-quarterly supply for only a month or two was sufficient to relieve the banks from the difficulties into which they were occasionally brought by extending their operations too far."

Banking on the whole was a very profitable business in those days. From 1792 to 1808 the Bank of Pennsylvania never divided less than eight per cent, and sometimes ten. In 1792 the Bank of North America divided fifteen per cent, the next year thirteen and one-half, and for the five succeeding years twelve per cent annually. Our commerce being exposed to frequent interruptions by belligerents, the necessity for borrowing was often so urgent as to make the banks masters of the situation, and money was not infrequently lent by them for two and three per cent a month. The business of banking was less openly conducted than at the present day. It was part of the policy of every bank to keep its transactions as carefully hidden as possible. It was long before people generally became sufficiently accustomed to these institutions, either to appreciate or admit their utility. Except a branch of the United States Bank, which was set up in Norfolk in 1799, no bank existed in Virginia until 1804. Yet a subsequent writer in the Richmond *Enquirer* declared that until this branch appeared there no people enjoyed greater happiness. "The desk of every agriculturist in Virginia had some gold or silver to spare if he were a prudent and industrious man, or he had something like money to spare in the hands of his merchant, who, in the days of which I am speaking, acted as a banker to his prospering customers. Nor was any interest paid upon such moneys as might be deposited in the hands of the merchant, because both planter and merchant considered themselves accommodated by the arrangement—the planter in having his money safely kept for him until he wanted to use it, and the merchant in having the use of the money until it was called for."

As for the need of banks to transmit funds from one place to another, he adds: "Nor was there the least inconvenience in transmitting money from one point to another through the merchants whose credit was then as good as the credit of the banks now, if not better. Banks have destroyed the credit and confidence which men had in one another."

The banks in the greater cities having comparatively large capitals, were conducted on principles which afforded greater safety to the public than the smaller institutions situated elsewhere, whose capital often to a considerable extent was fictitious, consisting partly in notes secured by stock and managed by persons "with whose skill, caution or integrity the public was very little acquainted." Yet the latter were the banks which had the most extensive circulation. In 1809 the three banks in Boston made the following return:

	CAPITAL.	CIRCULATION.	SPECIE.
Massachusetts.	$ 800,000	$139,850	$105,670
Union,	1,200,000	279,431	132,242
Boston,	1,800,000	226,940	161,270
	$3,800,000	$646,221	$399,182

At the same time, five other banks in the State of Massachusetts made the following return:

	CAPITAL.	CIRCULATION.	SPECIE.
Lincoln and Kennebec,	$200,000	$242,847	$20,920
Northampton,	75,000	122,363	19,377
Hallowell and Augusta,	200,000	166,123	23,664
Penobscot,	150,000	183,470	19,586
Berkshire.	75,000	83,060	7,682
	$700,000	$797,863	$91,229

These figures forcibly illustrate the difference between the safe and cautious method of conducting a banking business observed in the cities and the erratic and irresponsible method of operating outside them.

After the Bank of Massachusetts the next bank chartered in that State was the Union Bank, organized in 1792, with a capital of $1,200,000, of which $400,000 was subscribed by the State. In 1795 the Nantucket and Merrimac Banks were established. Up to 1799 but one more bank was chartered in Massachusetts. In that year a law was enacted prohibiting the establishment of unincorporated associations. In 1803 an act requiring semi-annual returns to be made by the banks to the Governor and Council was passed, and in 1805 an amendment required these returns to be sworn to. In 1805 sixteen banks were in operation. From 1805 to 1811 but one new bank was chartered. Two more were chartered in 1811. In all the charters granted by Massachusetts after 1793, provision was made for a State subscription, and in 1812 the State held about $1,000,000 out of the $8,000,000 of stock of the banks of the State. Nearly all the banks were re-chartered in 1811. In 1812 the State first imposed a tax on bank capital. In 1813 the system of compelling the redemption at par in Boston of the notes of the eastern banks, by assorting and returning the notes to the place of issue, was inaugurated by the New England Bank organized that year. This was the beginning of what was afterwards known as the Suffolk Bank system.

Up to June 11, 1812, the date of the declaration of war with Great Britain, nineteen banks were chartered by the Legislature of New York. Seven of these: the Bank of New York, Merchants', Mechanics', Union, and City Bank of New York City, the New York State Bank of Albany, and the Bank of Utica, are now National banks, and the Manhattan Company and Bank of America are the leading State banks.

During the period from 1791 to 1812 political feeling was bitter, and obtaining the charters of the banks organized during this time was, in many cases, the occasion of much strife and intrigue. Governor Tompkins, afterward Vice-President of the United States, in the year 1813 prorogued the Legislature, assigning as one reason for his action the attempt to secure a bank charter through the use of corrupt means. These charters were in the nature of special privileges, granted to particular persons, and all others were specially restrained by law from participating in the business of banking. A restraining act was passed in 1804 to compel private banking institutions to wind up their business, leaving a clear field to chartered corporations. This act prohibited any person, under a penalty of $1,000, from subscribing to, or becoming a member of any association for the purpose of receiving deposits, or from doing any business which incorporated banks, by their charters, were permitted to do.

The first institution in the State of Ohio in the nature of a bank was chartered under the name of the Miami Exporting Company, in 1803, immediately upon the admission of this State to the Union. It was chartered for forty years, with a nominal capital of $500,000, in shares of $100 each, payable five dollars in cash and the remainder in produce or merchandise. Although in forming a trading company, it issued bills and redeemed them in notes of other banks. The first regular bank was chartered in 1808, and was located in Marietta, with a capital of $500,000. During the same year another bank was established at Chillicothe, then capital of the State, with a capital of $100,000. From 1809 to 1816 four banks only were chartered in Ohio.

The first bank in the State of Illinois was established under its Territorial Government in 1813, at Shawneetown, and three years after was incorporated for a term of twenty years with a capital of $300,000. In 1835 its charter was extended to 1857 and its capital increased to $1,400,000 the additional capital being subscribed by the State.

The first serious explosion in the banking business in New England after the adoption of the Federal Constitution occurred in 1809. The notes of many banks outside of Boston were at a varying discount, running as high as five per cent, and the merchants and retail dealers in that city on whom the burden of depreciation fell combined for their own protection. They appointed a committee and raised a fund for the purpose of sending home the bills of banks outside of that city received in the course of their business and procuring their redemption and of bringing suits against banks neglecting or refusing payment. This step brought on a crisis. First, the Farmers' Exchange Bank—a large institution whose operations were among the most notable in the history of New England banking—suddenly failed, and "the shock upon the public was tremendous." The Berkshire Bank followed next. The discovery that banks could fail affected the credit of all, and in 1809 most of the country banks of New England having bills in circulation stopped payment. "It would probably be a moderate estimate to put the lost in New England by the bank failures of that period at $1,000,000."

When the charter of the first United States Bank expired its notes were withdrawn and the notes of State banks were issued in reckless profusion to supply their place. During the year 1811 and the two succeeding years one hundred and twenty new banks commenced business in the United States. In Pennsylvania the Legislature passed an act authorizing the wholesale creation of new banks on the loosest principles, which, fortunately, was vetoed by the Governor. The new banks of these three years added nominally about $30,000,000 to the banking capital of the country. But the real capital of nearly all of these new concerns was almost purely nominal, as, when a new bank was organized, its stock subscribed, and the first installment paid, stock notes were taken for the residue, which notes were discounted to meet all subsequent calls. As soon as it became known that this practice was generally followed the credit of all banks in circulation, save those whose reputation had been firmly established, was quite swept away and the issues of all except a comparatively small number of well-known banks began to depreciate. This increase of banking circulation came on the eve of the war with Great Britain during which period exports almost ceased, and the coasting and foreign trade of the whole country was practically annihilated. As but a small portion of this manufactured capital could be used in legitimate mercantile enterprise, considerable sums were invested in Government loans. The demand for money in this direction as the war progressed became so great that bank-notes rapidly multiplied. In New England, however, the banks did not subscribe so freely, because of the unpopularity of the war in that section. The banks of the interior, as well as those of New York, Philadelphia and Baltimore, expanded their issues with inexcusable indiscretion, to call it by no harsher name. The drain upon the country for specie for shipment to Europe was great, increasing, and perfectly well known. As is always the case this drain was felt first and with greatest stringency in those cities where the paper in circulation was most abundant and most discredited. At this time the laws of the New England States imposed a penalty of twenty-four per cent per annum on all banks suspending payment of their circulating notes. This regulation forced the weaker banks of that section to the wall, and assisted the stronger institutions in maintaining their notes in full credit after those of the banks of other sections had become greatly depreciated.

The capture of Washington in 1814 was followed by the failure of nearly all the banks of the middle and southern States. All had been drained of their specie. Those at Washington went first, ascribing their failure to the fact that they were plundered by the English invaders, though they had little for the enemy to take. Those at Baltimore gave way next. Then the six banks at Philadelphia suspended specie payments, and the next day those of New York followed the example. The New England banks, however, easily stood the pressure. Their issues of circulating paper were less, their individual strength was greater, they were better used to united action, and the local supply of specie was more abundant than in any other section of the Union. In the South and West the Bank of Nashville alone maintained specie payment of its paper until August 1815, "the sturdy honesty of whose directors," says Gouge, "amidst such general knavery, is no less praiseworthy than it is remarkable." The broken banks, though refusing to redeem their notes, professed their desire and ability to do so at an early day. At first business was not seriously interrupted by their suspension, for gold and silver remained the standard of value. Bills of doubtful credit were compared with these and the ratio of their depreciation fixed by this sound standard. Bank bills became a merchantable commodity and were commonly bought and sold for coin; their rate of discount was tabulated and regularly announced in the newspapers; they were even sold at auction, the purchaser paying therefor in specie. Though the people and the Government were subjected to considerable loss and more inconvenience from the employment of this depreciated paper, creditors received their just dues and business calculations could be made with reasonable safety so long as the specie standard was adhered to. But the unfortunate action of the then Secretary of the Treasury in directing that the depreciated paper of the State banks should be received without discount in payment of loans, customs duties, and other taxes, changed this almost in a moment. The suspended banks increased their issues, their depreciated currency became the standard, coin disappeared or was bought and sold as merchandise at a premium varying in different cities with the ratio of debasement of local bank-notes, and the difficulties of the Government and the business community immensely multiplied.

From 1815 to the resumption of specie payments in 1817, the condition of affairs was such as to place a direct premium on rascality in banking. During these years, under the suspension of the specie payments, while they were in a bankrupt condition, the minor State banks made larger dividends than ever before. All responsibility for their issues had ceased; they grew rich at the expense of the holders of their notes. It is no wonder they opposed a return to specie payments.

We have seen, in connection with the account given of the formation of the Second Bank of the United States, the part played by that bank and by the United States Treasury in bringing about, in 1817, a return to specie payments.

CHAPTER IX.

THE STATE BANKS FROM 1816 TO 1863.

When the Second United States Bank was created the various State banks continued to do business as before. The Government no longer kept its deposits with them, but it did not interfere with their affairs. Of course, the National bank with its vast resources overshadowed them; still they flourished and multiplied in number. The first noteworthy advance in the system of State banking occurred in New England in 1824. In February of that year an attempt was made to induce the banks of Boston to give the bills of country banks the same credit as the banks in the city gave to the notes of each other. If they were thus taken it would be necessary to send them home to be redeemed unless the country banks should choose to make an arrangement for their redemption in Boston. It was finally agreed among the banks (though not all of them came into the scheme), that each should receive at par in all payments from its customers the bills of all the banks in good credit in the New England States, thus making country money equal in value to Boston money, and saving to the customers of the city banks the tax previously imposed on them in the way of premium for Boston money. The bills thus received were not to be kept for any considerable length of time, nor to be paid out to supply the circulation of the city. Nor was it necessary for each bank to employ messengers to carry the bills home, for an agreement was made that the Suffolk Bank should do this business or procure their redemption in such manner as it saw fit. The country bills received by the other banks in Boston which were parties to the arrangements were paid over daily to the Suffolk Bank, and each received in lieu thereof Boston money at par. The bills thus received by the Suffolk Bank absorbed a considerable portion of its capital. To indemnify it for exchanging or redeeming the bills of the country banks, the allied banks each lent the Suffolk Bank, without interest, a sum of money which was held to be equivalent to the service performed. This plan of redemption was known as the Suffolk Bank system, and was of obvious benefit to the public in facilitating the transaction of business and in protecting a portion of the community from a constant tax and almost every one from occasional heavy losses. The general tendency of the arrangement was to give to each country bank the benefit of the principal local circulation of its own neighborhood, and to direct its bills homeward when they had wondered away. The excellence of the system is shown by the fact that it continued for so many years, and became so widely accepted throughout New England. It operated as a check to excessive issues of paper by any of the banks included in the association, as they could not make any large addition to the quantity of their notes in circulation without its being at once discovered by the Suffolk Bank. Discovery would of course be followed by a demand for increased security as a consideration for continuing the redemption of the bills of any bank which seemed to be inclined to resort to such a practice. Although there was at first some opposition to the Suffolk Bank system it came into nearly universal use in New England as early as 1825 and continued in successful operation down to the adoption of the National banking system.

The first comprehensive State law regulating banking was passed in Massachusetts in 1829. In 1837 there had been organized in that State one hundred and thirty-four chartered banks, of which thirty-two failed in the great panic of that year, with a loss of about thirty per cent of their entire indebtedness. From 1793 to 1836 but ten banks had failed in Massachusetts. As a result of the revulsion of 1837 that State adopted a system of official examinations which was carefully and judiciously adhered to, and which was equally helpful in maintaining the soundness and solvency of the banks and public faith and confidence in their management. A free-banking law was adopted in 1851, much like that which grew up in the State of New York, but only seven banks were organized under it, as the specially chartered banks then in existence were possessed of numerous and valuable privileges not conceded to those formed under the provisions of the general law. In October, 1865, all but one of the State banks of Massachusetts, save four which wound up and went out of business, had re-organized as National banks.

In New York the restraining act of 1804, aimed at the extinction of unincorporated banks, was followed in 1818 by even more stringent legislation. This enacted that no person, association of persons or body corporate, except such bodies corporate as were expressly authorized by law, should keep any office for the purpose of receiving deposits, or discounting notes or bills, or for issuing any evidence of debt to be loaned or put in circulation as money. Although many of the restrictive features of this law were salutary and are to-day part of the law of every State, its effect, as a whole, was in the direction of a monopoly of all forms of brokerage by the specially-chartered banks. The statute remained in force until 1837, only one year before the adoption of the free-banking act. The safety-fund system originated in New York and was authorized, on the recommendation of Governor Van Buren, by the Act of April 2, 1829. The distinctive feature of this system was the requirement that each bank operated under it should make an annual contribution of one-half of one per cent of its capital to a common fund to be held by the Treasurer of the State, such payments to be continued until each bank had thus deposited three per cent of its capital. This fund was to be used to redeem the circulating notes and to pay the other debts of any bank, joining the association, which might become insolvent. In case the fund should at any time become impaired by payments made from it, the banks were required to again make their annual contributions until each had once more on deposit three per cent of its capital stock. In practice the amount required to be deposited to the credit of the fund was found to be too small to afford any substantial protection or relief. When, during the panic of 1837, eleven banks belonging to the system failed, the whole fund amounted to but little more than five per cent of their debts for the payment of which it was pledged. The loss in this one instance to depositors and bill-holders of these banks was upward of $2,500,000, beside the total lost of their capital stock amounting to some $3,000,000 more. The deficiency of the safety fund was made good by an issue by the State of its six per cent bonds, this advance to be reimbursed by future payments by the banks into this fund. But in the end the State was a considerable loser by this transaction as the whole sum contributed by safety-fund banks to that fund down to 1848, when the scheme was finally abandoned, was but $1,876,000, little more than seventy-five per cent the debts of the eleven insolvent institutions. In 1842 the safety-fund law was amended so that the common fund became responsible only for the payment of the circulating notes of banks failing thereafter, it being argued that banks which enjoyed the exclusive privilege of furnishing a paper currency should be required to contribute something to a common fund to make that currency safe and stable; that a contribution of a moderate sum for this purpose was only reasonable and proper, but that there was neither propriety nor justice in requiring all the banks to contribute to a general fund for the benefit of the depositors or other general creditors of individual banks; and as there was no exclusive privilege to receive deposits or contract general debts there was no reason why the special fund should be applied to their liquidation. The original safety-fund system also operated as a bar to the formation of new banks, which led to many abuses and the creation of much cumbersome machinery for obtaining new charters. This was one strong incentive to the adoption by the State of New York of the free-banking system, which was created by the Act of April 13, 1838. By this system all the restrictions of banking privilelges to a favored class were abolished. Any number of persons were alowed to form banking associations, subject only to the common restrictions and penalties imposed by the general law. As originally enacted the law provided for the issue of circulating notes to these banks by the State, upon the deposit of stocks of the State of New York and of the United States at par, or of other States at their market price in amount sufficient to make them equal to a five per cent stock at par, or of bonds secured by mortgages on improved and productive real estate worth, exclusive of the building thereon, double the amount secured by the mortgage, and bearing interest at not less than six per cent. The issue of notes to each bank was to be equal to the amount of the deposit. From 1838 to 1843 twenty-nine of the banks organized on this plan failed, and a sale of the securities which they had deposited realized a sum sufficient to pay, averaging the whole, seventy-four per cent only of their outstanding circulating notes. Some paid nearly in full, others much less than the average. Losses in every instance occurred only in the case of those banks which had deposited the stocks of States other than New York. The Act was therefore amended so as to exclude the stocks of all States except New York, and these were required to be kept equal in amount, at market value, to a five per cent stock at par. In 1848 an amendment was adopted requiring all stocks deposited to bear six per cent interest and all bonds seven per cent, the mortgages securing the latter to be for but two-fifths of the value of the lands covered. In 1849 still another amendatory act required one-half the securities in all cases to consist of New York State stock, and provided that all other securities should be, or be made equal to, six per cent stock, to be received at not above par and at not more than their market value. The general policy of the New York free-banking system furnished the groundwork for the plan on which the present National banking law was built up. In 1840 the State of New York required its banks to redeem their notes at an agency to be established either in New York City, Albany, or Troy, as well as at the home office. The redemption at the agency was at a discount of one-half of one per cent, subsequently reduced to one-fourth of one per cent. This discount was, in practice, divided between the bank whose bills were redeemed and the redemption agency. Any bank neglecting to provide for such redemption of its notes was to be forced to wind up its business. The constitution of this State, adopted in 1846, prohibited the Legislature from granting any further special charters to banking corporations; and provided for formation of banking institutions under a general law. It also provided that after 1850 the stockholders in all banks issuing circulating notes should be responsible for all the debts of the bank, of every kind, in an amount equal to their stock in such bank. In case of the bank's insolvency bill-holders were preferred to all other creditors.

In Ohio but five banks were authorized before 1816. In that year six new banks were chartered by an omnibus act which required each new bank, as well as such of the old ones as should apply for an extension of charter, to set apart annually for the use of the State, such a part of its earnings as would, at the expiration of the term for which its charter was granted, amount to one twenty-fifth of its capital. By a law passed in 1825 this provision was so modified as to require each bank to pay to the State two per cent on all dividends theretofore paid and four per cent upon all such as should be thereafter declared. From 1816 to 1834 thirteen new banks were authorized. Branches of the Bank of the United States having been established at Chillicothe and Cincinnati, the Legislature proceeding upon the theory which then obtained in Ohio and other States that the State should participate in the profits of the banking corporations which it created, levied a lump sum or tax of $50,000 on each of these branches provided they should remain in business later than September 1, 1819. The bank contested this tax, however, and in the Supreme Court of the United States obtained a decision in its favor and denying the right of the States to tax its branches. In 1845 the safety-fund system was applied to a State bank then authorized. A sum equal to ten per cent of the circulating notes of the bank was to be paid to a board of control, to be by it invested in Ohio State or United States stocks, or in bonds secured by first mortgages on real estate of double the value of the security, to be deposited in the State Treasury. Sixty-three branches of this State bank were created, each of which was treated as an independent institution so far as depositing security and receiving the interest thereon was concerned. In case of the failure of any branch bank its own funds and securities, not deposited in the safety fund, were to be applied to the redemption of its circulation before the safety fund could be called on, thus giving bill-holders a first lien on all its assets. The safety-fund act was also applied to a portion of the banks previously existing, and the same statute authorized an independent banking system which provided for a deposit with the State Treasurer of United States or Ohio State stocks, to the full amount of the circulating notes to secure their payment. A free-banking law, modeled on that of New York, was passed in 1851, but the new Constitution, adopted later in the same year, materially restricted its operation. The revenue laws of Ohio, at this period, discriminated strongly against the banks, subjecting them to double and three-fold taxation, as compared with other forms of property and investment. In 1856 another State bank was created by law, largely on the lines of that of 1845, but with a clause attaching a personal liability to the ownership of the stock. Most of the banks organized under the law of 1851 were taxed into liquidation, and in 1856 upward of sixty banks in this State were in bankruptcy, more or less complete. In 1863 there were in Ohio fifty-six banks doing business under its laws, viz: Seven independent banks with an aggregate capital of $350,000; three free banks with $1,270,000; and the State Bank of Ohio with thirty-six branches and an aggregate capital of $4,054,000 and $7,246,000 circulation. The total capital of all the banks of the State, when the National banking law went into effect, was $5,674,000; circulation, $9,057,837; specie, $3,023,285.

Early banks in Indiana were few. But two were chartered previous to 1820. In 1834 the State Bank of Indiana was chartered with ten branches, each liable for the debt of all the others. Each share was to pay the State an annual tax of twelve and one-half cents, and was liable to all taxes assessed upon other forms of capital, with the proviso that in no event should taxes on these shares exceed one per cent in the aggregate. The cash capital of this bank was largely borrowed at the East upon the credit of the State, which not only took $1,000,000 of its stock directly, but also loaned its credit to individual stockholders to the extent of one-half their subscriptions, taking individual bonds secured upon real estate at one-half its value, for the re-payment of the sums so advanced. This bank paid dividends averaging twelve to fourteen per cent annually, and weathered the panic of 1837 without loss of capital or prestige. It went into liquidation in 1854 on the expiration of its charter, and returned to its stockholders nearly double the par value of their stock. The State of Indiana received about $3,000,000 from its investment of $1,000,000 in this institution, as well as payment in full of all sums for which it became surety. In 1851 Indiana adopted a new Constitution which prohibited the further creation of banking corporations except under a general law. The general banking act, adopted in 1852 in pursuance of this constitutional provision, required the deposit of stocks of that States or of the United States as security for the circulation of all banks formed thereafter. A new State bank chartered in Indiana in 1854, on the expiration of the charter of the first State bank, had a capital of $6,000,000, was excellently managed and passed through the panic of 1857 without suspending specie payments.

In Illinois a State bank was chartered in 1821 with a capital of $500,000. It was owned by the State. It had no real capital and was little, if any, better than the schemes for the emission of bills of credit to be lent to all comers, which flourished in the colonies during the last century. Of its notes $300,000 were issued and loaned to citizens of the State, not more than $1,000 to one person, upon real estate mortgage, for one year, at six per cent interest. These notes were made receivable for taxes and for all debts due the State and the bank. They rapidly depreciated and after passing for a time at twenty-five cents on the dollar, became wholly discredited and cease to circulate. In 1835 a new State bank was incorporated with a capital of $500,000, afterward increased to $2,000,000, which was also owned by the State and managed and controlled by the Legislature. It suspended specie payments during the panic of 1837-38 and never recovered sufficiently to resume. In 1843 this bank and the old Shawneetown bank in which the State had a controlling interest, were wound up under a law passed that year, which practically confiscated the property of private stockholders, depositors and bill-holders. The State took possession of its bonds amounting upward of $3,000,000, which these banks held as security for their bill-holders and depositors, and caused the same to be burned in the old State House Square at Springfield, in the presence of the Legislature. In 1843 a free-banking law was adopted, modeled on the provisions of the earliest free-banking acts of New York and Indiana. The securities deposited by the free banks in Illinois were almost wholly those of the extreme southern and south-western States, the values of which fluctuated so widely and continually as to deprive the bills secured thereby of any settled value. Under the Constitution of 1870 State banking ceased in Illinois so far as the creation of new banks is concerned.

In nearly all the southern and western States banks were incorporated, during the period under consideration, in which the State had an interest, partial or exclusive. Free-banking systems were also generally adopted, after 1850, with the provisions for the security and redemption of circulating notes, purely formal and useless in some and effective and substantial in others. The result in all the other States was like that in one or another of those whose experience is hereinbefore epitomized. Indiana and Louisiana managed their banks with increasing and conspicuous prudence and success. To award justly the palm for pre-eminent badness would be a task as difficult as unprofitable. We have noticed the case of those States which, by constitutional limitation, forbade the granting of special banking charters. Wherever obtainable these special charters were in great demand because of the laxness which universally characterized their provisions. The abuse of any State system which did not provide for the redemption at the State capital or other business center, of the bills of every bank authorized to do business within its limits, was easy and inevitable. A common plan was to obtain in one State a charter for a bank to be located at some obscure and inexcessible point where no occasion exists for any legitimate banking facilities, and to procure, on the deposit of doubtful and inadequate security, an issue of bank bills which were at once taken to a distant State to be put in circulation among a people having no means of procuring redemption. Charters issued in Georgia were sold to be used for putting a flood of worthless bank-notes in circulation in Illinois. Banks ostensibly located in New Jersey had all their business operations conducted in other states. The $notes of all banks except those located in large commercial cities, were always at a discount. At New York a discount of one-eighth of one per cent was charged on the bills of New England banks redeemable at the Suffolk bank. The common rate of discount on the bills of banks which redeemed their currency only over their own counters was from one to five per cent, and often greatly exceeded that rate. Five per cent on the entire circulation of all the banks in the United States is estimated to have been lost each year to the bill-holders by discount and brokerage. Losses by insolvency were much greater. The losses and vexation occasioned by the circulation of counterfeits and notes of broken banks was something incredible to one accustomed only to the currency of to-day.

In 1837 a general suspension of specie payments took place, occasioned by the revulsion and panic of that year. A partial resumption in 1838 was followed by a second suspension in 1839, which was especially disastrous in the West and South. The reckless management of the Bank of the United States, then operating under a charter from the State of Pennsylvania, was the principal occasion of this second crash. Whatever the previous merit or demerit of that bank may have been, its course at this time was such as to justify the most severe condemnation, as its policy was directed to forcing a run on, and suspension of, the New York banks in order to bring on another complete suspension. A general and final resumption of specie payments was not effected until 1842. In 1857 another panic caused another general suspension of payments by the banks. This revulsion, like so many others in this country, was occasioned by expansion and overtrading. The first actual shock was the failure of the Ohio Life and Trust Company, on August 24, 1857. This concern had borrowed largely, on call, in New York and had loaned its funds improvidently. Its liabilities were about $7,000,000, and its credit had been so high that its failure shook confidence in other institutions. A desire to test the foundations of credit followed by a general collapse. It had been the rule among banks to keep on hand specie to the amount one-third of outstanding bills. During the period of activity which preceded 1857 this wholesome rule had been greatly relaxed and few banks in the interior possessed a specie reserve exceeding one-twelfth the total of their circulating notes. The loss of the steamer *Central America* with a million in gold helped to create a momentary stringency in New York. Collections on interior points began to drag. Failures of banks, brokers and produce dealers became numerous, and on September 12 and 13 the banks at nearly all points south and west of New York suspended payment. On October 13, 1857, the New York banks suspended and the New England and Boston banks followed a few days later.

The panic forced a speedy liquidation of all inflated schemes and enterprises, and, as the country was at the bottom, in a genuinely prosperous condition, the recovery was prompt and easy. Imports stopped almost completely. Gold flowed in from Europe. The New Orleans banks, nine in number, had suffered least of all. But four of these suspended, and they for a few days only. The New York banks resumed in a body on December 12, and all others followed gradually and informally.

PART II.

THE DEPARTMENT OF THE TREASURY.

ITS HISTORY AND FUNCTIONS.

INTRODUCTION.

To give a comprehensive description within a limited space of the duties and procedure of a Department so extensive as the Treasury is a task beset with many difficulties. The seed that was planted in 1775, when the representatives of the struggling colonies appointed Continental Treasurers, has been a striking illustration of evolution from the simple to the complex, bearing fruit in the shape of an immense Department of Finance, which, in its manifold ramifications, giving employment to about 18,000 people, embraces every branch of the Government service.

The control and direction of the National finances; the customs service; the enforcement of the immigration laws; the survey of ocean coasts, lakes and rivers; the light-house establishment; the supervision and control of the national banks; the inspection of steam vessels; the enforcement of laws and regulations in relation to navigation; the designing, erection and custody of public buildings; the mints and assay offices; the marine-hospital service; the life-saving service; the compilation and publication of statistics relating to the Department; the manufacture, issue and redemption of currency; and the duties performed by the law officers in the construction and enforcement of laws, constitute in themselves a vast array of important and difficult functions. When to the foregoing is added the examination, revision and adjustment of all accounts, not only of the Department, but of every branch of the Legislative, Executive and Judicial Establishment, its magnitude and responsibility may be better appreciated.

It has been deemed best, out of the wealth of material that presents itself for selection, to give a history of the Department, a brief statement of the Duties of each Bureau, with the addition of details of business methods of those Bureaus with which bankers are usually brought in contact in their transactions with the Government; regulations in relation to coin and paper currency, bonds, drafts, warrants, and checks, and special items of interest relating to national banks and depositories. Much of this material is embodied in the circulars issued by the Department, but is here arranged in more convenient manner for reference, and being placed in permanent form, is less liable to meet the fate usually attending circulars. It has been the desire and intention to devote but little space to statistics, which, while valuable to the interested few, make but dreary reading to the general public. In the stead there has been given detailed statements of procedure in the manufacture, issue, redemption and destruction of paper currency, accompanied by illustrations, which it is hoped will prove of interest. Finally, a few articles have been included, which, while perhaps not strictly germane to the subject, have been the subject-matter of many inquiries from bankers and others.

An experience of many years devoted to the receipt, distribution and answer of correspondence of an important bureau has encouraged the hope that the selections of materials above outlined have been judicious, and that they may prove not only entertaining, but of some lasting benefit.

SYNOPSIS OF CONTENTS.

History of the Treasury Department.
History of the Treasury Seal.
Bureaus of the Department, titles of officers, and functions.
1. Secretary of the Treasury.
2. Supervising Architect.
3. Director of the Mint.
4. Chief of Bureau of Engraving and Printing.
5. Supervising Surgeon-General of Marine-Hospital Service.
6. General Superintendent of the Life-Saving Service.
7. Supervising Inspector-General of Steam-Vessels.
8. Chief of the Bureau of Statistics.
9. Light-House Board.
10. Superintendent of Immigration.
11. Commissioner of Navigation.
12. Superintendent of the Coast and Geodetic Survey.
13. Chief of the Secret Service Division.
14. Comptroller of the Treasury.
15. Auditor for the Treasury Department.
16. Auditor for the War Department.
17. Auditor for the Interior Department.
18. Auditor for the Navy Department.
19. Auditor for the State and Other Departments.
20. Auditor for the Post Office Department.
21. Treasurer of the United States.
22. Register of the Treasury.
23. Comptroller of the Currency.
24. Commissioner of Internal Revenue.

Solicitor of the Treasury (Department of Justice).
Solicitor of Internal Revenue (Department of Justice).

History of Office of Treasurer of the United States.
Issue and Redemption of Currency (Regulations).
    Issue of United States Notes.
        Treasury Notes of 1890.
        Silver Certificates.
        Gold Coin.
        Standard Silver Dollars.
        Subsidiary (Fractional) Silver Coin.
        Minor Coin.
    Redemption of United States Notes.
        Treasury Notes of 1890.
        Silver Certificates.
        National Bank Notes.
        Subsidiary (Fractional) Silver Coin.
        Minor Coin.
    Advertisements on Coins.
    Defaced Minor Coin.
    Registration free of charge (Currency for Redemption).
    Express Charges.
    Disposition of Counterfeit Money.
Refunding Certificates.
Gold Certificates.
Currency Certificates.
Interest Checks (Regulation).
    Closing and Opening of Transfer Books.
    Dates of Dividends and Payment of Checks.
    Duplicates.
    Change of Address.
    Indorsements
Transfer Checks (Regulations).
    Issue.
    Duplicates.
Treasury Drafts and Warrants (Regulations).
    Issue.
    Duplicates.
    Indorsements.

Gold Coins of the United States.
    Weight, fineness and alloy.
    Denomination now issued.
    Coinage discontinued.
Silver Coins of the United States.
    Weight, fineness and alloy.
    Denominations now issued.
    Coinage discontinued.
Minor Coins of the United States.
    Weight and alloy.
    Denominations now issued.
    Coinage discontinued.

Purchase of Uncurrent Gold Coin.
        Silver Coin.
Mutilated Minor Coin.
Light-Weight Gold Coin.
Legal Tender.
        Gold Coin.
        Standard Silver Dollars.
        Subsidiary Silver Coin.
        Minor Coin.
        United States Notes.
        Demand Treasury Notes.
        One and Two Year Notes of 1863.
        Compound Interest Notes.
        Treasury Notes of 1890.
        Columbian Half Dollars.
        Columbian Quarters.
Not Legal Tender.
        Gold Certificates.
        Silver Certificates.
        National Bank Notes.
        Trade Dollars.
        Fractional Currency.
        Foreign Gold Coin.
        Foreign Silver Coin.
        Continental Currency (?)
Legal Tender Cases in the Supreme Court.
"Outstanding Liabilities."
        Three-year-limit for Checks and Drafts.

Government Bonds.
        Titles and Amounts of Loans.
        Regulations.
                Redemption.
                To Secure Deposits.
                To Secure Circulation.
                Purchase.
                Transfer and Registry (Assignment).
                Exchange of Coupon for Registered
                Non-exchange of Registered for Coupon.
                Lost Registered Bonds.
                Lost Coupon Bonds, Coupons, and U. S. Notes.
                Destroyed and Defaced Bonds.
                Mutilated Coupons.
                Withdrawal of Bonds to secure Deposits.
                Withdrawal of Bonds to secure Circulation.

Disbursing Officers Checks.
        Duplicates.
        Pension Checks, (90 day limit).
Post Office Warrants.
        Duplicates.

National Banks.
    Number in Operation.
    The Organization of a National Bank.
    Reserve Cities.
        Lawful Money Reserve.
        Place for Redemption of Circulation.
        Additional Reserve Cities.
        Central Reserve Cities.
        List of Reserve Cities.
    National Bank Examiners.
        Appointment, Powers and Duties.
        Compensation.
    Semi-Annual Duty on Circulation.
        Duty.
        Return.
        How to ascertain Duty.
        "Notes in Circulation."
        Opinion of Attorney-General.
        New Banks.
        Banks in Liquidation.
        Payment of Duty.
    Amount Collected from Banks by Semi-Annual Duty.
    National Bank Redemption Agency.
        History.
        Duties.
        Expenses, how paid.
    National Bank Notes.
        Lost or Stolen.
        Manufacture and Issue.
        Redemption and Destruction.
        Bureau of Engraving and Printing.
            Engraving and Printing.
        Comptroller of the Currency.
            Issue of Notes.
        Treasurer of the United States.
            Redemption of Notes.
        Comptroller of the Currency.
            Redemption of Notes.
        Committee.
            Destruction of Notes.
    National Bank Depositaries.
        Applications for Designation.
        Regulations.
        Functions.
        Service rendered to Government.
        Number, and Bonds held.

United States Paper Currency.
    Manufacture, Issue, Redemption, and Destruction.
        Secretary of the Treasury.
            Government Paper Mill.
            Distinctive Paper.
        Bureau of Engraving and Printing.
            Engraving and Printing Sheet Currency.
        Treasurer of the United States.
            Sealing and Separating Sheet Currency.
            Issue of Notes.
            Redemption of Notes.
        Secretary of the Treasury.
            Re-Count of Redeemed Notes.
        Register of the Treasury.
            Re-Count of Redeemed Notes.
        Committee.
            Destruction of Notes by Maceration.

Advice as to Official Mail.
Annual Reports of Financial Officers.
Public Debt Statements.
Resumption of Specie Payments.
List of Sub-Treasuries, Mints, and Assay Offices.
Exemption of United States Bonds from Taxation.
Taxation of National Bank Notes and Treasury Notes.
United States Mint Tests for Gold and Silver Coins.
Conscience Fund.
Values of Foreign Coins.
Columbian Half Dollars.
Columbian ("Isabella") Quarters.
Revenues and Expenditures of Government.
Contents of Vaults in U. S. Treasurer's Office.
Amount of Money in Circulation.
Per Capita Circulation.
Population of the United States, (January 1, 1895).
Methods in the Erection of a Public Building.

Continental Currency.
    History.
    Why not redeemable.
    Counterfeiting.
    Decision of Comptroller.
    Legal Tender Qualities.

Fessenden on "Finance."
The Wiles of "Green Goods" Men.
Premiums on Coins, (non paid by Government).
State Bank Notes, (not redeemed by Government).
Confederate Notes, (not redeemed by Government).
Gold Coins Minted by Private Parties.
Origin of the Dollar Mark ($).

HISTORY OF THE TREASURY DEPARTMENT.

GERM: The germ of the Treasury department was planted July 29, 1775 (Journals of Congress, vol. 1, p. 173) when by a resolution of Congress, the management of the finances was intrusted to two Treasurers. BOARD OF TREASURY: By resolution of February 17, 1776 (Ibid. vol. 2, p. 66), a standing committee of five was appointed for superintending the Treasury (known as the Committee on Finance, or Board of Treasury). There was but little change in the character of the Department until 1779. SECRETARY OF THE TREASURY: On February 11, 1779 (Ibid. vol. 5, p. 51), Congress resolved "That a Secretary of the Treasury be appointed," and on May 29, 1779 (Ibid. p. 234), Robert Troup was elected "Secretary to the Board of Treasury."

WILLARD FORESTER WARNER.

On July 30, 1779 (Ibid. p. 301), Congress agreed to an "Ordinance for establishing a board of treasury." The Board was to consist of five members as heretofore, but there was a reorganization as to methods, functions and *personnel*. SUPERINTENDENT OF FINANCE: On February 20, 1781 (Ibid. vol. 7, p. 31), Robert Morris was elected by Congress as Superintendent of Finance. Congress vested the office with powers similar to those now held by the Secretary of the Treasury (Ibid. p. 31 *et sequitur*). BOARD OF TREASURY: Robert Morris, Superintendent of Finance, having signified his intention of retiring from said office (Ibid. vol. 9, p. 251) Congress resolved on May 28, 1784, that a Board consisting of three commissioners be appointed to superintend the Treasury and manage the finances of the United States, which shall be styled The Board of Treasury" (Ibid. p. 255). The Finance Department of the Government was managed by Commissioners until 1789, when the Congress created a Treasury Department. TREASURY DEPARTMENT ESTABLISHED: By the Act of September 2, 1789 (1 Stat., p. 65), the Treasury Department was established. This act provided for a Secretary of the Treasury, an Assistant to the Secretary of the Treasury, a Comptroller, an Auditor, a Treasurer and a Register.

SEAL OF TREASURY DEPARTMENT.

On September 26, 1778, the Continental Congress resolved "That a committee of three be appointed to prepare a seal for the treasury and for the navy; the members chosen were Mr. Witherspoon, Mr. G.

THE U. S. TREASURY, WASHINGTON, D. C.
South-west (Main) Front.

Morris, and Mr. R. H. Lee" (Journals of Congress No. 4 p. 567). The Navy at that time was under the jurisdiction of the Board of Admiralty, and the Treasury under that of the Committee on Finance, or Board of Treasury.

The said committee made a report as to the device for a seal for the Navy, but no record can be found of a report for the Treasury. A seal, however, was adopted, impressions of which may be found on original papers now in the files of the Office of the Register of the Treasury. Some minor changes have been made from time to time, but the seal adopted was substantially the same in device and legend as the seal of the Treasury Department at this day.

It may be interesting to state in this connection that Mr. Edward Stabler, of Sandy Springs, Montgomery County, Maryland (who was said to be one of the foremost die-sinkers and seal engravers of that period) was commissioned in 1849 to make a fac-simile of the original seal, which was nearly worn out. Mr. Stabler suggested some minor changes as improvements, but was informed that the design must be copied exactly "In accordance with the law." Diligent efforts have been made by numerous interested parties to locate the law referred to, but so far as I am informed, without avail.

The legend on the Treasury Department Seal is "Thesaur. Amer. Septent. Sigil.," being an abbreviation of the Latin sentence: "Thesauri

Americana Septentrionis Sigillum," meaning, The Seal of the Treasury of North America. The inference drawn from the history of those times would be that, in the event of success by the Colonies, the whole of North America would be represented by the symbol.

THE SECRETARY OF THE TREASURY.

The Secretary of the Treasury is charged by law with the management of the national finances. He prepares plans for the improvement of the revenue and for the support of the public credit; superintends the collection of the revenue, and prescribes the forms of keeping and rendering public accounts and of making returns; grants warrants for all moneys drawn from the Treasury in pursuance of appropriations made by law, and for the payment of moneys into the Treasury; and annually submits to Congress estimates of the probable revenues and disbursements of the Government. He also controls the construction of public buildings; the coinage and printing of money; the collection of statistics; the administration of the coast and geodetic survey, life-saving, light-house, revenue-cutter, steamboat-inspection, and marine-hospital branches of the public service, and furnishes generally such information as may be required by either branch of Congress on all matters pertaining to the foregoing. The routine work of the Secretary's office is transacted in the offices of the Supervising Architect, Director of the Mint, Chief of Bureau of Engraving and Printing, Supervising Surgeon-General of Marine Hospitals, General Superintendent of Life-Saving Service, Supervising Inspector-General of Steam Vessels, Bureau of Statistics, Light-House Board, and in the following divisions:

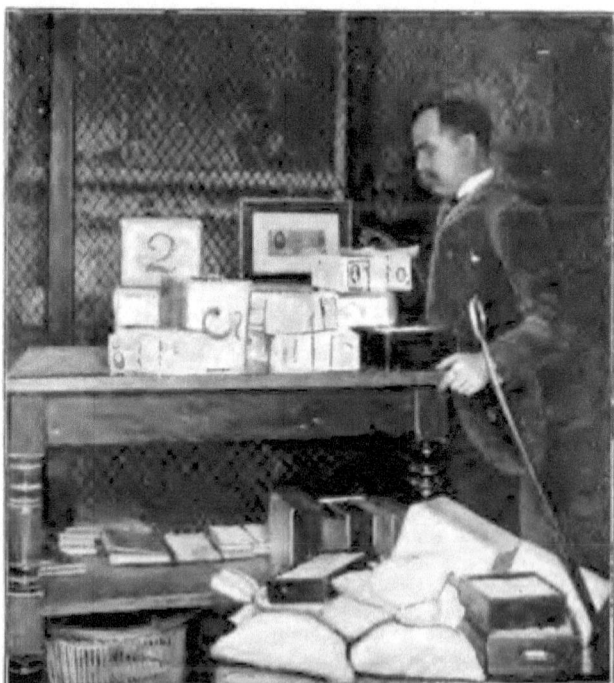

CASH ROOM VAULT (TREASURY DEPARTMENT).

CAPTAIN OF THE WATCH.
MAIN CORRIDOR TREASURY BUILDING.

Book-keeping and Warrants; Appointments; Customs; Public Moneys; Loans and Currency; Revenue Cutter; Stationery, Printing, and Blanks; Mails and Files; Special Agents; and Miscellaneous.

SUPERVISING ARCHITECT.

This officer is charged with the following duties: The preparation and duplication of plans for public buildings, the construction of the same, and with the repairs and preservation of such buildings, including marine-hospitals, the supply of heating apparatus, elevators, vaults, safes, locks, etc., therefore.

THE DIRECTOR OF THE MINT.

The Director of the Mint has general supervision of all the mints and assay offices of the United States. He prescribes rules, to be approved by the Secretary of the Treasury, for the transaction of business at the mints and assay offices. He regulates the distribution of silver coin and the charges to be collected of depositors. He receives for adjustment the accounts of the mints and assay offices, superintends their expenditures and annual settlements, and makes special examination of them when deemed necessary. All appointments, removals, and transfers in the mints and assay offices are subject to his approval. The purchase of silver bullion and the allotment of its coinage are made by the

REDEMPTION DIVISION (U. S. TREASURY).
KNIFE FOR CUTTING REDEEMED NOTES IN HALVES.

CASH ROOM.
PREPARING CURRENCY FOR SHIPMENT (TREASURY DEPT.)

Director, and, at his request, also transfers of the moneys in the mints and assay offices, and advances from appropriations for the mint service.

Tests of the weight and fineness of coins struck at the mints are made in the assay laboratory under his charge. The values of the standard coins of foreign countries are annually estimated for custom-house and other public purposes. Two annual reports are prepared by the Director, one for the fiscal year, and printed in the Finance Report of the Secretary of the Treasury, the other for the calendar year, on the statistics of the production of the precious metals.

CHIEF OF BUREAU OF ENGRAVING AND PRINTING.

DUTIES. The functions of the Bureau consist in the engraving and printing and otherwise preparing the United States currency, certificates of deposit, bonds, national currency, checks, miscellaneous drafts and warrants, internal revenue stamps, custom stamps and postage stamps.

SUPERVISING SURGEON-GENERAL MARINE HOSPITAL SERVICE.

The Supervising Surgeon-General is charged with the supervision of the marine hospitals and other relief stations of the service, and the care of sick and disabled seamen taken from the merchant vessels of the United States (ocean, lake and river), and from the vessels of the Revenue, Marine and Light-House Services. This supervision includes the purveying of medical and other supplies, the assignment of and orders to medical officers, the

Separating and trimming U. S. Notes received in sheets of 4 notes from Bureau of Engraving and Printing, in Issue Division U. S. Treasury Office

examination of requisitions, vouchers and property returns, and all matters pertaining to the service. Under his direction all applicants for pilot's licenses are examined for the detection of color-blindness. Ordinary seamen, on request of a master or agent, are examined physically to determine their fitness before shipment, and a like examination is made of the candidates for admission to the Revenue Marine Service and candidates for appointment as surfmen in the United States Life-Saving Service. He examines also and passes upon the medical certificates of claimants for pensions under the laws of the Life-Saving Service. Under the act of April 29, 1878, he is charged with the framing of regulations for the prevention of the introduction of contagious diseases and the prevention of their spread; and under the act of August 1, 1888, he is charged with the conduct of the quarantine service of the United States. He has the direction of laboratories established to investigate the cause of contagious diseases, and publishes each week an abstract of sanitary reports received from all parts of the United States and (through the State Department) from all foreign countries. Under the law of March 28, 1890, known as the Interstate quarantine law, he is charged with preparing the rules and regulations, under direction of the Secretary of the Treasury, necessary to prevent the introduction of certain contagious diseases from one State to another, and he has also supervision of the medical inspection of alien immigrants, which under the law of March 3, 1891, is conducted by the medical officers of the Marine Hospital Service.

GENERAL SUPERINTENDENT OF THE LIFE-SAVING SERVICE.

It is the duty of the General Superintendent to supervise the organization and government of the employes of the service; to prepare and revise regulations therefor as may be necessary; to fix the number and compensation of surfmen to be employed at the several stations within the provisions of law; to supervise the expenditure of all appropriations made for the support and maintenance of the Life-

BOND VAULT, U. S. TREASURER'S OFFICE.

Bonds held to secure circulation of National Banks; to secure deposits of public moneys with National Bank Depositories, and to secure trust funds (Miscellaneous).

Saving Service; to examine the accounts of disbursements of the district superintendents, and to certify the same to the accounting officers of the Treasury Department; to examine the property returns of the keepers of the several stations, and see that all public property thereto belonging is properly accounted for; to acquaint himself, as far as practicable, with all means employed in foreign countries which may seem to advantageously affect the interest of the service, and to cause to be properly investigated all plans, devices and inventions for the improvement of life-saving apparatus for use at the stations which may appear to be meritorious and available; to exercise supervision over the selection of sites for new stations the establishment of which may be authorized by law, or for old ones the removal of which may be made necessary by the encroachment of the sea or by other causes; to prepare and submit to the Secretary of the Treasury estimates for the support of the service; to collect and compile the statistics of marine disasters; to collect and compile the statistics of marine disasters contemplated by the act of June 20, 1874, and to submit to the Secretary of the Treasury, for transmission to Congress, an annual report of the expenditures of the moneys appropriated for the maintenance of the Life-Saving Service, and of the operations of said service during the year.

INTERIOR OF CASH ROOM (TREASURY DEPARTMENT).

SUPERVISING INSPECTOR-GENERAL OF STEAM VESSELS.

The Supervising Inspector-General superintends the administration of the steamboat inspection laws, presides at the meeting of the Board of Supervising Inspectors, receives all reports, and examines all accounts of inspectors. The Board of Supervising Inspectors meets in Washington annually, on the third Wednesday in January, to establish regulations for carrying out the provisions of the steamboat inspection laws.

BUREAU OF STATISTICS.

The Chief of the Bureau of Statistics collects and publishes the statistics of our foreign commerce, embracing tables showing the imports

REDEMPTION DIVISION (U. S. TREASURY).
Canceling machine punching 4 holes (one in each corner) of redeemed notes.

and exports, respectively, by countries and customs districts; the transit trade inwards and outwards by countries and by customs districts; imported commodities warehoused, withdrawn from, and remaining in warehouse; the imports of merchandise entered for consumption, showing quantity, value, rates of duty, and amounts of duty collected on each article or class of articles; number of immigrants, their nationality, occupation, etc., arriving from foreign countries, and the number of passengers departing for foreign countries; the inward and outward movement in our foreign trade and the countries whence entered and for which cleared, distinguishing the nationalities of the foreign vessels; also special information in regard to our internal commerce. The publication of the Bureau are as follows: Annual Report on Commerce and Navigation; Annual Report of Internal Commerce; Annual Statistical Abstract of the United States; Quarter-yearly Reports on Commerce, Navigation and Immigration; Monthly Summary Statements of Imports and Exports; Monthly Reports of Exports of Breadstuffs, of Provisions, of Petroleum, and Cotton; Monthly Reports of Total Values of Foreign Commerce and Immigration.

LIGHT HOUSE BOARD.

LIGHT HOUSE ESTABLISHMENT: By the Act of August 7, 1789, it was provided that all expense for the support, maintenance, and repairs of light houses, beacons, buoys and public piers, erected, placed, or sunk before the passing of said Act, should be defrayed out of the Treasury of the United States, provided such

ISSUE DIVISION (U. S. TREASURY OFFICE).
Employe in charge of sealing U. S. paper currency; 4,000 notes in each package which is delivered to the Reserve Vault.

light-houses, etc., should in the meantime be ceded to and vested in the United States, by the State or States in which they were located, together with the lands and tenements thereunto belonging, and together with the jurisdiction of the same. By this Act the Secretary of the Treasury was charged with the preparation of contracts for all materials and supplies, said contracts to be approved by the President, and with the fixing of the compensation of employes, to be appointed by the President.

LIGHT-HOUSE BOARD: The Light-House Board was organized by the Act of August 31, 1852, which required it to make a plan for the lighting of the coasts (ocean, lake and river) of the United States.

This report was made and submitted to Congress, by which it was in effect adopted. The plan provides, in brief, for lighting the whole coast-lines of the United States, including those of the Atlantic and Pacific, those of the lakes and of the larger rivers. "The President shall appoint two officers of the Navy, of high rank, two officers of the Corps of Engineers of the Army, and two civilians of high scientific attainments, whose services may be at the disposal of the President, together with an officer of the Navy and an officer of Engineers of the Army, as secretaries, who shall constitute the Light-House Board (R. S. Sec. 4653). "The Secretary of the Treasury shall be *ex-officio* president of the Light-House Board" (R. S. Sec. 4654).

REDEMPTION (U. S. TREASURY).
A "counter" engaged in the redemption of mutilated currency.

DUTIES OF THE BOARD: The Light-House Board, under the superintendence of the Secretary of the Treasury, discharges all administrative duties relating to: The construction, illumination, inspection, and superintendence of light-houses, light-vessels, beacons, buoys, sea-marks, and their appendages, and embracing the security of foundation of works already existing; procuring illuminating and other apparatus, supplies and materials of all kinds for building, and for rebuilding when necessary, and keeping in good repair the light-houses, light-vessels, beacons and buoys of the United States; has charge and custody of all the archives, books, documents, drawings, models, returns, apparatus, and other things appertaining to the Light-House Establishment; and has charge of the purchase of the necessary land for the erection of light-houses, where the proper site does not belong to the United States, out of the appropriations made.

The Atlantic coast-line is about 5,000 miles long, that of the Pacific about 1,500, that of the lakes about 3,000, that of the rivers about 5,500 miles, making a total of about 15,000 miles.

SUPERINTENDENT OF IMMIGRATION.

The Superintendent of Immigration is charged with the duties, under the control and supervision of the Secretary of the Treasury, of enforcing the laws in relation to immigration. These laws are embraced in the Acts of March 3, 1875, August 3, 1882, June 26, 1884, February 26, 1885, October 19, 1888, February 23, 1887, March 3, 1891, and March 3, 1893. The office of Superintendent of Immigration was created by section 7 of the Act of March 3, 1891. All inspection and other officers in the immigration service are assigned to duty by the Superintendent, their official duties and conduct are supervised by him, and all correspondence between the Department and the officers in the immigration service is conduced by the Superintendent.

Section 5 of the Act of March 3, 1893, provides that it shall be the duty of every inspector of arriving alien immigrants to detain for a special inquiry, under section 1 of the immigration act of March 3, 1891, every person who may not appear to him to be clearly and beyond doubt entitled to admission, and all special inquiries shall be conducted by not less than four officials acting as inspectors, to be designated in writing by the Secretary of the Treasury or the Superintendent of Immigration, for conducting special inquiries, and no immigrant shall be admitted upon special inquiry except after a favorable decision made by at least three of said inspectors, and any decision to admit shall be subject to appeal by any dissenting inspector to the Superintendent of Immigration, whose action shall be subject to review by the Secretary of the Treasury, as provided in section 8 of said immigration act of March 3, 1891. When an appeal is thus taken to the Superintendent of Immigration he will prepare and sign his decision in the case, and submit the same to the Secretary, who will indicate thereon with his signature his approval or disapproval. If the decision is approved it will be promulgated as written; if disapproved it will be promulgated as revised.

Immigration inspectors under the alien contract-labor laws are required, in connection with their regular duties, to render all assistance in their power to the enforcement of the United States customs laws, and to this end, whenever circumstances render this course practicable, they are subject to the immediate authority of the respective collectors of customs in the districts to which they are assigned.

THE COMMISSIONER OF NAVIGATION.

The Commissioner of Navigation is charged with general superintendendence of the commercial marine and merchant seamen of the United States, except so far as supervision is lodged with other officers of the Government. He is specially charged with the decision of all questions relating to the issue of registers, enrollments, and licenses of vessels and the filling of those documents, with the supervision of laws relating to the admeasurement, letters and numbers of vessels, and with the final decision of questions concerning the collection and refund of tonnage taxes. He is empowered to change the names of vessels, prepares annually a list of vessels in the United States, and reports annually to the Secretary of the Treasury the operations of the laws relative to navigation.

THE SUPERINTENDENT OF THE COAST AND GEODETIC SURVEY.

The Coast and Geodetic Survey is charged with the survey of the Atlantic, Gulf, and Pacific coasts of the United States, including the coasts of Alaska; the survey of rivers to the head of tide-water or ship navigation; deep-sea soundings, temperature and current observations along the said coasts and throughout the Gulf Stream and Japan Stream flowing off from them; magnetic observations and gravity research; determinations of heights by geodetic leveling, and of geographical positions by lines of trans-continental triangulation, which, with other connecting triangulations and observations for latitude, longitude, and azimuth, furnish points of reference for State surveys and connect the work on the Atlantic coast with that on the Pacific. Results of the survey are published in the form of annual reports, which include professional papers of value; bulletins which give information deemed important for immediate publication; notices to mariners, issued monthly; tide tables, issued annually; charts upon various scales, including harbor charts, general charts of the coast, and sailing charts; chart catalogues and Coast Pilots.

J. A. THATCHER.
PRESIDENT DENVER NATIONAL BANK, DENVER, COL.

SECRET SERVICE DIVISION.

This Division is charged with the following duties: The suppression of counterfeiting the obligations and coins of the Government; the suppression of the production or sale of all articles in imitation of the obligations or coins of the Government; investigation of all suspected fraudulent claims of back pay and bounty for the Auditor for the War Department; investigation of all suspected fraudulent or excessive claims for reimbursement of expenses incurred in last sickness and burial of pensioners for the Auditor for the Interior Department; investigating alleged frauds in seamen's back pay, bounty, and prize money for the Auditor for the Navy Department, and miscellaneous work relating to robbery and embezzlement of public funds.

THE COMPTROLLER OF THE TREASURY.

The Act of July 31, 1894, reorganizing the accounting offices of the Government, abolished the office of Second Comptroller of the Treasury and the Commissioner of Customs, and provided that hereafter the First Comptroller shall be known as the Comptroller of the Treasury. The Comptroller is not charged with the duty of revising accounts, except upon appeal from the settlements made by the Auditors, an appeal to be taken within one year by either the claimant, the head of the Department interested, or by the Comptroller himself. Upon the request of a disbursing officer, or the head of a Department, the Comptroller is required to give his decision upon the validity of a payment to be made, which decision, when rendered, shall govern the Auditors and the Comptroller in the settle-ment of the account involving payment; to approve, disapprove, or modify all decisions made by the Auditors making an original construction, or modifying an existing construction of statutes, and to certify his action to the Auditor. He shall transmit all decisions made by him forthwith to the Auditor or Auditors whose duties are affected thereby. By the regulations of the Department the Comptroller passes upon the sufficiency of authorities to indorse drafts and receive and receipt for money from the Government, upon the evidence presented in applications for duplicates or lost or destroyed United States bonds, drafts, checks, etc. The forms of keeping and rendering all public accounts (except those relating to the postal service), the recovery of debts certified by the Auditors to be due the United States, and the preservation, with their vouchers and certificates, of accounts finally adjusted, are under the direction of the Comptroller. Upon revision of accounts, appealed from the several Auditors to the Comptroller, his decision upon such revision is final and conclusive upon the executive branch of the Government.

AUDITOR FOR THE TREASURY DEPARTMENT.

The Auditor for the Treasury Department receives and examines all accounts of salaries and incidental expenses of the office of the Secretary of the Treasury and all bureaus and offices under his direction. All accounts relating to the customs service, public debt, internal revenue, Treasurer and Assistant Treasurers, mints and assay offices, Bureau of Engraving and Printing, Coast and Geodetic Survey, Revenue-Cutter Service, Life Saving Service, Light House Board, Marine Hospital, Public Buildings, Steam-boat-Inspection Service, Immigration Service, Bureau of Navigation, Secret Service, Alaskan Fur-Seal Fisheries, and all other business within the jurisdiction of the Department of the Treasury, and certifies the balances arising thereon to the Division of Bookkeeping and Warrants.

AUDITORS FOR THE WAR DEPARTMENT.

The Auditor for the War Department receives and examines all accounts of salaries and incidental expenses of the office of the Secretary of War and all bureaus and offices under his direction, all accounts relating to the military establishment, armories and arsenals, national cemeteries, fortifications, public buildings and grounds under the Chief of Engineers, rivers and harbors, the Military Academy, and to all other business within the jurisdiction of the Department of War, and certifies the balances arising thereon to the Division of Bookkeeping and Warrants, and sends a copy of each certificate to the Secretary of War. This office is not located in the Treasury Department, but in the "Winder Building" near the War Department as a matter of convenience.

THE AUDITOR FOR THE INTERIOR DEPARTMENT.

CHARLES WARREN.
CASHIER AMERICAN NATIONAL BANK, LOUISVILLE, KY.

The Auditor for the Interior Department shall receive and examine all accounts of salaries and incidental expenses of the office of the Secretary of the Interior, and of all bureaus and offices under his direction, and all accounts relating to Army and Navy pensions, Geological Survey, public lands, Indians, Architect of the Capitol, patents, census, and to all other business within the jurisdiction of the Department of the Interior, and certify the balances arising thereon to the Division of Bookkeeping and Warrants, and send forthwith a copy of each certificate to the Secretary of the Interior."

THE AUDITOR FOR THE NAVY DEPARTMENT.

The Auditor for the Navy Department examines and settles all accounts of the Navy Department, including the office of the Secretary of the Navy, and all offices and bureaus under his direction, certifying the balances arising thereon to the Secretary of the Treasury (Division of Bookkeeping and Warrants), sending a copy of each certificate to the Secretary of the Navy.

THE AUDITOR FOR THE STATE AND OTHER DEPARTMENTS.

The Auditor for the State and other Departments receives, examines and certifies the balances arising thereon to the Division of Bookkeeping and Warrants all accounts of salaries and incidental expenses of the offices of the Secretary of State, the Attorney-General, and the Secretary of Agriculture, and of all bureaus and offices under their direction; all accounts relating to all other business within the jurisdiction of the Department of State, Justice and Agriculture; all accounts relating to the diplomatic and consular service, the judiciary, United States courts, judgments of the United States courts, Executive Office, Civil Service Commission, Interstate Commerce Commission, Department of Labor, District of Columbia, Fish Commission, Court of Claims and its judgments, Smithsonian Institution, Territorial governments, the Senate, the House of Representatives, the Public Printer, Library of Congress, Botanic Garden, and accounts of all boards, commissions, and establishments of the Government not within the jurisdiction of any of the Executive Departments. He also examines and approves or disapproves all requisitions for advances of money made by all persons authorized to do so in any of the above-named Departments, commissions or establishments.

THE AUDITOR FOR THE POST-OFFICE DEPARTMENT.

The Auditor for the Post-Office Department examines and adjusts all accounts relating to the postal service, and his decisions on these are final, unless an appeal be taken in twelve months to the Comptroller. He superintends the collection of all debts due the United States for the service of the Post-Office Department, and all penalties imposed; directs suits and all legal proceedings in civil actions, and takes all legal means to enforce the payment of money due the United States for the service of the Post-Office Department. This office is not located in the Treasury Department, but in the Post-Office Department, as a matter of convenience.

THE TREASURER OF THE UNITED STATES.

The Treasurer of the United States is charged with the receipt and disbursement of all public moneys that may be deposited in the Treasury at Washington and the sub-treasuries at Boston, New York, Philadelphia, Baltimore, New Orleans, San Francisco, St. Louis, Chicago and Cincinnati, and in the national-bank United States depositaries; is trustee for bonds held to secure national-bank circulation and public deposits in national banks; is custodian of Indian trust-fund bonds; is agent for paying the interest on the public debt, and ex-officio commissioner of the sinking fund of the District of Columbia. The Treasury sub-divisions are:

CHIEF CLERK—Receives and distributes the official mail; has charge of the correspondence and the disposition and payment of the clerical force, and the custody of the records and files; and the issue of duplicate checks and drafts.

CASH DIVISION—For receipt and payment of public funds at Washington.

ISSUE DIVISION—Completion of new United States notes, gold and silver certificates, and count of silver, gold and minor coin.

REDEMPTION DIVISION—All currency except national-bank notes received and redeemed.

LOAN DIVISION—Interest checks prepared and bonds redeemed.

ACCOUNTS DIVISION—The accounts of the Treasury, the sub-treasuries, and the United States national-bank depositaries are kept.

NATIONAL BANK DIVISION—Has custody of bonds held for national bank circulation, for public deposits, and various public trusts, and makes collection of semi-annual duty.

NATIONAL BANK REDEMPTION AGENCY—Notes of national banks are redeemed and accounted for.

THE REGISTER OF THE TREASURY.

The Register of the Treasury signs and issues all bonds and sends to the Treasurer of the United States schedules showing the names of persons entitled to receive interest thereon. He examines and registers redeemed bonds, paid interest coupons, interest checks and interest bearing notes, legal tenders and fractional currency.

PRESIDENT STATE SAVINGS BANK, DETROIT, MICH.

THE COMPTROLLER OF THE CURRENCY.

The Comptroller of the Currency has, under the direction of the Secretary of the Treasury, the control of the national banks. The divisions of this Bureau are:

ORGANIZATION DIVISION—The organization of national banks.

ISSUE DIVISION—The preparation and issue of national-bank circulation.

REPORTS DIVISION—Examination and consolidation of the report of national banks.

REDEMPTION DIVISION—The redemption and destruction of notes issued by national banks.

THE COMMISSIONER OF INTERNAL REVENUE.

The Commissioner makes assessment of, and has general superintendence of the collection of all internal revenue taxes; employment of internal revenue agents; compensation and duties of gaugers, storekeepers, and other subordinate officers; the preparation and distribution of stamps, instructions, regulations, forms, blanks, hydrometers, stationery, etc.; and analysis of foods and drugs in the District of Columbia, and payment of bounty on sugar.

THE SOLICITOR.

The Solicitor of the Treasury takes cognizance of all frauds or attempted frauds on the customs revenue. He is charged by law with duties regarding the compromise of debts and with a supervision over suits for the collection of moneys due the United States, excepting those due under internal revenue laws. His approval is required of official bonds of United States Assistant Treasurers, Department disbursing clerks, collectors of internal revenue, the Secretary and the Chief Clerk of the Department of Agriculture. As the law officer of the Treasury Department many matters are referred to him for his examination and opinion arising under the customs, navigation, banking, and registry laws, and in the administration of the Department. He is also charged by law with the supervision of suits and proceedings arising out of the provisions of law governing national banking associations in which the United States and any of its agents or officers are parties; also, with the charge, release, and sale of lands acquired in payment of debt, excepting those acquired under internal revenue laws.

(NOTE:—The Solicitor of the Treasury is not an officer of the Treasury Department, but of the Department of Justice. As his functions pertain to the Treasury Department the office is located therein as a matter of convenience.)

SOLICITOR OF INTERNAL REVENUE.

The Act of July 13, 1866, (14 Stat., p. 170), created the office of Solicitor of Internal Revenue, as a part of the corps of the Internal Revenue Office, but by the Act of June 22, 1870, (16 Stat., p. 162), organizing the Department of Justice, the Solicitor was formally trasferred to that Department. Although an officer of the Department of Justice his office is located in the Treasury Department, as a matter of convenience, his duties being intimately connected, as the title indicates, with the office of the Commissioner of Internal Revenue.

DUTIES OF THE SOLICITOR:—He is the law officer and law adviser of the Commissioner of Internal Revenue. He is charged with duties of a miscellaneous nature involving advice upon points of law, but his principal functions, as defined by law, are in connection with comprise cases, as follows: "The Commissioner of Internal Revenue, with the advice and consent of the Secretary of the Treasury, may compromise any civil or criminal case arising under the internal revenue laws instead of commencing suit thereon; and, with the advice and consent of the said Secretary and the recommendation of the Attorney-General, he may compromise any such case after a suit thereon has been commenced. Whenever a compromise is made in any case there shall be placed on file in the office of the Commissioner the opinion of the Solicitor of Internal Revenue, or of the officer acting as such, with his reasons therefor with a statement of the amount of tax assessed, the amount of additional tax or penalty imposed by law in consequence of the neglect or delinquency of the person against whom the tax is assessed, and the amount actually paid in accordance with the terms of the compromise." (Revised Statute, Section 3229).

A. C. JOBES.
CASHIER KANSAS NATIONAL BANK, WICHITA, KANSAS.

HISTORY OF THE OFFICE OF TREASURER OF THE UNITED STATES.

JOINT TREASURERS (CONTINENTAL). Under date of July 29, 1775, (Journals of Congress, vol. 1, p. 173), it was resolved "That Michael Hillegas and George Clymer, Esqrs., be *joint Treasurers* of the United Colonies. By the same resolution (Ibid., p. 174), they were styled *Continental Treasurers*. CONTINENTAL TREASURER: Under date of August 6, 1776, (Ibid., vol. 2, p. 299), it was resolved that for future there be only one Continental Treasurer, Mr. G. Clymer, one of the joint Treasurers, being appointed a delegate to Congress by the Convention of Pennsylvania. TREASURER OF THE UNITED STATES: By the resolution of September 6, 1777, (Ibid., vol. 3, p. 301), additional compensation was "allowed to Michael Hillegas, Esq., *Treasurer of the United States*, from the 6th day of August, 1776, when Mr. Clymer resigned the office of joint Treasurer." On March 22, 1785, (Ibid., vol. 10, p. 96), mention is made of Michael Hillegas, Esquire, *Continental Treasurer*."

Mr. Hillegas held the office of Treasurer continuously from July 29, 1775, to September 11, 1789. The first entry to be found on the records in the office of the Register of the Treasury is under date of April 16, 1776, (see "Waste-Book). The last entry on the original ledger accounts, also in the Office of the Register, prior to the date of the commission of Mr. Meredith, is under date of August 28, 1789.

TREASURY DEPARTMENT ESTABLISHED. — THE TREASURER—By the act of September 2, 1789, (1 Stat., p. 65), the Treasury Department was established. It was provided that, among other officers, there should be a Treasurer. The first incumbent under said act was Samuel Meredith, whose commission bore the date of September 11, 1789, (see U. S. Treasury Register).

ISSUE AND REDEMPTION OF CURRENCY.

(Based upon Treasury Department circular No. 162 of November 1, 1894).

The following regulations govern the issue, redemption, and exchange of the paper currency and the gold, silver, and minor coins of the United States and the redemption of national bank notes by the Treasurer of the United States:

ISSUE OF UNITED STATES PAPER CURRENCY. The Treasurer will forward new United States notes, Treasury notes of 1890, or silver certificates, by express, at the expense of the consignee, at Government contract rates, or by registered mail, registration free, at the risk of the consignee, in return for such notes or certificates unfit for circulation, national bank notes, fractional silver coin, or minor coin, received for redemption.

Silver certificates are issued by the Treasurer or Assistant Treasurers upon a deposit of standard silver dollars.

ISSUE OF GOLD COIN. Gold coin is issued in redemption of United States notes, in sums not less than $50, by the Assistant Treasurers in New York and San Francisco, and in redemption of Treasury notes of 1890, in like sums, by the Treasurer and all the Assistant Treasurers.

ISSUE OF STANDARD SILVER DOLLARS. Standard silver dollars are issued by the Treasurer and Assistant Treasurers in redemption of silver certificates and Treasury notes of 1890, and are sent by express, at the expense of the Government, in sums or multiples of $500, for silver certificates or Treasury notes of 1890 deposited with the Treasurer or any Assistant Treasurer.

ISSUE OF FRACTIONAL SILVER COIN. Upon the deposit of an equivalent sum in United States currency or national bank notes with the Treasurer or any Assistant Treasurer or national bank depositary, fractional silver coin will be paid in any amount by the Treasurer or Assistant Treasurers in the cities where their several officers are, or will be sent by express, in sums of $200 or more, at the expense of the Government, or by registered mail, at the risk of the consignee, in packages of $50, registration free, from the most convenient Treasury office, to the order of the depositor. For this purpose drafts may be sent to the Treasurer or the Assistant Treasurer in New York, payable in their respective cities to the order of the officer to whom sent.

ISSUE OF MINOR COIN. Minor coin is issued under the following regulations of the Director of the Mint:

Five-cent nickel and one-cent bronze pieces will be furnished in the order of application from the United States Mint at Philadelphia, Pa., to points reached by the United States and connecting express companies, free of transportation charges, in sums of $20, or multiples thereof, except New York, Boston, Baltimore, Philadelphia, Cincinnati, Chicago, St. Louis, New Orleans,

JAS. W. ENGLISH,
PRESIDENT AMERICAN TRUST & BANKING CO., ATLANTA, GA.

and San Francisco, upon receipt and collection by the Superintendent of that Mint of a draft on New York or Philadelphia payable to his order. To points not reached by express companies, delivery under contract with the Government being impracticable, these coins will be sent by registered mail at applicant's risk, registry fee to be paid by the Government.

A supply of these coins will be kept on hand by the Assistant

Treasurers of the United States at New York, Boston, Philadelphia, Baltimore, Cincinnati, Chicago, St. Louis, New Orleans and San Francisco, and application for them should be made to the sub-treasuries.

Minor coin is not forwarded by express to applicants by the Treasurer or Assistant Treasurers, nor is it forwarded by the mint at Philadelphia to applicants in cities where there are sub-treasuries.

The Treasurer and Assistant Treasurers will pay out for lawful money any minor coin not needed in the current business of their offices, but in no case should drafts be sent to them for it.

ISSUE OF THE TREASURER'S TRANSFER CHECKS. Subject to the convenience of the Treasury, and provided that the express charges on remittances have been prepaid, the Treasurer will issue transfer checks on the Assistant Treasurers, payable to the order of the sender or his correspondent, for United States notes and Treasury notes of 1890 unfit for circulation or national bank notes sent to Treasurer for redemption, or for fractional silver coin or minor coin sent in multiples of $20 to the Treasurer or Assistant Treasurer, but not for silver certificates sent for redemption.

REDEMPTION OF PAPER CURRENCY.

BY TREASURER AND ASSISTANT TREASURERS. United States notes, fractional currency notes, gold certificates, silver certificates, and Treasury notes of 1890, are redeemable by the Treasurer, and when not mutilated so that less than three-fifths of the original proportions remains, by the several Assistant Treasurers, at face value.

UNITED STATES NOTES are redeemable in coin, in sums not less than $50, by the Assistant Treasurers in New York and San Francisco.

TREASURY NOTES OF 1890 are redeemable in coin, in sums not less than $50, by the Treasurer and all the Assistant Treasurers.

SILVER CERTIFICATES are redeemable in standard silver dollars only, or exchangeable for other silver certificates.

NATIONAL BANK NOTES are redeemable in lawful money of the United States by the Treasurer, but not by the Assistant Treasurers.

LESS THAN THREE-FIFTHS OF NOTES. United States notes, fractional currency notes, gold certificates, silver certificates, Treasury notes of 1890, and national bank notes, when mutilated so that less than three-fifths, but clearly more than two-fifths, of the original proportions remains, are redeemable by the Treasurer only, at one-half the face value of the whole note or certificate. Fragments not clearly more than two-fifths are not redeemed, unless accompanied by the evidence required in the following paragraph:

AFFIDAVITS. Fragments less than three-fifths are redeemed at the face value of the whole note when accompanied by an affidavit of the owner or other persons having knowledge of the facts that the missing portions have been totally destroyed. The affidavit must state the cause and manner of the mutilation, and must be sworn and subscribed to before an officer qualified to administer oaths, who must affix his official seal thereto, and the character of the affiant must be certified to be good by such officer or some other having an official seal. Signatures by mark (X) must be witnessed by two persons who can write, and who must give their places of residence. The Treasurer will exercise such discretion under this regulation as may seem to him needful to protect the United States from fraud. Fragments not redeemable are rejected and returned.

RETURNS FOR PAPER CURRENCY.

For remittances received under the Government contract:

SUB-TREASURY CITIES. For remittances from a place where there is a sub-treasury, returns will be made in new United States paper currency by express, at the expense of the consignee, at Government contract rates; or, subject to the convenience of the Treasury, in the Treasurer's transfer checks on the subtreasury in the place from whence the remittance is received.

OTHER PLACES. For remittances from a place where there is no sub-treasury returns will be made in new United States paper currency by express, at the expense of the consignee, at Government contract rates; or in fractional silver coin, at the expense of the Government for transportation, in sums or multiples of $200.

NO EXCHANGE. No exchange for remittances of currency to the Treasurer for redemption under the Government contract will be furnished either by transfer checks or shipments of currency.

REDEMPTION OR EXCHANGE OF SILVER AND MINOR COIN.

ASSORTMENT. Fractional silver coin and coins of copper, bronze, or copper-nickel may be presented in sums or multiples of $20,

J. J. SULLIVAN.
CASHIER CENTRAL NATIONAL BANK, CLEVELAND, OHIO.

assorted by denominations in separate packages, to the Treasurer or an Assistant Treasurer for redemption or exchange into lawful money, and standard silver dollars for exchange into silver certificates only. When forwarded by express, the charges should be prepaid.

OLD AND NEW DESIGN. Depositors of fractional silver coin will obtain quicker returns and aid the Department in retiring the old issues from circulation, if they will present coins of the old designs and the new in separate packages.

NOT RECEIVED. No foreign, mutilated, or defaced silver coins or coins to which paper or any other substance has been attached as an advertisement or for any other purpose, will be received. Reduction by natural abrasion is not considered mutilation.

DEFACED MINOR COIN. Minor coin that is so defaced as not to be readily identified, or that is punched or clipped, will not be redeemed or exchanged. Pieces that are stamped, bent, or twisted out of shape, or otherwise imperfect, but showing no material loss of metal, will be redeemed.

TRANSMISSION TO THE TREASURER.

MAKING UP PACKAGES. United States notes, gold certificates, silver certificates, Treasury notes of 1890, and national bank notes should be sent in separate remittances. The notes should be assorted by denominations and inclosed in paper straps, not more than 100 notes to each strap, and the straps should be marked with the amount of their contents. Not more than 8,000 notes should be put in one package.

INVENTORY. An inventory, giving the amount of each denomination of notes, the total amount in the package, the address of the party sending, and the disposition to be made of the proceeds, should be inclosed with each package, and a letter of advice sent by mail.

PACKAGES BY EXPRESS. The package, if sent by express, should be sealed up in stout paper and addressed to the "Treasurer of the United States, Washington, D. C." The wrapper should be plainly marked with the owner's name and address, the amount and kind of currency inclosed, and, if the sender desires the benefit of the Government contract, with the words "under Government contract with the United States Express Company."

REGISTRATION FREE OF CHARGE. It is the duty of postmasters to register free of charge all letters on which the postage has been fully prepaid, addressed to the Treasurer, containing currency of the United States for redemption. It is recommended that all such letters be registered as a protection against loss.

REMITTANCES BY MAIL. Remittances of money by mail should be addressed to the "Treasurer of the United States, Washington, D. C." Such remittances and returns therefore by mail are invariably at the risk of the owners. All communications to the Treasurer in regard to packages lost in the mail are referred for investigation to the Chief Post-Office Inspector, Post Office Department, Washington, D. C., to whom any subsequent inquiry should be addressed.

EXPRESS CHARGES.

GOVERNMENT CONTRACT. The Government contract with the United States Express Company for the transportation of moneys and securities extends to all points accessible through established express lines reached by continuous railway communication, in all the States and Territories of the United States, excepting Alaska, Arizona, California, Idaho, Nevada, New Mexico, Oregon, Utah, and Washington, but does not embrace sea, river, or stage transportation of any kind.

RATES. The contract rates for the transportation of all kinds of paper currency to or from Washington are:

W. J. HAYES.
OF W. J. HAYES & SONS, BANKERS, CLEVELAND–BOSTON–NEW YORK.

Between Washington and points in the territory of the United States Express Company and reached by it, 20 cents per $1,000 or fractional part thereof over $500; sums of $500 or fractional part thereof, 10 cents.

Between Washington and points in the territory of another express company excepting points in Texas, Arkansas, Colorado, Kansas, Nebraska, Montana, North Dakota, South Dakota, Wyoming, and the Indian and Oklahoma Territories, 60 cents per $1,000 or fractional part thereof over $500; sums of $500 or fractional part thereof, 40 cents.

Between Washington and points in Colorado, Kansas, and Nebraska, 75 cents per $1,000 or fractional part thereof over $500; sums of $500 or fractional part thereof, 50 cents.

Between Washington and points in Texas, Arkansas, Montana, North Dakota, South Dakota, Wyoming, and the the Indian and Oklahoma Territories, $1 per $1,000 or fractional part thereof over $500; sums of $500 or fractional part thereof, 65 cents.

EXPRESS CHARGES PAID BY GOVERNMENT. Express charges are paid by the Government, at contract rates, on standard silver dollars sent by the Treasurer or Assistant Treasurer in sums or multiples of $500, or fractional silver coin in sums of $200 or more, and on minor coin sent from the mint at Philadelphia in sums or multiples of $20.

ON CURRENCY SENT FOR REDEMPTION. On United States notes, gold certificates, silver certificates, Treasury notes of 1890, or national bank notes, sent for redemption, and on any kind of lawful money sent for credit of the 5 per cent. redemption fund, the charges, if not prepaid, are deducted from the proceeds at contract rates.

ON RETURNS IN CURRENCY. On United States notes, gold certificates, silver certificates, or Treasury notes of 1890, returned for United States currency or national bank notes redeemed, the charges are deducted at contract rates.

ON SILVER AND MINOR COIN. On standard silver dollars, fractional silver coin, and minor coin, sent for exchange or redemption the charges must be prepaid by the sender.

ON TRANSFERS OF FUNDS. On transfer of funds from national bank depositaries, under letters of instruction, the charges must be paid by the depositaries.

CONTROL OF RATES. The Treasurer has no control over rates exacted when the charges are prepaid, or for the transportation outside of the territorial limits of the contract.

EXPRESS CHARGES INCLOSED. No charge is made for the amount of express charges inclosed with a remittance when separately noted on the wrapper. Packages should always be marked with the exact amount of the contents.

GENERAL INFORMATION.

ASSORTMENT OF CURRENCY BY KINDS AND DENOMINATIONS. Paper currency presented for redemption or exchange or for credit of the Treasurer at the offices of the Assistant Treasurers must be assorted by kinds and denominations, and inclosed in paper straps, the straps not to contain more than 100 notes each, and to be plainly marked with the amount of the contents.

STAMPING COUNTERFEIT MONEY. The act of June 30, 1876, (19 Statutes, 64), requires "that all United States officers charged with the receipt or disbursement of public moneys, and all officers of national banks, shall stamp or write in plain letters the word 'counterfeit,' 'altered,' or 'worthless' upon all fraudulent notes issued in the form of and intended to circulate as money which shall be presented at their places of business; and if such officers shall wrongfully stamp any genuine note of the United States or of the national banks, they shall, upon presentation, redeem such notes at the face value thereof."

DISPOSITION OF COUNTERFEIT MONEY. Counterfeit notes or coins found in remittances to this office are returned to the sender canceled for the purpose of enabling him to make reclamation, and after such use they must be returned to the Treasurer for transfer to the Secret-Service Division of the Treasury Department.

REFUNDING CERTIFICATES.

The Act of February 26, 1879, (20 Statutes, 321), authorized the Secretary of the Treasury to issue, in exchange for lawful money of the United States, certificates of deposit, of the denomination of ten dollars, bearing interest at the rate of 4 per cent. per annum, and convertible at any time, with accrued interest, into the 4 per cent. bonds described in the refunding act.

The said Act made no provision for their payment in money. After July 1, 1907, when the 4 per cent. bonds become redeemable at the option of Government, holders of certificates, if the Secretary so directs, may receive in cash their face value with interest accrued to that date. No money can be accepted in the conversion of these certificates to make up the amount required for the issue of a bond; only their face value and the accrued interest can be applied.

Parties sending certificates for conversion should state whether registered or coupon bonds are desired, and should forward the certificates to the Treasurer, who will furnish the necessary data for the issue of bonds by the Secretary. Any excess of interest is returned by check to the remittor.

ORRIN BUMP,
PRESIDENT OLD SECOND NATIONAL BANK, BAY CITY, MICHIGAN

GOLD CERTIFICATES.

FIRST AUTHORIZED. The issue of Gold Certificates was authorized by Section 5 of the Act of March 3, 1863, (12 Stat., p. 709). as follows:

That the Secretary of the Treasury is hereby authorized to receive deposits of gold coin and bullion with the Treasurer or any Assistant

Treasurer of the United States, in sums not less than twenty dollars, and to issue certificates therefor, in denominations of not less than twenty dollars each, corresponding with the denominations of the United States notes. The coin and bullion deposited for or representing the certificates of deposit shall be retained in the Treasury for the payment of the same on demand. And certificates representing coin in the Treasury may be issued in payment of interest on the public debt, which certificates, together with those issued for coin and bullion deposited, shall not at any time exceed twenty per centum beyond the amount of coin and bullion in the Treasury; and the certificates for coin or bullion in the Treasury shall be received at par in payment for duties on imports."

It will be observed that under the foregoing Act the Secretary was authorized, but not required, to issue certificates on deposits of gold coin and bullion. Their issue under this Act was discontinued during the fiscal year ending June 30, 1879.

PRESENT AUTHORITY. By Section 12 of the Act of July 12, 1882, (22 Stat., p. 165), their issue was "authorized and directed," as follows:

"That the Secretary of the Treasury is authorized and directed to receive deposits of gold coin with the Treasurer or Assistant Treasurer of the United States, in sums not less than twenty dollars, and to issue certificates therefor in denominations of not less than twenty dollars each, corresponding with the denominations of United States notes. The coin deposited for or representing the certificates of deposit shall be retained in the Treasury for the payment of the same on demand. Said certificates shall be receivable for customs, taxes, and all public dues, and when so received may be re-issued; and such certificates, as also silver certificates, when held by any national banking association, shall be counted as part of its lawful reserve; and no national banking association shall be a member of any clearing house in which such certificates shall not be receivable in the settlement of clearing house balances: PROVIDED, That the Secretary of the Treasury shall suspend the issue of such gold certificates whenever the amount of gold coin and gold bullion in the Treasury reserved for the redemption of United States notes falls below one hundred millions of dollars; * * * *."

ONE HUNDRED MILLION RESERVE. In accordance with the provisions of the foregoing Act the issue of gold certificates was suspended on April 14, 1893, the gold coin and bullion in the Treasury "reserved for the redemption of United States notes" having fallen below the amount of one hundred million dollars.

CURRENCY CERTIFICATES.

(Act of June 8, 1872).

R. S. Section 5193. "The Secretary of the Treasury may receive United States notes on deposit, without interest, from any national banking associations, in sums of not less than ten thousand dollars, and issue certificates therefor in such form as he may prescribe, in denominations of not less than five thousand dollars, and payable on demand in United States notes at the place where the deposits were made. The notes so deposited shall not be counted as part of the lawful money reserve of the association; but the certificates issued therefor may be counted as part of its lawful money reserve, and may be accepted in the settlement of clearing-house balances at the places where the deposits therefor were made."

R. S. Section 5194. "The power conferred on the Secretary of the Treasury, by the preceding section, shall not be exercised so as to create any expansion or contraction of the currency. And United States notes for which certificates are issued under that section, or other United States notes of like amount, shall be held as special deposits in the Treasury, and used only for the redemption of such certificates."

INTEREST CHECKS. 4 PER CENT. CONSOLS OF 1907.

CLOSING AND OPENING OF TRANSFER BOOKS. The Books of the Department are closed to the transfer of stock on the evening of the last day of February, May, August, and November, and re-opened for transfer and exchange on the morning of the first day of April, July, October, and January. In case stock is transferred while the books are closed, the interest will be declared in favor of the payee of the old bonds.

DATES OF DIVIDENDS AND PAYMENT OF CHECKS. The quarterly dividends of interest, due on the first day of January, April, July, and October, are paid by checks, which are mailed on or before those dates to holders of stock or to parties designated by the holders to receive them. Checks can be drawn only in the names of the payees inscribed on the face of the stock.

5 PER CENT. BONDS OF 1904.

CLOSING AND OPENING OF TRANSFER BOOKS. The Books of the Department are closed to the transfer of stock on the evening of the fifteenth of January, April, July, and October, and re-opened for transfer and exchange on the morning of the first day of February, May, August, and November.

DATES OF DIVIDENDS AND PAYMENT OF CHECKS. The quarterly dividends of interest, due on the first day of February, May, August, and November, are paid by checks, which are mailed on or before those dates to holders of stock or to parties designated by the holders to receive them. Checks can be drawn only in the names of the payees inscribed on the face of the stock.

4½ PER CENT. FUNDED LOAN OF 1891, (CONTINUED AT 2 PER CENT.)

CLOSING AND OPENING OF TRANSFER BOOKS. The Books of the Department are closed to the transfer of stock on the evening of the last day of January, April, July, and October, and re-opened for transfer and exchange on the morning of the first day of March, June, September, and December.

DATES OF DIVIDENDS AND PAYMENT OF CHECKS
The quarterly dividends of interest, due on the first day of March, June, September, and December, are paid by checks, which are mailed on or before those dates to holders of Stock or to parties designated by the holders to receive them. Checks can be drawn only in the names of the payees inscribed on the face of the stock.

PACIFIC RAILWAY BONDS.

CLOSING AND OPENING OF TRANSFER BOOKS. The Books of the Department are closed to the transfer of this stock on the evening of the last day of May and November, and re-opened for transfer and exchange on the morning of the first day of July and January.

DATES OF DIVIDENDS AND PAYMENT OF CHECKS. The semi-annual dividends of interest, due on the first day of January and July, are paid by checks, which are mailed on or before those dates to holders of stock or to parties designated by the holders to receive them. Checks can be drawn only in the names of the payees inscribed on the face of the stock.

3.65 DISTRICT OF COLUMBIA FUNDING BONDS.

CLOSING AND OPENING OF TRANSFER BOOKS. The Books of the Department are closed to the transfer of this stock on the evening of the 21st day of January and July, and re-opened for transfer and exchange on the morning of the first day of succeeding months.

DATES OF DIVIDENDS. The dividends of interest are payable semi-annually, at the office of the Treasurer U. S. or the Assistant Treasurer U. S. in New York, on the first day of February and August by checks, which are sent by mail on those dates to holders of stock or to parties designated by them to receive their checks. The check can be drawn only in the name of the payee inscribed on the face of the stock.

GENERAL REGULATIONS AS TO INTEREST CHECKS.

FOUR MONTHS LIMIT: For a period of four months from date of issue, checks are payable at the offices of the Treasurer U. S., and any Assistant Treasurer U. S.; after that time they are payable only at the U. S. Treasury in Washington.

DUPLICATE CHECKS. Upon request being made for a duplicate, payment of the original check will be stopped, and, upon satisfactory proof of its loss, a bond of indemnity will be prepared in this office, and transmitted for execution. Upon the return of the bond executed according to instructions, and its approval by the Comptroller of the Treasury, a duplicate check will be issued, provided *forty-five days* have elapsed from the date of the original. Foreign holders of stock will be required, under the ruling of this Department, to execute such a bond with two sureties resident in the United States.

SCHEDULES. Schedules, from which the checks are written and mailed, giving the name and address of each payee, the amount of bonds held by him, and the interest due thereon, are prepared quarterly in the office of the "Register of the Treasury, Washington, D. C.," to whom all communications relating thereto should be addressed.

CHANGE OF ADDRESS. Requests to change the post-office address of a person entitled to receive interest-checks should give the title of the loan and the last post-office address, and be sent to the Register of the Treasury. The address should be given in full, and include the street and number.

INDORSEMENTS. 1. The name of the payee, as indorsed, must correspond with that on the face of the check. If the name as written on the check is spelled incorrectly, the check should be returned to the Treasurer U. S. for correction, unless the spelling corresponds with that on the face of the bonds, in which case both check and bonds should be forwarded to the Register of the Treasury for correction.

ARTHUR D. BISSELL,
PRESIDENT PEOPLE'S BANK, BUFFALO, N. Y.

2. Payees and indorsees must indorse by their own hands; officials, officially, with full title; firms, the usual firm signature by a member of the firm, not by a clerk or other person for the firm.

3. Stamped indorsements and signatures in pencil are not accepted.

4. Indorsements by mark (X) must be witnessed by two persons who can write, and who must give their places of residence.

5. When the Secretary of the Treasury has been notified that the payee of bonds are infants, checks issued in payment of interest thereon

are delivered and paid only to the guardian of such infants who must file with the Auditor of the Treasury Department evidence, (1) of guardianship; (2) that his authority is in force; and (3) of the identity of his ward with the payee of the bonds. Neither the father nor the mother of the infant has the right to indorse such interest-checks.

6. Interest-checks are paid upon the indorsement of any one of several joint holders, co-attorneys, guardians, executors, administrators, or trustees; but in a transfer of stock, or in the execution of a power of attorney to collect interest, all must join.

7. Indorsements by an agent, attorney, guardian, executor, administrator, or trustee of an estate, are not recognized unless evidence of authority has been filed with the Auditor for Treasury Department. In the four last-named cases the certificate, under seal, of the Probate Court is required.

8. Evidence of authority to indorse checks payable to corporations or societies, *except in the case of Cashiers of National Banks*, must be furnished the Auditor for Treasury Department in the form of a certified copy, under seal, of an extract from the by-laws showing the authority of the officer to indorse for the corporation or society, and giving his name and the date of his election, or in the form of a resolution adopted by the official board of such corporation or society, designating by name and title the officers empowered to collect interest. *The same evidence is required to cover indorsements by Presidents, Vice-Presidents, and assistant Cashiers of National Banks.* If the corporation or society have no seal, the instrument must be acknowledged before a notary public or other competent officer under his seal.

9. When a check is payable to an officer of an institution, as, for instance, "John Smith, Cashier of the First National Bank of Smithville, Ohio," authority for any other individual to indorse must be given by the officer named in the check.

10. In transmitting to the Auditor for Treasury Department powers of attorney, letters testamentary, letters of administration, or other evidence of authority for indorsements, notice should be given that officer at which of the following named officers checks will be presented for payment under such powers, viz: Washington, New York, Boston, Philadelphia, Baltimore, Cincinnati, Chicago, St. Louis, New Orleans, and San Francisco.

NOTE. District of Columbia checks are payable only at Washington and New York.

11. Checks paid on indorsements not in accordance with the above requirements are returned to the parties through whose hands they have passed for collection, with reclamation for the amounts.

TRANSFER CHECKS.

The Treasurer's transfer checks are issued by the Redemption Division in return for United States notes and Treasury notes of 1890 received for redemption, by the Loan Division in the redemption of United States bonds; by the Cashier in redemption of subsidiary silver coin or minor coin, and in various other cases; and by the National

Bank Redemption Agency in return for national bank notes sent for redemption. Said checks are drawn on the Assistant Treasurers of the United States at Boston, New York, Philadelphia, Baltimore, Cincinnati, Chicago, St. Louis, New Orleans, and San Francisco.

DUPLICATES. Upon request being made for a duplicate, payment of the original check will be stopped, and, upon satisfactory proof of its loss, a bond of indemnity will be prepared in this office, and transmitted for execution. Upon the return of the bond executed according to instructions, and its approval by the Comptroller of the Treasury, a duplicate check will be issued, provided *forty-five days* have elapsed from the date of the original.

TREASURY DRAFTS AND WARRANTS.

Treasury drafts were drawn by the Treasurer of the United States, based upon warrants drawn by the Secretary of the Treasury, countersigned by the Comptroller, and recorded by the Register. The drafts were drawn upon the Treasurer U. S., an Assistant Treasurer U. S., or a national bank designated as a depository of public moneys of the United States. By recent provisions of law the issue of Treasury drafts ceased on December 31, 1894, and on January 1, 1895, the issue of TREASURY WARRANTS commenced in their stead.

DUPLICATES. Upon request being made for a duplicate, payment of the original will be stopped, and, upon satisfactory proof of its loss, a bond of indemnity will be prepared in this office, and transmitted for execution. Upon return of the bond executed according to instructions, and its approval by the Comptroller of the Treasury, a duplicate will be issued, providing *forty-five days* have elapsed from the date of the original.

INDORSEMENT AND PAYMENT OF TREASURY DRAFTS AND POST-OFFICE DEPARTMENT WARRANTS.

(Department Circular No. 87 of June 7, 1893.)

Treasury drafts and Post-Office warrants must not be paid until the indorsements conform to the following regulations:

1. The name of the payee, as indorsed, must correspond in spelling with that on the face of the draft; no guarantee of an indorsment, imperfect in itself, can be accepted. If the name of a payee, as written on the face of a draft, is spelled incorrectly, the draft should be returned to the Treasurer U. S. for correction.

2. Indorsements by mark (X) must be witnessed by two persons who can write, giving their places of residence.

3. Indorsements by executors, administrators, guardians, or other fiduciaries must be accompanied by certified copies, under seal, of letters testamentary, letters of administration, of guardianship, or other evidence of fiduciary character, as the case may be.

4. Payees and indorsees must indorse by their own hands; officials, officially with full title; firms, the usual firm signature by a member of the firm, not by a clerk or other person for the firm.

5. Every indorsement must be by the proper written (not printed) signature of the person whose indorsement is required.

6. Powers of attorney for the indorsements of drafts in payment of claims must be executed as required by section 3477 of the Revised Statutes of the United States. The letter of attorney must state the number, date, and amount of the draft, also the number and kind of warrant on which the draft is issued; must be signed by the constituent in the presence of at least two attesting witnesses subsequently to the date of the draft, and be acknowledged by him before a notary public, and certified by such officer under his hand and official seal; or, when not before a notary public, the acknowledgment must be before an officer having authority to take acknowledgments of deeds within the State or Territory in which it is taken, which authority must be shown by a certificate as to the official character and signature of such officer and setting forth that he is duly authorized to take acknowledgments of deeds, made by the clerk of a court or record of such State or Territory, under the seal of the court, or by some other officer of the State or Territory authorized to make such certificate, under his official seal.

If executed in a foreign country, the acknowledgment must be before a notary public, and certified under his hand and official seal, or before a consul or minister of the United States, under the seal of the legation or consulate.

The official taking the acknowledgment must certify that the letter of attorney was read and fully explained to the constituent at the time of acknowledgment, and that said constituent is personally well known to him to be the identical person named in and who subscribed his name to said power of attorney.

7. Evidence of authority to indorse for incorporated or unincorporated companies must have been previously filed *with the First Comptroller of the Treasury*, or accompany drafts drawn or indorsed to the order of such companies or associations. Such evidence should be in the form of an extract from the by-laws or records of the company or association showing the authority of the officer to indorse and receive and receipt for moneys for the company, and giving his name and the date of his election or appointment, and the period for which he was elected or appointed, and that such authority shall be binding on the company until notice of revocation has been filed *with the First Comptroller of the Treasury*, which extract must be verified by a certificate under seal signed by the president and secretary, or by one of these officers and not less than two of the directors; which certificate must state that such authority remains unrevoked and unchanged. If the company have no seal, the extract should be certified as correct by a notary public or other competent officer under his seal. When a resolution is adopted at a special meeting of directors, it must be shown that all had notice of the time and place of such meeting, and that a quorum assented to the resolution.

The evidence of authority to indorse required in paragraph 7, above, may be dispensed with in the case of drafts or checks not exceeding in amount the sum of twenty-five dollars ($25), payable to a corportion or company which necessarily employs a number of local agents in the transaction of its business—such as railroad, telegraph, steamboat, express, transfer, turnpike, hotel, newspaper, gas, and ice companies—when it is impracticable to obtain the indorsement of the secretary, treasurer, or other principal officer of such corporation or company: *Provided*, that the draft or check be indorsed by a local agent of such corporation or company who is authorized to receive and collect money on behalf of the same, and that this indorsement as such agent be guaranteed by a bank, or by some other responsible and satisfactory guarantor.

8. In cases where an individual or a co-partnership is doing business under a company title, the affidavit of the owner or of at least two members of the co-partnership will be required, showing the fact of ownership, and in the case of co-partnerships, naming the member of the co-partnership who is authorized to indorse and receive and receipt for moneys for the owners.

CLARENCE W. HAMMOND,
CASHIER PEOPLE'S BANK, BUFFALO, N. Y.

9. The indorsement of all the joint holders or co-trustees, executors, administrators, guardians, or other fiduciaries will be required on drafts, and in the execution of a power to a third party to collect all must join. In case of the death of either, the survivors will be recognized as having full authority, upon due proof of such death and survivorship.

NOTE. Since this circular, the latest on the subject, was issued, the official designation of the First Comptroller of the Treasury has been changed to Comptroller of the Treasury, the office of Second Comptroller of the Treasury having been abolished.

GOLD COINS OF THE UNITED STATES.

FINENESS AND ALLOY. The standard for gold coins of the United States shall be such that of one thousand parts by weight nine hundred shall be of pure metal and one hundred of alloy: The alloy of the gold coins shall be of copper, or of copper and silver; but the silver shall in no case exceed one-tenth of the whole alloy. (R. S. Section 2514.)

NOW ISSUED.

$20—Double Eagle. Authorized by the Act of March 3, 1849, (9th Stat., p. 397). Standard weight of the double-eagle, or twenty dollar piece, five hundred and sixteen grains. (R. S. Section 3511.)

$10—Eagle. Authorized by the Act of April 2, 1792, (1 Stat., p. 248). Standard weight of the eagle, or ten-dollar piece, two hundred and fifty eight grains. (R. S. Section 3511.)

$5—Half Eagle. Authorized by Act of April 2, 1792, (1 Stat., p. 248). Standard weight of the half-eagle, or five-dollar piece, one hundred and twenty-nine grains. (R. S. Section 3511.)

$2½—Quarter Eagle. Authorized by the Act of April 2, 1792, (1 Stat., p. 248). Standard weight of the quarter-eagle, or two and a half dollar piece, sixty-four and a half grains. (R. S. Section 3511.)

COINAGE DISCONTINUED.

$3 Piece. Authorized by the Act of February 21, 1853, (10 Stat., p. 161). Standard weight of the three-dollar piece, seventy-seven and four-tenths grains. (R. S. Section 3511.) Coinage discontinued by the Act of September 26, 1890, (26 Stat., p. 485).

$1 Piece. Authorized by the Act of March 3, 1849, (9 Stat., p. 97.) "The gold coins of the United States shall be a one-dollar piece, which, at the standard weight of twenty-five and eight-tenths grains, shall be the unit of value * * * *." (R. S. Section 3511.) Coinage discontinued by the Act of September 26, 1890, (26 Stat., p. 485).

SILVER COINS OF THE UNITED STATES.

FINENESS AND ALLOY. The standard for silver coins of the United States shall be such that of one thousand parts by weight nine hundred shall be of pure metal and one hundred of alloy. The alloy of silver coins shall be of copper. (R. S. Section 3514.)

NOW ISSUED.

STANDARD SILVER DOLLARS. Authorized by the Act of April 2, 1792, (1 Stat., p. 248). Coinage discontinued by the Act of February 12, 1873, (R. S. Section 3513). Coinage re-authorized by the Act of February 28, 1878, (20 Stat., p. 25).

The Act of February 28, 1878, (R. S. Supplement, p. 152) provides:

"That there shall be coined, at the several mints of the United States, silver dollars of the weight of four hundred and twelve and a half grains, Troy of standard silver, as provided in the Act of January eighteenth, eighteen hundred thirty-seven, on which shall be the devices and superscriptions provided by said act; * * * ."

NOTE—The provisions of the Act of 1837, ch. 3, (5 Stat., L., 137), here referred to, are as follows:

"Section 8. That the standard for both gold and silver coins of the United States shall hereafter be such, that of the one thousand part by weight, nine hundred shall be of pure metal, and one hundred of alloy; and the alloy of the silver coins shall be copper. * * * ."

"Section 9. That of the silver coins, the dollar shall be of the weight of four hundred and twelve and one-half grains; * * * ."

HALF DOLLARS. Authorized by the Act of April 2, 1792, (1 Stat., p. 248). The weight of the half-dollar shall be twelve grams and one-half of a gram. (R. S. Section 3513).

QUARTER DOLLARS. Authorized by the Act of April 2, 1792, (1 Stat., p. 248). The weight of the quarter-dollar shall be one-half of the weight of said half-dollar. (R. S. Section 3513).

DIMES. Authorized by the Act of April 2, 1792, (1 Stat., p. 248). The weight of the dime shall be one-fifth of the weight of the said half-dollar. (R. S. Section 3513.)

COINAGE DISCONTINUED.

TRADE DOLLARS. Authorized by the Act of February 12, 1873, (R. S. Section 3513.) The weight of the trade dollar shall be four hundred and twenty grains troy. (Ibid.) Coinage suspended by Secretary of the Treasury February 22, 1878. By Act of March 3, 1887, (24 Stat., p. 635) the authority to coin was repealed, and it was provided that for a period of six months they should be received by the Treasurer or any Assistant Treasurer in exchange for silver dollars or subsidiary coins. This period having expired they are not now redeemable but are purchased by the Mints as bullion in the same manner as other uncurrent silver coin.

TWENTY CENT PIECES. Authorized by the Act of March 3, 1875, (18 Stat., p. 473.) There shall be coined at the Mints a coin of silver of the denomination of twenty cents, and of the weight of five grams. (Ibid.) Coinage discontinued by the Act of May 2, 1878, (20 Stat., p. 47).

HALF DIMES. Authorized by the Act of April 2, 1792, (1 Stat., p. 248). To be of the value of one-twentieth of a dollar, and to contain eighteen grains and nine-sixteenths part of a grain of pure, or twenty grains and four-fifth parts of a grain of standard silver. (Ibid.) Coinage discontinued by the Act of February 12, 1873. (R. S. Section 3513.

THREE CENT PIECES. Authorized by the Act of March 3, 1851, (9 Stat., p. 591). To be composed of three-fourths silver and one-fourth copper, and to weigh twelve grains and three-eighths of a grain. (Ibid.) Coinage discontinued by the Act of February 12, 1873, (R. S. Section 3513.)

MINOR COINS OF THE UNITED STATES.
NOW ISSUED.

FIVE CENT NICKEL. Authorized by the Act of May 16, 1866, (14 Stat., p. 47). The alloy for the five cent piece shall be of copper and nickel, to be composed of three-fourths copper and one-fourth nickel. The weight of the piece of five cents shall be seventy-seven and sixteen hundredths grains troy. (R. S. Section 3515).

ONE CENT BRONZE. Authorized by the Act of April 22, 1864, (13 Stat., p. 54). The alloy of the one cent piece shall be ninety-five per centum of copper and five per centum of tin and zinc, in such proportions as shall be determined by the Director of the Mint. The weight of the one-cent piece shall be forty-eight grains. (R. S. Section 3515.)

COINAGE DISCONTINUED.

THREE CENT NICKEL. Authorized by the Act of March 3, 1865, (13 Stat., p. 517.) The alloy for the three cent pieces shall be of copper and nickel, to be composed of three-fourths copper and one-fourth nickel. The weight of the three cent piece shall be thirty grains. (R. S. Section 3515). Coinage discontinued by the Act of September 26, 1890. (26 Stat., p. 485).

TWO CENT BRONZE. Authorized by the Act of April 22, 1864, (13 Stat., p. 54). The standard weight to be ninety-six grains, or one-fifth of one ounce troy, to be composed of ninety-five per centum of copper, and five per centum of tin and zinc. (Ibid). Coinage discontinued by the Act of February 12, 1873. (R. S. Section 3515.)

ONE CENT COPPER. Authorized by the Act of July 6, 1787. Authorized to be coined (by the United States Mint) by the Act of April 2, 1792 (1 Stat., p. 248). To be of the value of the one hundredth part of a dollar, and to contain eleven penny-weights of copper. (Ibid). Coinage discontinued by the Act of February 21, 1857. (11 Stat., p. 63).

ONE CENT NICKEL. Authorized by the Act of February 21, 1857, (11 Stat., p. 163). The standard weight to be seventy-two grains, or three twentieths of one ounce troy, and to be composed of eighty-eight per centum of copper and twelve per centum of nickel. (Ibid). Coinage discontinued by the Act of April 22, 1864. (13 Stat., p. 54).

HALF CENT COPPER. Authorized by the Act of April 2, 1792, (1 Stat., p. 248). To be of the value of half a cent, and to contain five penny-weights and half a penny-weight of copper. (Ibid). Coinage discontinued by the Act of February 21, 1857. (11 Stat., p. 63.)

PURCHASE OF UNCURRENT GOLD COINS.

(Department Circular No. 114 of July 15, 1892).

Mutilated or otherwise uncurrent United States gold coins, of any denomination, will be received at any of the mints or assay offices of the United States, and the value of the fine gold contained will be paid to the depositor at the rate of $20.67 per ounce fine, or $18.60 per ounce standard (.900 fine).

Returns for mutilated coins will be made by check payable to the order of the depositor, unless remittances by express or registered mail are preferred. In either case the payments will be at the depositor's expense and risk.

PURCHASE OF UNCURRENT SILVER COINS.

(Department Circular No. 15 of January 30, 1892.)

The Superintendents of the Mints at Philadelphia, San Francisco, New Orleans, and Carson will purchase, when presented in sums of three dollars and upwards, mutilated and uncurrent United States silver coin at the price fixed by the Director of the Mint for silver contained in gold deposits.

Uncurrent coins should be transmitted to the mints by registered mail or express (charges prepaid). The value will be returned in the same manner at the seller's expense and risk.

NOTE. Mutilated minor coin (copper, bronze, or copper-nickel) will neither be redeemed nor purchased.

LIGHT(WEIGHT) GOLD COINS.

The Secretary of the Treasury, under date of July 9, 1886, issued the following instructions to the Treasurer:

PRESIDENT FIRST NATIONAL BANK, KALAMAZOO, MICH.

"You are hereby instructed on and after August 1, 1886, to reject, and place a distinguishing mark upon all gold coins of the United States presented at your counters for deposit, which may be found below the standard weight and limit of tolerance provided by law for the single piece. Although the law makes such coins a legal tender 'at valuation in proportion to their actual weight,' it is found to be impracticable for public officers, generally, who receive them to determine the exact valuation.

"The true value of light weight gold coins can only be ascertained at the United States Mints at Philadelphia, New Orleans, and San Francisco, and the United States Assay Office at New York, where they will be received, their value determined, and proper amount of coins of legal weight, or a check therefor, returned.

"This action is taken to avoid the necessity of testing the same coin more than once, experience having shown that when a light weight coin is handed back to a depositor without placing thereon some distinguishing mark, a cashier or teller may in the course of business handle and reweigh the same coin several times."

On August 23, 1886, the foregoing instructions were so modified as to authorize the placing of a distinguishing mark on all gold coins which fall below the "least current weight," as shown by the set of least current weights provided for the purpose, instead of below the "standard weight and limit of tolerance."

UNITED STATES CURRENCY.—LEGAL TENDER.

DEFINITION OF THE TERM LEGAL TENDER. "Money of a character which by law a debtor may require his creditor to receive in payment in the absence of any agreement in the contract or obligation itself." (Bouvier's Law Dictionary).

GOLD COINS. The gold coins of the United States are a legal tender in all payments at their nominal value when not below the standard weight and limit of tolerance provided by law for the single piece, and, when reduced in weight below such standard and tolerance, are a legal tender at valuation in proportion to their actual weight. (Act of February 12, 1873, 17 Stat., p. 426, R. S., Section 3585).

STANDARD SILVER DOLLARS are a legal tender at their nominal value for all debts and dues, public and private, except where otherwise expressly stipulated in the contract. (Act of February 28, 1878, 20 Stat., p. 25).

SUBSIDIARY SILVER COIN. The silver coins of the United States of smaller denominations than one dollar are a legal tender in all sums not exceeding ten dollars, in full payment of all dues, public and private. (Act of June 9, 1879, 21 Stat., p. 457).

MINOR COIN (coin of copper, bronze, or copper-nickel). Minor coins are a legal tender at their nominal value for any amount not exceeding twenty-five cents in any one payment. (Act of February 12, 1873, 17 Stat., p. 426).

UNITED STATES NOTES (known as legal tender notes, or "Greenbacks.") They are a legal tender in payment of all debts, public and private, within the United States, except duties on imports and interest on the public debt. (Act of March 3, 1863, 12 Stat., p. 711, R. S., Section 3588).

Section 3 of Act of January 14, 1875, (18 Stat., p. 296), provided that, on and after January 1, 1879, the Secretary of the Treasury should redeem, in coin, the United States legal tender notes then outstanding, on their presentation for redemption at the office of the Assistant Treasurer U. S., New York, in sums of not less than fifty dollars.

Treasury Department circular letter No. 141, of December 21, 1878, addressed to Officers of Customs, authorized them, by reason of the foregoing Act, to receive United States notes in payment of duties on imports, on and after January 1, 1879.

DEMAND TREASURY NOTES authorized by the Act of July 17, 1861, (12 Stat., p. 259), and the Act of February 12, 1862, (12 Stat., p. 338), are lawful money and a legal tender in like manner as United States notes. (R. S., Section 3589).

ONE AND TWO YEAR NOTES OF 1863. These notes, redeemable one year from date and two years from date, bearing interest at five per centum per annum, are a legal tender for their face value, exclusive of interest. (Act of March 3, 1863, 12 Stat., p. 710)

COMPOUND INTEREST NOTES. These notes were payable at any time after three years from date, and bearing interest not exceeding seven and three-tenths per centum, payable in lawful money at maturity, or, at the discretion of the Secretary of the Treasury, semi-annually; and such of them as should be made payable, principal and interest, at maturity, to be a legal tender to the same extent as United Sates notes for their face value, excluding interest. (Act of June 30, 1864, 13 Stat., p. 218).

TREASURY NOTES OF 1890 are a legal tender in payment of all debts, public and private, except when otherwise expressly stipulated in the contract, and are receivable for customs, taxes, and all public dues. (Act of July 14, 1890, 26 Stat., p. 289).

COLUMBIAN HALF DOLLARS are a legal tender to the same extent as subsidiary silver coin, i. e., ten dollars in any one payment. (Act of August 5, 1892, 27 Stat., p 389).

COLUMBIAN QUARTERS are a legal tender to the same extent as subsidiary silver coin, i. e., ten dollars in any one payment. (Act of March 3, 1893, 27 Stat., p. 586).

UNITED STATES CURRENCY.—NOT LEGAL TENDER.

GOLD CERTIFICATES are not a legal tender. They are receivable for customs, taxes, and all public dues. (Act of July 12, 1882, 22 Stat., p. 165).

SILVER CERTIFICATES are not a legal tender. They are receivable for customs, taxes, and all public dues. (Act of February 28, 1878, 20 Stat., p. 25).

NATIONAL BANK NOTES are not a legal tender. They are receivable at par in all parts of the United States in payment of taxes, excises, public lands, and all other dues to the United States, except duties on imports; and also for all salaries and other debts and demands owing by the United States to individuals, corporations, and associations within the United States, except interest on the public debt, and in redemption of the national currency. (Act of June 3, 1864, 13 Stat., p. 106, R. S., Section 5182).

TRADE DOLLARS are not a legal tender. By the Act of February 12, 1873, (17 Stat., p. 424), they were legal tender at their nominal value for any amount not exceeding five dollars in any one payment, but under date of July 22, 1876, (19 Stat., p. 215), it was enacted that the trade dollar should not thereafter be a legal tender.

The Act of March 3, 1887, (24 Stat., p. 634), provided that all trade dollars should be presented for redemption within a period of six months after the passage of said Act. Said coins are not now redeemable, but will be purchased as bullion in the same manner as mutilated or other uncurrent silver coin, by the United States Mints at Philadelphia, New Orleans, Carson, and San Francisco.

FRACTIONAL CURRENCY is not a legal tender. NOTE. It was receivable for postage and revenue stamps, and also in payment of

CASHIER FIRST NATIONAL BANK, KALAMAZOO, MICH.

any dues to the United States less than five dollars, except duties on imports. (Act of March 3, 1863, 12 Stat., p. 711).

FOREIGN GOLD COINS are not a legal tender in payment of debts. (Act of February 21, 1847, 11 Stat., p. 163, R. S., Section 3584).

FOREIGN SILVER COINS are not a legal tender in payment of debts. (Act of February 21, 1857, 11 Stat., p. 163, R. S., Section 3584).

CONTINENTAL CURRENCY. The question has been raised and disputed as to whether what was called the "Continental Currency," issued during the War of the Revolution by the old government, was or was not a legal tender. The facts appear to be that while the Continental Congress did not by any ordinance attempt to give it that character, they asked the States to do so, and all seem to have complied except Rhode Island. The Continental Congress only enacted that the man who refused to take the money should be deemed an enemy of his country. ("The National Loans," by Rafael A. Bayley, Treasury Department; prepared for the Tenth Census).

LEGAL TENDER CASES. Against constitutionality, Hepburn v. Griswold, 8 Wall, 603. For constitutionality, Knox v. Lee, 12 Wall, 457; Parker v. Davis, 12 Wall, 559.

OUTSTANDING LIABILITIES.

THREE-YEAR-LIMIT FOR CHECKS AND DRAFTS. Treasury drafts, disbursing officers' checks, etc., outstanding more than *three years from the date of issue*, are, at the end of each fiscal year, deposited to the credit of the Treasurer U. S. on account of appropriation "Outstanding Liabilities." They are covered into the Treasury by what are known as COVERING-IN-WARRANTS to the credit of said appropriation, and to the personal credit of the payees of said drafts and checks, to await proper claims for their payment.

Drafts and checks of this nature should be sent to the Secretary of the Treasury, who will have them examined by the proper accounting officer, and then referred to the Auditor for the Treasury Department for examination and settlement.

GOVERNMENT BONDS.

(From Public Debt Statement January 2, 1895.)

	AM'T ISSUED	OUTSTANDING JANUARY 1, 1895.
Funded Loan of 1891, Acts of July 14, 1870, and Jan. 20, 1871, at 4½ per cent., continued at 2 per cent., Option, U. S., Interest payable to M., J., S., and D................ (4½s)	$250,000,000	$ 25,364,500
Funded Loan of 1907, Acts of July 14, 1870, and Jan. 20, 1871, at 4 per cent., redeemable July 1, 1907, Interest payable to J., A., J., and O...............	740,883,500	559,622,150
Refunding Certificates, Act of Feb. 26, 1879, at 4 per cent., interest payable to J., A., J., and O............	40,012,750	56,480
Loan of 1904, Act of Jan. 14, 1875, at 5 per cent., redeemable Feb. 1, 1904, interest payable to F., M., A., and N...............	94,125,000	94,125,000
Aggregate of Interest-Bearing Debt, exclusive of United States Bonds issued to Pacific Railroads as stated below...............	$1,125,021,250	$679,168,130

BONDS ISSUED IN AID OF THE CONSTRUCTION OF THE SEVERAL PACIFIC RAILROADS.

NAME OF RAILWAY.	PRINCIPAL OUTSTANDING JAN. 1, 1895.
Central Pacific..	$ 25,885,120
Kansas Pacific...	6,303,000
Union Pacific...	27,236,512
Central Branch, U. P..	1,600,000
Western Pacific...	1,970,560
Sioux City and Pacific..	1,628,320
Totals...	$ 64,623,512

REGULATIONS AS TO GOVERNMENT BONDS.

BONDS FOR REDEMPTION. Should be sent to the Secretary of the Treasury.

BONDS TO SECURE DEPOSITS. Should be sent to the Treasurer.

BONDS TO SECURE CIRCULATION. Should be sent to the Comptroller of the Currency.

BONDS FOR PURCHASE. Should be sent to the Secretary of the Treasury, but not until offer has been made to, and accepted by, that officer.

BONDS FOR ASSIGNMENT (TRANSFER AND REGISTRY). Where it is desired to assign or transfer bonds on the books of the Treasury Department, they should be sent to the Register of the Treasury.

COUPON BONDS TO BE EXCHANGED INTO REGISTERED BONDS. Should be sent to the Secretary of the Treasury.

REGISTERED BONDS CANNOT BE EXCHANGED INTO COUPON BONDS.

LOST REGISTERED BONDS. In case of the loss of registered bonds send notice with numbers and description, to the Secretary of the Treasury, who will direct that the lost bonds be entered upon the caveat list.

LOST COUPON BONDS, U. S. NOTES, AND COUPONS. The Government cannot, and will not, undertake to protect the owners.

DESTROYED AND DEFACED BONDS. Address all communications on these subjects to the Secretary of the Treasury.

MUTILATED COUPONS. Will not be paid at the Sub-Treasuries, but must be sent to the Treasurer U. S.

WITHDRAWAL OF BONDS HELD TO SECURE CIRCULATION. Send correspondence on this subject to the Comptroller of the Currency.

WITHDRAWAL OF BONDS HELD TO SECURE DEPOSITS. Address all correspondence on this subject to the Secretary of the Treasury.

DISBURSING OFFICERS' CHECKS.

DUPLICATE CHECKS. R. S. Section 3646 (as amended by Act of February 16, 1885). Whenever any original check is lost, stolen, or destroyed, disbursing officers and agents of the United States are authorized, after the expiration of six months, and within three years from the date of such check, to issue a duplicate check; and the Treasurer, assistant treasurers, and designated depositaries of the United States are directed to pay such duplicate checks, upon notice and proof of the loss of the original checks, under such regulations in regard to their issue and payment, and upon the execution of such bonds, with sureties, to indemnify the United States, as the Secretary of the Treasury shall prescribe. This section shall not apply to any check exceeding in amount the sum of two thousand five hundred dollars.

R. S. Section 3647. In case the disbursing officer or agent by whom such lost, destroyed, or stolen original check was issued, is dead, or no longer in the service of the United States, it shall be the duty of the proper accounting officer, under such regulations as the Secretary of the Treasury shall prescribe, to state an account in favor of the owner of such original for the amount thereof, and to charge such amount to the account of such officer or agent.

BONDS OF INDEMNITY. Bonds of Indemnity are furnished by the Secretary of the Treasury in these cases only; Where the Bond is for the issue of an interest check or Treasury draft, address the Treasurer of the United States.

PENSION CHECKS NOT PAID IN 90 DAYS. All pension checks not presented for payment within 90 days from the date of issue must be sent to the Secretary of the Treasury (and not to the U. S. Treasurer) for authorization of payment. If presented at the office on which drawn without compliance with this requirement *payment will be refused.*

CASHIER THE WISCONSIN NATIONAL BANK, MILWAUKEE, WIS

POST OFFICE WARRANTS.

Post Office Warrants are drawn by the Third Assistant Postmaster General, and countersigned by the Auditor for the Post Office Department and the Treasurer of the United States. Said warrants are drawn on the Treasury and the various Sub-Treasuries.

DUPLICATES. Applications should be addressed to the Auditor for the Post Office Department, who will furnish the blank bond of indemnity and give the necessary instructions.

NUMBER OF NATIONAL BANKS IN OPERATION.

(From Report of Comptroller of Currency, 1894).

The records of the Bureau show that on October 31 the total number of national banks in operation was 3,756, with an authorized capital stock of $672,671,365, represented by 7,955,076½ shares of stock owned by 287,842 shareholders, thus giving to each bank in the system an average capital stock of $179,692, with 2,117 shares and 76 shareholders.

In this total number of banks in the system Pennsylvania leads with 406; New York follows with 334; Massachusetts is next with 267, and the three following in order of numbers are Ohio, 246; Texas, 218; and Illinois, 217. In the item of capital stock Massachusetts is first, with $97,992,500, with the several States following next in the order named, viz.: New York, $87,346,060; Pennsylvania, $74,168,390; Ohio, $45,240,100; Illinois, $38,506,000; Texas, $23,255,000; Connecticut, $22,791,070, and Missouri, $20,840,000.

On October 2, 1894, the date of their last report of condition, the total resources of the 3,755 banks then reporting were $3,473,922,055.27, of which their loans and discounts aggregated $2,007,122,191.30, and money of all kinds in bank, $412,428,192.45. Of their liabilities, $1,728,418,819.12 represented individual deposits, $334,121,082.10 surplus and net undivided profits, and $172,331,978 circulating notes outstanding. The total amount of circulation of national banks October 31, as shown by the books of the office, was $207,472,603, a net decrease during the year of $1,741.563, and a gross decrease of $8,614,864 in circulation secured by a deposit of bonds.

THE ORGANIZATION OF A NATIONAL BANK. When any person advises the office of the Comptroller of the Currency that he contemplates organizing a bank, he is written to and requested to file there a formal notice setting forth the name of the place in which it is proposed to locate the bank, the title by which the bank is to be known, and the names of five or more of the persons who propose to take stock therein. The object of this notice is to enable the Comptroller to reserve for the persons the title selected so as to prevent the confusion and difficulties that would arise from the selection of a title which could not be approved. When this notice is filed, the persons, if they so desire, are furnished with blank forms to be used in affecting an organization, and the title which they have selected, if it is approved, is reserved for them for a reasonable period. The forms sent include articles of association, organization certificate, certificate upon which officers and directors are to set forth the facts of which it is necessary for the Comptroller to inform himself before authorizing the bank to begin business; oaths of directors, and order for circulating notes. When these papers are returned to this office executed, they are carefully examined to see that they are in due form, and if any errors are found therein these errors are pointed out and the papers sent back to the corporation for correction or completion, as the case may be. If all the papers are found duly correct, this fact is certified to the bond clerk, who then sends to the Register of the Treasury, for transfer upon the books of the Department, the bonds which have been forwarded to this office for the account of the bank.

When this transfer has been made, and the bonds have been deposited with the Treasurer, the certificate of the Comptroller, authorizing the bank to begin business, is issued.

RESERVE CITIES.

"LAWFUL-MONEY RESERVE" PRESCRIBED. Every national banking association in either of the following cities: Albany, Baltimore, Boston, Cincinnati, Chicago, Cleveland, Detroit, Louisville, Milwaukee, New Orleans, New York, Philadelphia, Pittsburg, Saint Louis, San Francisco, and Washington, shall at all times have on hand, in lawful money of the United States, an amount equal to at least twenty-five per centum of the aggregate amount of its notes in circulation and its deposits; and every other association shall at all times have on hand, in lawful money of the United States, an amount equal to at least fifteen per centum of the aggregate amount of its notes in circulation and of its deposits. Whenever the lawful money of any association in any of the cities named shall be below the amount of twenty-five per centum of its circulation and deposits, and whenever the lawful money of any other association shall be below fifteen per centum of its circulation and deposits, such association shall not increase its liabilities by making any new loans or discounts otherwise than by discounting or purchasing bills of exchange payable at sight, nor make any dividend of its profits until the required proportion, between the aggregate amount of its outstanding notes of circulation and deposits and its lawful money of the United States, has been restored. And the Comptroller of the Currency may notify an association, whose lawful money reserve shall be below the amount above required to be kept on hand, to make good such reserve and if such association shall fail for thirty days thereafter so to make good its reserve of lawful money, the Comptroller may, with the concurrence of the Secretary of the Treasury, appoint a receiver to wind up the business of the association, as provided in section fifty-two hundred and thirty-four. (R. S. Section 5191).

WHAT MAY BE COUNTED TOWARDS THE "LAWFUL-MONEY" RESERVE. Three-fifths of the reserve of fifteen per centum required by the preceding section to be kept, may consist of balances due to an association, available for the redemption of its circulating notes, from associations approved by the Comptroller of the Currency, organized under the act of June three, eighteen hundred and sixty-four, or under this Title, and doing business in the cities of Albany, Baltimore, Boston, Charleston, Chicago, Cincinnati, Cleveland, Detroit, Louisville, Milwaukee, New Orleans, New York, Philadelphia, Pittsburg, Richmond, Saint Louis, San Francisco, and Washington. Clearinghouse certificates, representing specie or lawful money specially deposited for the purpose, of any clearing-house association, shall also be deemed to be lawful money in the possession of any association belonging to such clearing-house holding and owning such certificate, within the preceding section. (R. S., Section 5192).

The Secretary of the Treasury may receive United States notes on deposit, without interest, from any national banking association, in sums of not less than ten thousand dollars, and issue certificates therefor in such form as he may prescribe, in denominations of not less than five thousand dollars, and payable on demand in United States notes at the place where the deposits were made. The notes so deposited shall not be counted as part of the lawful-money reserve of the association; but the certificates issued therefor may be counted as part of its lawful-money reserve, and may be accepted in the settlement of clearing-house balances at the places where the deposits therefor were made. (R. S., Section 5193).

That the Secretary of the Treasury is authorized and directed to receive deposits of gold coin with the Treasurer or assistant treasurers of the United States, in sums not less than twenty dollars, and to issue certificates therefor in denominations of not less than twenty dollars each, corresponding with the denominations of the United States notes. The coin deposited for or representing the certificates of deposit shall

J. A. THATCHER.
PRESIDENT DENVER NATIONAL BANK, DENVER, COL.

be retained in the Treasury for the payment of the same on demand. Said certificates shall be receivable for customs, taxes, and all public dues, and when so received may be re-issued; and such certificates, as also silver certificates, when held by any national-banking association, shall be counted as part of its lawful reserve; and no national banking association shall be a member of any clearing-house in which such certificates shall not be receivable in the settlement of clearing-house balances: *Provided*, That the Secretary of the Treasury shall suspend the issue of such gold certificates whenever the amount of gold coin and gold bullion in the Treasury reserved for the redemption of United States notes falls below one hundred million dollars; and the provisions of section fifty-two hundred and seven of the Revised Statutes shall be applicable to the certificates herein authorized and directed to be issued. (Section 12 of Act of July 12, 1882).

PLACE FOR REDEMPTION OF CIRCULATING NOTES. Each association organized in any of the cities named in section fifty-one hundred and ninety-one shall select, subject to the approval of the Comptroller of the Currency, an association in the city of New York, at which it will redeem its circulating notes at par; and may keep one-half of its lawful-money reserve in cash deposits in the city of New York. But the foregoing provision shall not apply to associations organized and located in the city of San Francisco for the purpose of issuing notes payable in gold. Each association not organized within the cities named, shall select, subject to the approval of the Comptroller, an association in either of the cities named, at which it will redeem its circulating notes at par. The Comptroller shall give public notice of the names of the association selected, at which redemption are to be made by the respective associations, and of any change that may be made of the association at which the notes of any association are redeemed. Whenever any association fails either to make the selection or to redeem its notes as aforesaid, the Comptroller of the Currency may, upon receiving satisfactory evidence thereof, appoint a receiver, in the manner provided for in section fifty-two hundred and thirty-four, to wind up its affairs. But this section shall not relieve any association from its liability to redeem its circulating notes at its own counter, at par, in lawful money on demand. (R. S. Section 5195).

ADDITIONAL RESERVE CITIES. That whenever three-fourths in number of the national banks located in any city of the United States having a population of fifty thousand people shall make application to the Comptroller of the Currency, in writing, asking that the name of the city in which such banks are located shall be added to the cities named in sections fifty-one hundred and ninety-one and fifty-one hundred and ninety-two of the Revised Statutes, the Comptroller shall have authority to grant such request, and every bank located in such city shall at all times thereafter have on hand, in lawful money of the United States, an amount equal to at least twenty-five per centum of its deposits, as provided in section fifty-one hundred and ninety-one and fifty-one hundred and ninety-five of the Revised Statutes. (Act of March 3, 1887).

CENTRAL RESERVE CITIES. That whenever three-fourths in number of national banks located in any city of the United States having a population of two hundred thousand people shall make application to the Comptroller of the Currency, in writing, asking that such city may be a central reserve city, like the city of New York, in which one-half of the lawful-money reserve of the national banks located in other reserve cities may be deposited, as provided in section fifty-one hundred and ninety-five of the Revised Statutes, the Comptroller shall have authority, with the approval of the Secretary of the Treasury, to grant such request, and every bank located in such city shall at all times thereafter have on hand, in lawful money of the United States, twenty-five per centum of its deposits, as provided in section fifty-one hundred and ninety-one of the Revised Statutes. (Act of March 3, 1887).

LIST OF CITIES, CENTRAL RESERVE. (1) New York City, (2) Chicago, (3) St. Louis. OTHER RESERVE CITIES. (1) Boston, (2) Albany, (3) Brooklyn, (4) Philadelphia, (5) Pittsburg, (6) Baltimore, (7) Washington, (8) New Orleans, (9) Louisville, (10) Cincinnati, (11) Cleveland, (12) Detroit, (13) Milwaukee, (14) Des Moines, (15) St. Paul, (16) Minneapolis, (17) Kansas City, (18) St. Joseph, (19) Lincoln, (20) Omaha, (21) San Francisco.

NATIONAL BANK EXAMINERS.

APPOINTMENT, POWERS, AND DUTIES. The Comptroller of the Currency, with the approval of the Secretary of the Treasury, shall, as often as shall be deemed necessary or proper, appoint a suitable person or persons to make an examination of the affairs of every banking association, who shall have power to make a thorough examination into all the affairs of the association, and, in doing so, to examine any of the officers and agents thereof on oath; and shall make a full and detailed report of the condition of the association to the Comptroller. (R. S. Section 5240).

COMPENSATION. All persons appointed to be examiners of national banks not located in the redemption cities specified in section five thousand one hundred and ninety-two of the Revised Statutes of the United States, or in any one of the States of Oregon, California, and Nevada, or in the Territories, shall receive compensation for such examination as follows. For examining national banks having a capital less than one hundred thousand dollars, twenty dollars; those having a capital of one hundred thousand dollars and less than three hundred thousand dollars, twenty-five dollars; those having a capital of three hundred thousand dollars and less than four hundred thousand dollars, thirty-five dollars; those having a capital of four hundred thousand dollars and less than five hundred thousand dollars, forty dollars; those having a capital of five hundred thousand dollars and less than six hundred thousand dollars, fifty dollars; those having a capital of six hundred thousand dollars and over, seventy-five dollars; which amount shall be assessed by the Comptroller of the Currency upon, and paid by, the respective association so examined, and shall be in lieu of the compensation and mileage heretofore allowed for making said examinations; and persons appointed to make examinations of national banks in the cities named in section five thousand one hundred and ninety-two of the Revised Satutes of the United States, or in any one of the States of Oregon, Califorinia, and Nevada, or in Territories, shall receive such compensation as may be fixed by the Secretary of the Treasury upon the recommendation of the Comptroller of the Currency; and the same shall be assessed and paid in the manner hereinbefore provided. (Ibid).

SEMI-ANNUAL DUTY ON CIRCULATION.

DUTY. There is due from every national bank, in the months of January and July of each year, a tax or duty of one-half of one per

F. W. HAYES,
PRESIDENT PRESTON NATIONAL BANK, DETROIT, MICH.

centum upon the average amount of its notes in circulation during the six months preceding each January and July. (Section 5214, R. S.)

RETURN. In order to ascertain the amount of duty due, every national bank must, within the first ten days of January and July of each year, make a return to the Treasurer of the United States, upon blanks furnished by him, of *the average amount of its notes in circulation for the six months next preceding the first day of January and July*. This return must be subscribed and sworn to by the President or Cashier of the bank, and a failure to so make it subjects the bank to a penalty of two hundred dollars.

HOW TO ASCERTAIN THE AVERAGE CIRCULATION. To ascertain the average amount of notes in circulation, the following directions should be closely followed:

If the duty is due in January, add together the daily balances of notes in circulation of each day, beginning with the first day of the last preceding July and including December 31. Divide the sum thus obtained by 184, the number of days from July 1 to December 31, and the quotient will be the average amount of notes in circulation for the six months preceding January 1.

If the duty is due in July, a similar calculation is made, beginning with the first day of the last preceding January and including June 30, but dividing the sum by 181, the number of days from January 1 to June 30, except in leap years, when the divisor will be 182. For each Sunday and holiday the balance of the preceding business day should be counted.

The same result may be obtained by banks making a weekly statement instead of daily statements, by adding together the weekly balances and dividing the sum by the number of weeks in the half year, which will be $25\frac{5}{7}$ or 26 for the first six months, and $26\frac{2}{7}$ for the last six months. For each day in any fractional part of a week, counting the one-seventh of the weekly balance next preceding such fractional part.

"NOTES IN CIRCULATION." Extract from opinion of the Attorney-General, rendered December 2, 1894.

"Bank notes signed and actually paid out over the country, or otherwise so dealt with as to become liabilities of the bank, are "notes in circulation." But notes merely held in the vaults of the bank, whether signed or unsigned, and notes so signed and held and carried on the books of the bank are not its "notes in circulation." For the same reason, notes that have been obligations of the bank but cease to be so and return and remain in the bank for whatever period, are not, during such period its "notes in circulation."

NEW BANKS. If a bank is organized between the first days of January and July or between July first and January first, or has no notes in circulation on the first day of January or July, then the calculation should begin on the day the bank first put any of its notes in circulation, and continued to and including June 30th or December 31st, as the case may be *and the sum divided by the full number of days, 181 or 184*.

BANKS IN LIQUIDATION. The liability ceases upon the deposit of lawful money to retire the notes, and a bank in liquidation, upon depositing such lawful money, begins the calculation in the same manner as above explained and continues it to the day of deposit of the lawful money, always dividing by the full number of days in the semi-annual period.

PAYMENT OF DUTY. Payment of duty must be made in one of the following ways, viz.:

1st. By a remittance to the Treasurer U. S. of the amount in lawful money or notes of nationl bank or by a draft on New York City, for which the Treasurer will issue his certificate of deposit in duplicate and send the *duplicate* to the bank.

2d. By depositing the amount due with an Assistant Treasurer of the United States or with a national bank depositary, for which the Assistant Treasurer or depositary will issue to the bank a certificate of deposit in *triplicate*, the original of which the bank should send to the Secretary of the Treasury, the duplicate to the Treasurer of the United States, and retain the triplicate as its voucher.

SEMI-ANNUAL DUTY COLLECTED FROM NATIONAL BANKS.

(From Treasurer's Report, 1894).

On Circulation, fiscal years	1864 to 1894, inclusive,	$75,834,997.17
On deposits,	"	"	1864 to 1883,	"	60,940,067.16
On capital,	"	"	1864 to 1883,	"	7,855,887.74

$144,630,952.07

NOTE. The tax on capital and deposits of National Banking Associations was repealed by the act of March 3, 1883. (22 Stat., p. 488, Supplement R. S., p 404).

NATIONAL BANK REDEMPTION AGENCY.

(Expenses Reimbursed by National Banks.)

By Section 3 of the Act of June 20, 1874, (18 Stat., p. 123), it was provided that the notes issued by national banks might be presented to the Treasurer U. S for redemption, etc. By the Act of March 3, 1875 (Ibid., p. 399), for the purpose of carrying into effect the provisions of the first named act, an appropriation was made for the force so employed in the Office of the Treasurer.

DUTIES. The business of the National Bank Redemption Agency consists in carrying into effect the provisions of the Acts of Congress approved June 20, 1874, (18 Stat., p. 123), July 12, 1882, (22 Stat., p 162), and July 14, 1890, (26 Stat., p. 289), and Section 5222 and 5229 of the Revised Statutes, relating to the redemption of national bank notes at the Treasury of the United States, of which the following are the principal features.

Section 3 of the Act of Congress approved June 20, 1874, (18 Stat, p. 123), provides that every national bank shall keep on deposit in the Treasury of the United States a sum of lawful money equal to 5 per centum of its circulation, to be held and used for the redemption of its notes; that the circulating notes of the banks shall be redeemed by the Treasurer on presentation and charged to the respective associations by which they were issued; that the redeemed notes shall be forwarded to the banks of issue, but if any of the notes are unfit for circulation they shall be delivered to the Comptroller of the Currency for destruction and replacement with new notes; and that the banks shall re-imburse to the Treasury the charges for transportation and the costs of assorting the notes redeemed. Section 4 of the same act provides that any bank may

FRED'K PABST,
PRESIDENT THE WISCONSIN NATIONAL BANK, MILWAUKEE, WIS.

deposit lawful money and take up the bonds on deposit for the security of an equal amount of circulation, and that this amount of its notes shall be redeemed at the Treasury and destroyed. Section 3 of the Act of March 3, 1875, (18 Stat., p. 399), requires the Secretary of the Treasury to reimburse the Treasury to the full amount expended in carrying into affect the provisions of the Act of June 20, 1874. By Section 6, 8, and 9, of the Act of July 12, 1882, (22 Stat., p. 162), these provisions are modified in some particulars, and each bank is required at the end of three years from the date of the extension of its corporate existence, to deposit lawful money with the Treasurer sufficient to redeem the remainder of the circulation which was outstanding at the date of the extension. The laws relating to the redemption of the notes of banks in voluntary liquidation or insolvent are embodied in the Revised Statues (Section 5220 to 5242.)

THE EXPENSES OF THE AGENCY. The expenses of the Agency, including the salaries of the employes; the charges for transporting the notes to Washington in sums or multiples of $1,000, and for the return of the notes fit for circulation to the banks of issue; and all other incidental expenses, are passed upon by the accounting officers of the Treasury, and paid in the first instance out of regular appropriations. After the close of each fiscal year the amount so expended is reimbursed to the Treasury, as provided in Section 3 of the Act of March 3, 1875, (18 Stat., p. 399), by deposit as a miscellaneous receipt, and assessed upon the several banks in proportion to their circulation redeemed. The assessments are computed in the Agency and charged on its books to the 5 per cent. account of the banks. An advice is sent to each bank assessed, showing the amount of its notes redeemed and the rate and amount of the assessment.

LOST OR STOLEN NATIONAL BANK NOTES. The Act of July 28, 1892, (27 Stat., p. 322) provides. "That the provisions of the Revised Statutes of the United States, providing for the redemption of national bank notes, shall apply to all national bank notes that have been or may be issued to, or received by, any national bank, notwithstanding such notes may have been lost by or stolen from the bank and put in circulation without the signature or upon the forged signature of the president or vice-president and cashier."

MANUFACTURE, ISSUE, REDEMPTION, AND DESTRUCTION OF NATIONAL BANK NOTES.

ENGRAVING AND PRINTING OF NATIONAL BANK NOTES.

Requisition is made on the chief of Bureau of Engraving and Printing by the Comptroller of the Currency for a plate and impressions for a new bank. The chief makes an order on the engraving division for the new face-plate. The engraving division makes the face-plate of the appropriate title for the new bank, daily depositing it, in its various stages of preparation at the close of the work, with the custodian of dies, rolls, and plates. The impressions comprise a plate printed tint, with a surface-printed charter number of bank subsequently placed on it, forming the back, a plate-printed face, and surface-printed seal and charter number on face. The tints of each denomination of all banks are alike, varying only as to the State or Territory in which the bank is located. To facilitate the preparation of the currency when ordered for the separate banks, the tints are prepared and kept in the vault division as stock in advance of such orders. When the Comptroller of the Currency makes an order on the chief of Bureau for a new plate for a national bank, in the event of its being the first organized in its State or Territory, the order includes the tint-plates, and the tints are prepared there from to accomodate the future orders of the same bank, and of any others that may be subsequently organized in the same State. On an order of the chief of Bureau the engraving division makes the tint-plate and deposits it with the custodian of dies, rolls, and plates. The paper for the tints is furnished by the Secretary of the Treasury on requisition of the wetting branch, and prepared for printing. On order of the chief of Bureau the plate branch draws the plate from the custodian of dies, rolls, and plates, and assigns it to a printer, who draws the paper from a wetting branch and prints the tints. These are passed to the examining division, wet counted, dried, arranged after drying, examined, counted, packed and deposited with the vault keeper for safe-keeping until redeemed for face printing. Pending the preparation of the face-plate and nearing its completion the chief of Bureau makes an order on the plate branch to print the faces, and on the surface branch to print the seals and charter numbers on the faces and the charter numbers combined with tints to form the back. When the order is received to print the faces, the wetting branch draws the tints on requisition on the examining division, and prepares them to receive the face printing. The plate branch draws the face-plate from the custodian of dies, rolls, and plates, assignes a printer, who draws the paper from the wetting branch and prints the faces. The printed faces are passed to the examining division, where they are wet-counted, dried, arranged after drying, examined, recounted, pressed, and again counted. They are then forwarded to the numbering division, where they are counted, trimmed, and recounted, receive the bank number, are examined and counted, receive the Treasury number, examined and counted, and delivered to the surface branch. In the surface branch the work is counted on its receipt, and a requisition made on the custodian of dies, rolls, and plates for the charter number and seal forms. The charter number is printed on the back, and the impressions examined and counted. The seal is printed on the face, and the work again examined and counted, and then packed and transmitted to the vault keeper for delivery to the Comptroller of the Currency, at which point the work is finally disposed of by the Bureau.

ISSUE OF NATIONAL BANK NOTES.

COMPTROLLER OF THE CURRENCY. This officer makes requests on the Bureau of Engraving and Printing, in compliance with orders from the banks, for the preparation of engraved plates for the national banks and the printing of their circulating notes therefrom, to supply not only the first issue to them, but also to replace the destruction of their notes as they occur.

When this "incomplate currency" is received from the Bureau of Engraving and Printing, it is examined, tested, and counted, a record of the same is entered on the books, and the reserve supply is stored in the vaults in sealed packages. The required amount are issued to the banks, (after being counted and recorded in the proper books), in sealed packages, with receipts for the same, which are forwarded to the banks, signed and returned by them, and filed in the office.

HERBERT L. O'BRIEN
CASHIER PRESTON NATIONAL BANK, DETROIT, MICH.

TREASURER OF THE UNITED STATES.

PROCEDURE IN REDEMPTION OF NATIONAL BANK NOTES. The notes are forwarded by banks for redemption mostly through the United States Express Company, under a contract with the United States for their transportation, and are received and receipted for by the Superintendent of the Redemption Agency, in sealed packages. Small sums are received by mail, and from some other sources.

These packages, with all sums coming from other sources, are delivered to the express clerk, and are by him entered upon a register, the entry consisting of the name and address of the sender, the amount marked upon the wrapper of the package, the date of the sender's advice, and the serial number of the remittance. The footing of this register for each day shows the amount received for redemption.

The packages are delivered by the express clerk singly to the counters, who receipt for them on the register. It is the duty of the the counters to open the package, count the contents, rejecting all notes not the genuine issue of a national bank, put up the notes, each denomination separately, in straps marked with the remittance number, the amount in the strap, the counter's signature, and the date of the count, and to prepare a report the result of the count by filling in a blank form. The notes, with the counter's report, are then delivered to the first assortment clerk, who verifies the amount by inventorying the sums marked on the straps, and gives his receipt on a book supplied to the counter. When the count of one package is completed, and the money delivered, the counter receives another package, and so on until all the remittances on hand have been disposed of.

The first assortment clerk, from the counter's reports, makes entry of the result of the count of each remittance upon a register, setting out the number of the remittance, the amount claimed by the sender, the amount of the proceeds, and by items the additions and deductions reconciling the count with the amount marked on the package. The footing of this register show the result of the whole count for each day. The counted notes remaim in the custody of the first assortment clerk, being placed in a safe, which is locked up by the Superintendent until the morning of the next business day, when they are apportioned among the first assorters, who give their receipts an a book.

The first assorters severally verify the amounts receipted for by making an inventory of the parcels and counting the notes in each strap. Their next duty is to assort the notes into groups of banks according to an alphabetical arrangement by location of all the banks that have circulation outstanding. The number of groups at this time is seventy-two, averaging about seventy banks each. The assortment being finished, the notes in each group are counted and put up in straps, each strap being marked with the number of the group, the amount, the assorter's signature, and the date. Finaly an inventory of the straps is made to reconcile the total with the amount receipted for, and the notes are delivered to the second assortment clerk, who also makes an inventory by strap, and gives his receipt on a book in the assorter's hands.

The grouped notes are locked up in the custody of the second assortment clerk in the manner already described, and on the next business day this clerk distributes the notes by groups in the assorters' straps, according to the group numbers marked on the straps makes into bundles the amounts in the groups, severally, and prepares a schedule of these amounts. The notes are then transferred by the Teller to the vault of the Agency, where the bundles are checked off by the Superintendent and placed in compartments assigned to the groups severally.

Each day the notes that have accumulated in a number of groups—usually five—are taken out of the vault by the Superintendent and the Teller and delivered to the second assortment clerk, who opens the bundles, verifies the contents of each by inventory, and assorts the notes of each group in the assorters' straps by denominations. He enters the several sums by denominations and groups in a book, and the money is locked up in his custody in a safe by the Superintendent. The following day the accumulations in the next consecutive groups are taken out of the vault in the same way, and so on. The intervals between successive handling of money in the same group depend upon the number of groups handled each day.

Next morning the second assortment clerk delivers the notes in his hands, arranged by denominations as described, to the second assorters, taking receipts on his book. The second assorters first verify by count the correctness of the sums receipted for, then assort the notes by bank issue, and finally count out the amounts found for each bank. In the final count the notes that under the various provisions of law are required to be destroyed are separated from those fit for circulation that are to be returned to the banks of issue, and those of the series of 1882 from the old series. The notes in the various lots are put up in different straps, which are marked with the number of the bank in the group, the amount, the assorter's signature, and the date. The correctness of the count is then verified by an inventory and the notes are delivered to a maker-up, who receipts for them after satisfying himself that the inventory is correct. The amounts delivered to the several makers-up are placed under lock in a safe until the next business day.

It is the duty of a maker-up to distribute the notes of the group in his charge according to the marks on the straps, to make a schedule for each class of the notes of each bank, showing the amount of each denomination and the total, and to fill in a printed list of the banks in the group with the totals shown by the schedules. The footings of the resulting colums of figures enable him to test the correctness of his work. The notes thus prepared in packages, with the schedules accompanying are then transferred to the delivery clerk and receipted for. A book in which the amounts of the packages have been entered also goes with the money.

The delivery clerk places the packages in the hands of the provers, one or more at a time to the same person, taking receipts, for verification of the work of the assorter and maker-up. This completed, the prover signs and dates the schedule, securely ties the notes that are to be returned to the bank of issue, and carries the parcel to the desk of the sealer, who wraps and seals it under the prover's eye, first cancelling the notes that are to be destroyed by cutting off the lower corners. The package is then returned by the prover to the delivery clerk, who gives his receipt. On the day following the making up of a group the notes are delivered from the Agency to the United States Express Company or the Comptroller of the Currency, according to the classification of the parcels, the delivery clerk taking receipts in favor of the Treasurer of the United States as redemption agent on blank form previously prepared

The exceptions to this course are in the case of banks whose redemption account is overdrawn, and of amounts less than the minimum sum put into a package. In the former case the delivery is suspended until the account is made good, and in the latter the notes are returned.

H. J. HOLLISTER
CASHIER OLD NATIONAL BANK, GRAND RAPIDS, MICH.

COMPTROLLER OF THE CURRENCY.

REDEMPTION OF THE NATIONAL BANK CURRENCY.

National Bank Currency is received by the Redemption Division, either direct from the bank of issue, the United States Treasurer, or the National Bank Redemption Agency. The daily receipts of packages of currency, which come sealed, are subject to count. The packages received are entered on a register, arranged alphabetically and numerically, and entered in counter's receipt books for their verification. A schedule is made of each package and series of currency contained therein, which gives charter-number and name of bank and number and value of notes. After verification the currency is returned to the clerk in charge of the register who gives his receipt therefor to the counters. The schedules are examined and name of agent marked on face of package and face of schedule. The packages are then checked by the register and the schedules delivered to another clerk, whose duty it is to make the certificate of destruction, which contains the aforementioned information. After checking, the packages are arranged according to agents, counted and verified by number of certificate for each agent, and placed in boxes in the vault preparatory to destruction the next day. The schedules made by the counters are used by the bookkeepers of the division to make their entries, and after being verified are filed. The certificates are used by the clerks in making up each day's destruction, and are finally forwarded to the banks of issue.

COMMITTEE ON DESTRUCTION.

DESTRUCTION OF MUTILATED NATIONAL BANK NOTES: Under the provisions of the National Bank Act (Section 5184, Revised Statues) a committee is appointed to witness and certify to the destruction of mutilated National bank notes. The committee consists of four persons, one appointed by the Secretary of the Treasury, one by the Comptroller of the Currency, one by the Treasurer of the United States, and one by the association.

This committee meets daily at 2 p. m. in the Redemption Division of the Office of the Comptroller of the Currency. One member reads from the certificate the name of the bank, one calls the amount from the slip on the package of money, the third checks the amount on the book in the presence of the bank's agent; after which this money is placed in the macerator for destruction, and the certificates are signed by the committee representing the Secretary of the Treasury, the Treasurer U. S., the Comptroller of the Currency, and the bank's agent. The said certificates are then forwarded to the various banks represented, there being from two hundred to three hundred certificates daily. The Macerator is located in the sub-basement of the Treasury Building. The notes are reduced to pulp by the combined action of steam, alkalies, and knives; and the pulp is sold under contract.

NATIONAL BANK DEPOSITARIES.

APPLICATION FOR DESIGNATION AS UNITED STATES DEPOSITARY: Any National Bank desiring to make application for designation as United States Depositary, should address the Secretary of the Treasury, who will give all necessary information and instructions.

REGULATIONS AS TO U. S. DEPOSITARIES: All national banking associations, designated for that purpose by the Secretary of the Treasury, shall be depositaries of public money, except receipts from customs, under such regulations as may be prescribed by the Secretary; and they may also be employed as financial agents of the Government; and they shall perform all such reasonable duties, as depositaries of public moneys and financial agents of the Government as may be required of them. The Secretary of the Treasury shall require the associations thus designated to give satisfactory security, by the deposit of United States bonds and otherwise, for the safe keeping and prompt payment of the public money deposited with them, and for the faithful performance of their duties as financial agents of the Government. And every association so designated as receiver or depositary of the public money shall take and receive at par all of the national currency bills, by whatever association issued, which have been paid into the Government for internal revenue, or for loans or stocks. (Section 5153 R. S.)

FUNCTIONS OF DEPOSITARIES: The national banks serve a very useful purpose, both to the Government and the public, more especially in localities where there is not a Sub-Treasury, by acting, when so authorized by the Secretary of the Treasury, as depositaries of public moneys and financial agents of the United States. For their services in this regard they receive no direct compensation, and are, moreover, required to give satisfactory security for the faithful performance of their duties and the safe custody and prompt payment of all public moneys intrusted to them, by a deposit with the Treasurer of a sufficient amount of United States bonds. (See Section 5153 R. S.)

SERVICE RENDERED TO GOVERNMENT: As Government depositaries, the national banks have received, stored in their vaults, and accounted for $5,356,625,891, without expense to the Government. (Report of Comptroller of the Currency, 1894). It may be added that the Government has never lost a cent of deposits of public moneys in National Bank Depositaries, while the savings in the transportation of funds during a period of thirty years must have amounted to a very considerable sum.

NUMBER OF DEPOSITARIES: On January 1, 1895, the number of national banks designated as depositaries was 157. The amount of bonds held by said banks to secure deposits of public moneys, on the same date, was $15,001,000.

MANUFACTURE, ISSUE, REDEMPTION AND DESTRUCTION OF UNITED STATES PAPER CURRENCY.
SECRETARY OF THE TREASURY.

GOVERNMENT PAPER MILL: This mill, where the distinctive paper for United States notes, gold and silver certificates, bonds, checks and drafts is made, is under the supervision of an employe of the Loans and Currency Division, detailed as superintendent by the Secretary of the Treasury. The distinctive paper shipped by the superintendent of the mill to the Treasury Department is under the custody of the Loans and Currency Division, where it is examined and counted.

DISTINCTIVE PAPER: The examination and count of the distinctive paper for United States securities and for the printing of internal revenue stamps is a critical one, involving the detection and exclusion of all sheets inferior in quality or weight to the paper adopted as the standard sheet, or which contain imperfections of any kind. In the case of silk-threaded paper the examination must exclude all paper where the silk is not completely inclosed between the two surfaces of the paper.

A. E. F. WHITE,
V-PRESIDENT PRESTON NATIONAL BANK, DETROIT, MICH

ISSUE OF DISTINCTIVE PAPER: The demand for all kinds of securities has its origin, so far as the Department is concerned, in the office from which the security is issued, the head of that office or bureau making his requisitions upon the Secretary for the number of printed impressions required from time to time to supply the demand.

LOANS AND CURRENCY DIVISION: This Division, having charge of the examination, count, and custody of distinctive paper, is the medium through which a requisition is sent. An order for the printing is prepared and signed by the Secretary. The amount of paper required to fill the requisition, with a percentage allowed for work spoiled, is placed by denominations to the credit of the Bureau of Engraving and Printing, and against this credit that bureau is allowed to draw from time to time for printing the securities ordered.

BUREAU OF ENGRAVING AND PRINTING.

ENGRAVING AND PRINTING SHEET, CURRENCY, ETC.

MISCELLANEOUS (OFFICE) DIVISION. The office receives the requisitions of the Departments for the work of the Bureau, and in compliance therewith gives the necessary order in writing to the superintendents of the several divisions and sees that they are properly carried out. It makes the estimates, subject to the approval of the Secretary of the Treasury, purchases the supplies, and prepares the designations for employment. The office receives, files, and answers communications, keeps all the general accounts of the Bureau, and reports daily to the Secretary of the Treasury, by classes and denominations, the blank distinctive paper received and delivered printed, and monthly reports compiled from the division, daily reports of the receipts, deliveries, and balances of paper, for comparison and check with the paper account against the Bureau kept in the Secretary's office, division of loans and currency.

ENGRAVING DIVISION. The work of this division is engraving new dies and plates for plate printing and new forms for surface printing the securities, etc., and keeping them in good printing order. New engravings are made only on the written order of the chief of the Bureau. The superintendent directs the preparation of models, to be approved by the Department for which the work is intended, and also all the processes of engraving, until the work is finished. The engraved stock is classified as plates, forms, rolls, dies, shells, etc., and numbered, each piece being designated and known by its class and separate serial number. All the engraved stock is held in safety vaults by the custodian of dies, rolls, and plates, a direct representative of the Secretary of the Treasury, independent of the Bureau. The custodian keeps a record of the engraved stock, and, on requisition of the superintendent, delivers during the day the pieces required for additional processes of engraving. He receives it all back at the close of work, giving the superintendent a receipt for each piece and makes a daily report to the Secretary of the Treasury that all the engraved stock delivered during the day has been correctly returned. The engraving division keeps a record of every piece of engraving handled, showing the name of the workman through whose hands each piece passed and the nature of the work bestowed upon it. Each workman at the close of the day delivers to the superintendent the piece remaining in his hands, and is not permitted to leave the building at any time without a certificate that all the engraved stock handled by him has been returned.

PRINTING DIVISION. Wetting Branch—The printing division comprises several branches under the general supervision of the superintendent of printing, and the work in the respective branches is under the immediate supervision of a separate superintendent. In the wetting branch the paper is prepared for plate printing. All the impressions representing values and the checks are printed on a distinctive paper manufactured exclusively for, and under the supervision of the officers of the Treasury Department. The superintendent of the wetting branch is furnished with a copy of the printing orders and makes daily requisitions on the Secretary of the Treasury for the paper needed. The paper is received in packages, usually of 1,000 sheets each, and is counted on receipt to verify the filling of the requisition. It is then passed through the wetting process. The wetting requires a separation and count of the paper in sections of from ten to forty sheets each, according to the character of the paper and its requisite condition for printing. The sections, which have been placed between cotton cloths saturated with water, are shifted, taken out of cloths and counted, and stacked in their wet condition ready for delivery to the printers. If more than one plate printing is required on the same sheet, the paper is again received in its printed form from the examining division to be prepared as before for the next printing. The individual plate printers are charged in this branch with the paper delivered to them daily for each job of work and credited with the paper returned unprinted. Employes are not permitted to leave the building without a certificate from the superintendent that the work is correctly balanced. An account is kept and a daily report made to the office by class and denomination of the number of sheets received, delivered, and on hand.

Plate branch—Hand-presses.—Plate-printing on the hand-presses is executed in this branch. No work is printed except on the written order of the chief of the Bureau. The superintendent daily assigns certain classes and denominations of printing to the individual printers, who draw from the wetting branch the paper to correspond with the job, and after counting it, give their individual receipts for it. By requisition on the custodian of dies, rolls, and plates, the superintendent obtains the necessary plates, and appropriately distributes them among the printers, holding each printer accountable for the return of his plate at the close of work. Attached to each press is an automatic register, by which every revolution of the press capable of printing an impression from the plate in the hands of the printer is exactly indicated to the register clerk, who makes a daily report to the office of the advance made in the register from the preceeding day. The printing of the day is collected from the printers in packages of one hundred and two hundred sheets each, entered in their pass-books, and delivered to the examining division, to be counted and recorded in the entry-book to the credit of the printer. At the close of work each day the accounts of the wetting branch, examining division, and register Clerks are compared and checked by the superintendent of printing, to show that the paper delivered for printing and the printed impressions received from the printers agree and correspond with the register account, and the custodian of dies, rolls, and plates reports that all the plates and forms delivered for printing during the day have been returned to him. No printer is permitted to pass from the building during the day without a certificate showing the return of his paper and a check showing the return of his plate.

Plate branch.—Steam-presses—Plate-printing on the presses operated by steam is executed in this branch. It is under the supervision of a seperate superintendent, and its methods are substantially the same as those of the plate branch hand-presses.

CASHIER HACKLEY NATIONAL BANK, MUSKEGON, MICH.

Surface branch.—The surface printing on typographic presses is executed in this branch. No work is printed except on the written order of the chief the Bureau. The presses are known by number, and in this branch the work is assigned to the press instead of the printer, one press-man having charge of one or more presses. The work consists of printing seals and charter numbers on the faces and charter numbers on the backs, of national currency, indorsements, addresses, etc., on checks, and tints on distinctive paper for internal-revenue and customs stamps, etc. The distinctive paper is drawn from the wetting branch, the national currency from the numbering division, and the checks from the binding division, and receipted for in each case by the superintendent. The engraved forms from which the printing is executed are drawn from the custodian of dies, rolls, and plates, the superintendent making the requisition, and taking a receipt for each piece returned at the close of work. The sheets are counted on their receipt, fed on the press, examined, and counted. Automatic registers are on the presses indicating the number of impressions printed. The register count is checked with the superintendent's account of each day, and no employe is permitted to leave the building without a certificate of the superintendent that the work account is correctly balanced. A daily report by classes and denominations is made to the office of the number of sheets received, delivered, and on hand.

EXAMINING DIVISION. In this division the plate printed work is carefully examined by experts with a view to eliminating and withholding from the further process all mutilated or imperfect impressions. The sheets requiring no additional wetting for further printing are also pressed by placing two together between pressing boards, and in lots of about a thousand, subjecting them to heavy hydraulic pressure to restore the even surface of the paper roughened by the wetting. The impressions printed in the plate branches come to this division fresh from the press to be wet-counted, are entered to the credit of the printers whose initials are printed on the margins of the sheets, spread on racks and conveyed to the drying-room to remain during the night. The surface printed tints are also received, counted, and delivered to the vault division to be held as stock subject to be drawn on requisition by the wetting branch to prepare them for additional printing in the plate branch. After the plate-printed impressions have been dried they are arranged in classes, each printer's work separately, and examined. A report is made of the number of sheets spoiled by each printer, and showing the nature of the defect as a basis of charge against the printer's pay account when the number of sheets exceeds a stated percentum of allowance for spoilage. The imperfect impressions are canceled and delivered to the vault division for final delivery to the Secretary of the Treasury for destruction. The perfect plate-printed impressions required for further plate printing are delivered to the vault division to be held subject to requisition by the wetting branch to prepare them for the additional printing. Those requiring no further plate printing are pressed and counted, and, if other processes are to be applied to them, they are delivered to the proper operating division. If no other process is required they are packed, and delivered to the vault division for delivery to the department for which they are intended. Employes are not permitted to leave the building without a certificate from the superintendent that the work account is correctly balanced. An account is kept by class and denomination, and a daily report made to the office of the number of impressions received, delivered, and on hand.

NUMBERING DIVISION. In this division all the securities, notes, certificates, checks, stamps, etc., requiring the process, are, with automatic machines, numbered on each subject of the sheet.

The numbers on the securities, notes, stamps, or checks of a particular issue or series begin at one on the first issue and continue in uninterrupted sequence, and represent the order and extent of the issue of any series. The sheets are received from the examining and binding divisions and counted on their receipt. After numbering they are examined as to the accuracy of the numbers and again counted. The sheets requiring seals and charter numbers imprinted on them by the surface process are machine-trimmed on the two sides to fit them to an accurate register on the surface-printing presses. The sheets requiring further processes are delivered to the proper operating division. Those that are finished are delivered to the vault division for final delivery to the department for which they are intended. Employes are not permitted to leave the building without the superintendent's certificate that the work is correctly balanced. An account is kept of the serial numbers placed on all the securities, notes, certificates, checks, stamps, etc., by class and denomination, and a daily report is made to the office of the number of sheets received, delivered, and on hand.

BINDING DIVISION. In this division all the checks and the stamps requiring the process are bound. Certain stamps are also gummed and pressed, and, after gumming, perforated; others are perforated without being gummed. There are other processes, such as needling, triming, and separating. The sheets are received from the examining division and numbering division and surface branch. They are counted on their receipt and passed through the various processes by the workmen and operatives under the supervision of the superintendent. All the bound sheets are examined as to the sequence of numbers in the volume, and all the unbound sheets are counted. The finished sheets are delivered to the vault division for final delivery to the department for which they are intended. Employes are not permitted to leave the building without a certificate from the superintendent that the work account is correctly balanced. An account is kept in the division and a daily report made to the office by class and denomination of the number of sheets received, delivered, and on hand.

VAULT DIVISION. The superintendent of this division receives from the several operating divisions the unfinished work for safekeeping when not undergoing any process, and receives the completed notes, securities, stamps, etc., and delivers them to the several Bureaus of the Treasury and other departments; and receives and delivers the imperfect impressions to the Secretary of the Treasury, and takes receipts and sees that the entries on the receipt book are accurately made and properly signed. The receipts obtained by the vault division are prepared in the office from the schedules of the divisions on account of which the deliveries are made, and are verified by the daily reports.

SECURITY WAGON. At stated times each day an inclosed and locked steel-lined truck or "security wagon" is used by this division to carry the paper from the office of the Secretary of the Treasury to the wetting branch, and also to deliver the securities, notes, stamps, etc. Emplyes are assigned by the superintendent to accompany the truck for protection; otherwise the employes are not permitted to leave the building without a certificate from the superintendent that the division account is correct.

TREASURER OF THE UNITED STATES.
SEALING AND SEPARATING SHEET CURRENCY.

RECEIPT OF SHEET CURRENCY: The notes are received from the Bureau of Engraving and Printing at 8:30 a. m. each business day, and the packages are carefully checked off and receipted for by the Division Chief, or his assistant, subject to count. Forty-eight (48) packages of 1,000 sheets each are now received daily.

PRESIDENT HACKLEY NATIONAL BANK, MUSKEGON, MICH.

The packages are at once numbered from 1 to 48, in the order in which the notes run numerically, in order to facilitate the arranging of the packages later in the day, and are then given to the sheet counters for verification in the order in which they are required in the Press Room, and is for the purpose of doing away with the necessity of rearranging the seals in the forms.

SEALING: In the meantime the presses, six in number, are being prepared for the process of sealing. As soon as a sufficient number of bundles have been counted to start the presses they are at once sent to the Press Room. When the sealing takes place the bundles are strapped and returned to the Separating Room, and others take their place. The packages just sealed are immediately given to the sheet counters (who are not permitted to count back their own work) when the third count is given. The second count is made in the Press Room by an automatic register attached to each press. During this third count the sheet counters are not only required to see that they have 1,000 sheets, and that they are all sealed, but must watch for imperfections of every description, more especially those resulting from the process of sealing.

The packages are now placed in a case constructed for the purpose, there to remain until all of the 48,000 sheets have been sealed, when they are arranged in the order in which the bundles were numbered upon their receipt from the Bureau of Engraving and Printing, packed in a box constructed for their reception, the box locked and taken to the Cashier's vault, where it is left until the next day; then taken out and delivered to the Issue Division, where the packages are placed in the immediate vicinity of the separating machines, and the process of separating and trimming begun.

SEPARATING: The separator takes a package of sheets and placing herself at the machine, feeds it sheet by sheet until all the 1,000 sheets have been passed through, separated, and trimmed ready for circulation, pausing a moment at the end of each 25 sheets (100 notes) to enable the receiver, who sits on the opposite side of the machine, to place a strap around the notes and pass the package to the note counter assigned to the machine, who makes the final count, sees that the notes are numerically arranged, removes for exchange such notes as have been thrown out for imperfections, substitutes perfect notes which are furnished at the time for the purpose, placing on the back of the strap the numbers of the substitute notes, the strap having already been stamped on its face, calling attention to the substitution; and so on until the entire 4,000 notes have been counted and are ready to go to the package sealer. She now turns over to the person keeping the record and exchange box a ticket which gives an exact description of the package, the names of those through whose hands it has passed, with the number of notes rejected marked thereon, the reasons, and who is responsible, receiving therefor a label which describes the package as a whole, which, with the bundle of money, is turned over to the package sealer.

PACKAGE SEALER: The package sealer sees that the bundle contains 40 packages, places the bundle in a press constructed for the purpose, compresses it to the smallest compass possible, ties it, wraps, seals, and labels it.

VAULT CLERK. When the package sealer has the whole 48 bundles ready he delivers them to the Vault Clerk and takes his receipt in a book especially prepared for the purpose.

This gives in detail the course which a single bundle of sheets takes from the moment it is received from the Bureau of Engraving and Printing up to the time when it is sealed, separated, trimmed, counted, packed and ready for the custody of the Vault Clerk.

It may be proper to add that this Division is daily handling 384,000 notes in process of completion, the denominations ranging from one dollar to one thousand.

ISSUE OF UNITED STATES PAPER CURRENCY.

CASH DIVISION. This division is a part of the office of the Treasurer of the United States, is under the immediate direction of the Cashier of the Treasury, and is charged, among other duties, with the receipt of all United States Notes, Treasury Notes of 1890, Gold Certificates, Silver Certificates, and Currency Certificates made and issued by the Government. A record is kept by kind, denomination, and number of all currency received, through the Issue Division of the Treasurer's Office, from the Bureau of Engraving and Printing, for deposit in the Reserve Vault, and of all currency withdrawn therefrom to take the place of unfit currency destroyed. Transfers of new currency are made to the various Sub-Treasuries. Returns for currency sent for redemption are made, when requested, in new currency, to the Banks and individuals by whom it was sent. Tickets showing the name and address of the Banks or individuals to whom the currency is to be shipped and the amount thereof are received from the Redemption Division, currency is drawn from the vault, and such amounts as are directed by the tickets are placed in strawboard shipping-boxes, which are wrapped, sealed, and addressed, and delivered to the United States Express Company for transmission. A record is kept of each note shipped, by kind, denomination and number.

REDEMPTION OF UNITED STATES PAPER CURRENCY.

EXPRESS CLERK: The express clerk receives from the Chief the packages of money transmitted for redemption and delivers them to the counters, taking a receipt for each one, after having entered in his register—in numerical order— the name and address of the sender, the amount marked on the outside of the wrapper, and the express charges to be deducted; he also makes a statement daily at the close of business of the uncounted money on hand, showing the amount of each package and the name of the counter or person having it in charge.

MONEY COUNTERS. Closely allied to the Express Clerk's desk are the money counters, who, each in turn, receives from him a package of money for count. This she takes to her desk, examines the seals to see that they are intact and have not been tampered with in transmission, notes the markings on the outside, then opens the package and compares the contents with the outside markings, taking care to report all overs, shorts, counterfeits, raised notes, pieced notes, or other errors. She then assorts the money into its different kinds and denominations, places it in paper straps properly marked, makes a written statement showing the contents of the package, its errors, etc., has the money cancelled, and returns it with the statement to the Teller, who gives her a receipt.

The counters are under the superintendence of experienced persons, who, in addition to other duties, carefully verify all errors, see that a record of them is made, and report matters of importance to the Chief.

TELLER: The teller receives from the counters the contents of each remittance after being counted, together with a statement showing the name of the sender, the amounts and kinds of money found, and a record of all errors (if any) discovered. He compares the money

VICE-PRESIDENT HACKLEY NATIONAL BANK, MUSKEGON, MICH.

with the statement, seeing that each item is properly entered and returned. He makes a detailed entry in his cash books and forwards the statement first to the Express Clerk for entry in his register, and then to the Settlement Clerks, as a basis for making returns to the sender of the remittance. He makes a daily statement showing the amount and kinds of money in his possession at the close of business.

At the opening of business each day the Teller delivers to the Delivery Clerk the money counted and got ready for destruction the preceding day; to the Odds Clerk the money not yet made up into full packages; to the Discount Clerk the mutilated notes that have been redeemed at less than full value; to the Cash Division the new money fit for reissue and the coin; and to the National Bank Redemption Agency the national bank notes found.

ODDS CLERK: The Odds Clerk receives from the Teller the odd money found in the preceding day's count, that is, the money of which there is less than $50 of a kind and denomination, and after combination returns what full money she can make up to the Teller.

DISCOUNT CLERK: The Discount Clerk receives from the Teller the money discounted during the day and holds it subject to the orders of the Chief.

DELIVERY CLERK: The Delivery Clerk prepares the redeemed money received from the Teller for destruction. He first assorts it into its kinds and denominations and makes an inventory of each, which is copied into a record kept for that purpose. A copy of this is also prepared for the use of the Destruction Committee, which, after being certified by them, is forwarded to the accounting officers of the Department in settlement of the Treasurer's redemption account.

The Delivery Clerk places marks and labels on each package of money, so that an error can always be traced, cuts it in two parts, lengthwise, on a knife prepared for that purpose, and delivers the upper half to the Office of the Register of the Treasury and the lower half to the Office of the Secretary of the Treasury, in each of which a recount and examination is made.

COMMITTEE ON DESTRUCTION.

DESTRUCTION OF UNITED STATES SECURITIES: The committee to witness and certify to the destruction of United States securities is composed of four persons, one representing the Secretary of the Treasury, one the Register of the Treasury, one the Treasurer U. S., and one especially appointed by the Secretary of the Treasury as a special witness. The committee is authorized by the Act of March 17, 1862 (12 Stat., p. 370).

All U. S. securities that are sent to the Treasurer U. S. for redemption are classified by denominations, counted, proved, and entered in a book for that purpose. They are then made up into lots by issues and denominations, after which they are cut in two from end to end—the upper half being sent to the Register of the Treasury and the lower half to the Office of the Secretary of the Treasury for recount to verify the count of the Treasurer's Office, after which each half is entered in a book in the respective offices, corresponding with the book of the Treasurer's Office.

These securities are then turned over to the committee for destruction, which committee meets three mornings of each week at 9 o'clock, in the Committee Room of the Secretary's Office and there checks the lowes halves by denominations from slips for that purpose into boxes said boxes being securely locked. The committee then goes to the Register's Office and there checks the upper halves of the same lots from the slips used in checking the lower halves; if the committee is then satisfied that all is correct, the boxes are taken to the Bureau of Engraving and Printing and the securities are placed in the macerator, which is then locked and sealed in their presence. The securities thus placed in the macerator are reduced to pulp by the combined action of steam alkalies, and knives; and the pulp is sold under contract.

ADVICE AS TO OFFICIAL MAIL.

DO NOT ADDRESS LETTERS TO THE "TREASURY DEPARTMENT." If letters are addressed to the "Treasury Department" they are invariably sent to the office of the Secretary, while, in thousands of cases, they are intended for other officers. The duties of each Bureau are herein clearly set forth, showing to whom correspondence on any subject should be addressed.

E. B. EVANS.
CASHIER GERMAN NATIONAL BANK, OSKOSH, WIS.

DO NOT SEND STAMPS, STAMPTED OR SELF-ADDRESSED ENVELOPES. They are unnecessary, are not used by the Department, and occasion a great deal of trouble. In some Bureaus the practice is to return the stamps and envelopes, in others the stamps are sold and the proceeds deposited in the Treasury.

ANNUAL REPORTS OF FINANCIAL OFFICERS: Report on finances, by the Secretary of the Treasury; report of the Director of the Mint (and also report on "Production of Precious Metals in the United States."); report of Comptroller of the Currency, in two volumes, (the second volume giving a detailed statement as to each National Bank); report of the Treasurer of the United States, and report of Treasurer as *ex-officio* Commissioner of the Sinking Fund of the District of Columbia.

Applications for copies of any of said reports should be addressed to the Bureau by which it is issued, as each Bureau is charged with the distribution of its own reports.

PUBLIC DEBT STATEMENT: This statement is issued on the first of each month by the Division of Book-keeping and Warrents, Office of the Secretary of the Treasury. Applications for said statement, and all correspondence on the subject, should be addressed to the Secretary of the Treasury.

RESUMPTION OF SPECIE PAYMENTS: " * * * * and on and after the first day of January, anno Domini eighteen hundred and seventy-nine, the Secretary of the Treasury shall redeem, in coin, the United States legal-tender notes then outstanding on their presentation for redemption, at the office of the Assistant Treasurer of the United States in the city of New York, in sums of not less than fifty dollars." (Section 3 of Act of January 14, 1875, 18 Stat., p. 296, Supplement R. S., p. 58.)

Section 3 of the Act of March 3, 1887, (24 Stat., p. 560), is as follows: That Section 3 of the Act of January 14, 1875, entitled "An Act to provide for the resumption of specie payments, be, and the same is, hereby amended by adding after the words "New York" the words "and the city of San Francisco, California."

LIST OF SUB-TREASURIES, MINTS, AND ASSAY OFFICES.

Location.	Title of Officer in Charge.
Sub-Treasuries.	
Baltimore	Assistant Treasurer U. S.
Boston	Assistant Treasurer U. S.
Chicago	Assistant Treasurer U. S.
Cincinnati	Assistant Treasurer U. S.
New Orleans	Assistant Treasurer U. S.
New York	Assistant Treasurer U. S.
Philadelphia	Assistant Treasurer U. S.
Saint Louis	Assistant Treasurer U. S.
San Francisco	Assistant Treasurer U. S.
Mints.	
Carson City, (Nev.)	Superintendent
New Orleans	Superintendent
Philadelphia	Superintendent
San Francisco	Superintendent
Denver, (Equipped as Assay Office)	Assayer in charge

Assay Offices.

Boise City, (Idaho)	Assayer in charge
Charlotte, (N. C.)	Assayer in charge
Helena, (Mon.)	Assayer in charge
New York	Superintendent
Saint Louis	Assayer in charge

EXEMPTION OF UNITED STATES BONDS FROM TAXATION.

Section 3701 of the Revised Statutes provides as follows: "All stocks, bonds, Treasury notes, and other obligations of the United States, shall be exempt from taxation by or under State or municipal or local authority." This section makes the exemption from taxation binding only upon "State or municipal or local authority," but according to the express terms of the act of Congress of July 14, 1870, the bonds and the interest thereon of the funded loans which are thereby authorized—namely, the loan of 1881, the loan of 1891, and the four-per-cent consols of 1907—"shall be exempt from the payment of all taxes or duties of the United States, as well as from taxation in any form by or under State, municipal or local authority; and the said bonds shall have set forth and expressed upon their face the above specified conditions."

TAXATION OF NATIONAL BANK NOTES AND TREASUARY NOTES.

The act of August 13, 1894, (Statutes, 53d Congress, 2d session p. 278), provides: That circulating notes of national banking associations and United States legal tender notes and other notes and certificates of the United States payable on demand circulating or intended to circulate as currency and gold, silver or other coin shall be subject to taxation as money on hand or on deposit under the laws of any State or Territory: *Provided*, that any such taxation shall be exercised in the same manner and at the same rate that any such State or Territory shall tax money or currency circulating as money within its jurisdiction.

Sec. 2. That the provisions of this Act shall not be deemed or held to change existing laws in respect of the taxation of national banking associations.

UNITED STATES MINT TEST FOR GOLD AND SILVER COINS.

For gold coins: Strong nitric acid 6½ drachms; muriatic acid 15 drops or ¼ drachm; water 5 drachms. For silver coins: Nitrate of silver 2¼ grains; nitric acid 30 drops; 1 ounce of water.

The liquid should be used near the edge of the coin or where it is most worn.

CONSCIENCE FUND.

An account designated as the "Conscience Fund," was opened by the Register of the Treasuay, to show from time to time the receipts of moneys by the United States Government from unknown persons. These moneys are covered into the General Treasury as a Miscellaneous Receipt, and may be used like other assets of the Treasury for any purpose that Congress may deem proper.

The account was opened in 1811, and up to January 1, 1895, there has been received, in small and large sums, the aggregate amount 271,448.70.

Remittances are received almost weekly—occasionally the receipts are two or three cases a week—and, as a rule, the letters are not signed. Frequently they are forwarded by clergymen at the request of penitents. As nearly all the communications are anonymous acknowledgements are always made through the local press of Washington.

VALUES OF FOREIGN COINS.

By Section 25 of the Act of August 28, 1894 (Statutes, 53rd Congress, 2nd session, p. 552) the Director of the Mint was required to estimate quarterly, on the first day of January, April, July, and October, the value of the standard coins in circulation of the various nations of the world. The following table is the estimate contained in Circular No. 1, of January 1, 1895:

COUNTRY.	Standard.	Monetary unit.	Value in terms of U. S. gold dollar	Coins
Argentine Republic	Gold and silver	Peso	$0.96.5	Gold: argentine ($4.82,4) and ½ argentine. Silver: peso and divisions
Austria-Hungary	Gold	Crown	.20,3	Gold: former system—4 florins ($1.92,9), 8 florins ($3.85,9), ducat ($2.28,7) and 4 ducats ($9.15,8). Silver: 1 and 2 florins. Gold: present system—20 crowns ($4.05,2), 10 crowns ($2.02,6)
Belgium	Gold and silver	Franc	.19,3	Gold: 10 and 20 francs. Silver: 5 francs.
Bolivia	Silver	Boliviano	.45,5	Silver: boliviano and divisions.
Brazil	Gold	Milreis	.54,6	Gold: 5, 10, and 20 milreis. Silver: ½, 1, and 2 milreis
British Possessions N. A. (except Newfoundland).	Gold	Dollar	1.00	
Central Amer. States—Costa Rica, Guatemala, Honduras, Nicaragua, Salvador	Silver	Peso	.45,5	Silver: peso and divisions.
Chile	Gold and silver	Peso	.91,2	Gold: escudo ($1.82,4), doubloon ($4.56,1), and condor ($9.12,9). Silver: peso and divisions.
China	Silver	Tael { Shanghai Haikwan (Customs) Tientsin Chefoo }	.67,3 .74,9 .71,4 .70,4	
Colombia	Silver	Peso	.45,5	Gold: condor ($9.64,7) and double-condor. Silver: peso.
Cuba	Gold and silver	Peso	.92,6	Gold: doubloon ($5.01,7). Silver: peso
Denmark	Gold	Crown	.26,8	Gold: 10 and 20 crowns
Ecuador	Silver	Sucre	.45,5	Gold: condor ($9.64,7) and double-condor. Silver: sucre and divisions
Egypt	Gold	Pound (100 piasters)	4.94,3	Gold: pound (100 piasters), 5, 10, 20, and 50 piasters. Silver: 1, 2, 5, 10, and 20 piasters
Finland	Gold	Mark	.19,3	Gold: 20 marks ($3.85,9), 10 marks ($1.93).
France	Gold and silver	Franc	.19,3	Gold: 5, 10, 20, 50, and 100 francs. Silver: 5 francs.
German Empire	Gold	Mark	.23,8	Gold: 5, 10, and 20 marks.
Great Britain	Gold	Pound sterling	4.86,6½	Gold: sovereign (pound sterling) and ½ sovereign.
Greece	Gold and silver	Drachma	.19,3	Gold: 5, 10, 20, 50, and 100 drachmas. Silver: 5 drachmas
Haiti	Gold and silver	Gourde	.96,5	Silver: gourde.
India	Silver	Rupee	.21,6	Gold: mohur ($7.10,5). Silver: rupee and divisions.
Italy	Gold and silver	Lira	.19,3	Gold: 5, 10, 20, 50, and 100 lire. Silver: 5 lire
Japan	Gold and silver*	Yen { Gold Silver }	.99,7 .49,1	Gold: 1, 2, 5, 10, and 20 yen Silver: yen
Liberia	Gold	Dollar	1.00	
Mexico	Silver	Dollar	.49,5	Gold: dollar ($0.98,3), 2½, 5, 10, and 20 dollars. Silver: dollar (or peso) and divisions
Netherlands	Gold and silver	Florin	.40,2	Gold: 10 florins. Silver: ½, 1, and 2½ florins.
Newfoundland	Gold	Dollar	1.01,4	Gold: 2 dollars ($2.02,7)
Norway	Gold	Crown	.26,8	Gold: 10 and 20 crowns
Peru	Silver	Sol	.45,5	Silver: sol and divisions
Portugal	Gold	Milreis	1.08	Gold: 1, 2, 5, and 10 milreis
Russia	Silver†	Ruble { Gold Silver }	.77,2 .35,4	Gold: imperial ($7.71,8), and ½ imperial ($3.86). Silver: ¼, ½, and 1 ruble
Spain	Gold and silver	Peseta	.19,3	Gold: 25 pesetas. Silver: 5 pesetas
Sweden	Gold	Crown	.26,8	Gold: 10 and 20 crowns
Switzerland	Gold and silver	Franc	.19,3	Gold: 5, 10, 20, 50, and 100 francs. Silver: 5 francs.
Tripoli	Silver	Mahbub of 20 piasters	.43,1	
Turkey	Gold	Piaster	.04,4	Gold: 25, 50, 100, 250, and 500 piasters
Venezuela	Gold and silver	Bolivar	.19,3	Gold: 5, 10, 20, 50, and 100 bolivars. Silver: 5 bolivars

* Gold the nominal standard. Silver practically the standard
† Coined since January 1, 1886. Old half-imperial = $3.98,6.
‡ Silver the nominal standard. Paper the actual currency, the depreciation of which is measured by the gold standard

COLUMBIAN HALF DOLLARS.

The Act of August 5, 1892 (27 Stat., p. 389), provided for the coinage of silver half dollars not to exceed five million (5,000,000) pieces, to be known as the Columbian half dollar, struck in commemoration of the World's Columbian Exposition. The said act authorized the Secretary of the Treasury to pay the same to the World's Columbian Exposition, for labor done, materials furnished, and services performed in prosecuting the work of preparing the Exposition for opening.

JOHN A. KING,
PRESIDENT FORT DEARBORN NATIONAL BANK, CHICAGO, ILL.

"Only about $750,000 were sold at the Fair, while nearly $1,250,000 more were paid out at their face value by the Fair Management. There were $570,880 of the coin which never left the Philadelphia Mint until now. There was $1,795,980 in the possession of the Government a short time ago, a large number finding their way back to the Treasury during the recent money panic. The officers of the Fair proposed at one time to pay the cost of transportation and recoinage of the half dollars which had not been sold to the public, in order to protect the rights of those who had bought the souvenirs at a premium. The sum of $41,000 was deposited with the Treasurer last December for these expenses, but the Government insisted on a further deposit of $17,000 to pay for the recoinage of the souvenirs which had never left the Philadelphia Mint, and to this the Managers demurred. The Director of the Mint had considerable correspondence on the subject with Mr. James W. Ellsworth, the Chairman of the Finance Committee, with the result that the deposit of $41,000 was withdrawn and the entire mass of souvenirs left to be treated as the Secretary of the Treasury might see fit. * * * It may be mentioned here that all the Columbian half dollars now being put in circulation bear the date 1893. There were $2,501,052.50 coined in that year, and $475,000 in 1892. The latter still sell at a premium." (Dickerman's Counterfeit Detector, November, 1894.)

The question has often arisen as to whether people are compelled to accept the Columbian half dollars, but there should be no doubt on the subject, as the Act authorizing their coinage provided that "All provisions of law relative to the coinage, legal-tender quality, and redemption of the present subsidiary silver coins shall be applicable to the coins issued under this Act."

Subsidiary silver coins are a legal tender in the amount of ten dollars in any one payment, and are redeemable, when presented in sums or multiples of twenty dollars, by the Treasurer or any Assistant Treasurer U. S.

Columbian half dollars are paid out only in exchange for gold coin or gold certificates, and will be sent by express at the expense of the Government in sums of $200 or more for like amounts of gold coin of current weight or gold certificates deposited with the Treasurer U. S. or any Assistant Treasurer.

A less sum than $200 will be sent by express at the cost of the consignee, or by registered mail in amounts of $50 at risk of consignee, registration free, as may be directed.

ISABELLA QUARTERS.

The Act of March 3, 1893, (27 Stat., p. 586), provides that "Ten thousand dollars of the appropriation for the Board of Lady Managers shall be paid in souvenir coins of the denomination of twenty-five cents, and for that purpose there shall be coined at the Mints of the United States silver quarter dollars of the legal weight and fineness, not to exceed forty thousand pieces * * * and all provisions of law relative to the coinage, legal-tender quality, and redemption of the present subsidiary silver coins shall be applicable to the coins herein authorized to be issued; * * *"

"There were $10,005.75 of Columbian quarter dollars coined and disposed of, none of which are in general circulation so far as we can learn." (Dickerman's Counterfeit Detector, November, 1894.) Said coins have the same legal-tender qualities and are redeemable in like manner as Columbian half dollars.

Applications for Isabella quarters must be made to the Board of Lady Managers of the World's Columbian Exposition, Chicago, Illinois.

REVENUES AND EXPENDITURES OF THE GOVERNMENT.

(Home Report of Treasurer, U. S., 1894.)

REVENUES AND EXPENDITURES.

The net ordinary revenues and expenditures for the fiscal years ending June 30, 1893 and 1894, were as shown in the following table:

	1893.	1894.	Increase.	Decrease.
REVENUES.				
Customs	$203,355,016.73	$131,818,530.62		$71,536,486.11
Internal revenue	161,027,623.93	147,111,232.81		13,916,391.12
Sale of public lands	3,182,089.78	1,673,637.30		1,508,452.48
Miscellaneous sources	18,254,898.34	17,118,618.52		1,136,279.82
Total	385,819,628.78	297,722,019.25		88,097,609.53
EXPENDITURES.				
Civil and miscellaneous:				
Customs, light-houses, public buildings, etc.	19,308,233.09	20,316,268.90	$918,035.90	
Internal revenue	14,866,436.78	16,308,849.71	1,442,412.93	
Interior civil (lands, patents, etc.)	9,751,506.22	8,911,054.85		840,451.37
Treasury proper (legislative, executive, and other civil)	50,507,363.69	49,160,804.19		1,346,559.50
Diplomatic (foreign relations)	1,997,042.90	1,702,307.31		294,735.59
Judiciary	7,212,216.68	5,544,599.11		1,667,617.57
War Department	49,641,773.47	54,567,929.85	4,926,156.38	
Navy Department	30,136,084.43	31,701,293.79	1,565,209.36	
Interior Department (Indians and pensions)	172,702,905.14	151,470,766.48		21,232,138.66
Interest on public debt	27,264,392.18	27,841,405.64	577,013.46	
Total	383,477,954.49	367,525,279.83	9,428,828.03	25,381,502.69
Net decrease				15,952,674.66
Surplus	2,341,674.29			72,144,934.87
Deficiency		69,803,260.58		

CONTENTS OF VAULTS IN U. S. TREASURER'S OFFICE.

(Approximate.)

VAULT.	AMOUNT.	DESCRIPTION.
1	$103,740,000	Standard silver dollars.
2	48,000,000	Standard silver dollars.
2	3,680,000	Gold coin.
2	600,900	Fractional silver, $529,000; minor coin, $71,900.
3	3,500,000	National bank notes received for redemption.
4	1,000,000	Mixed moneys received daily for redemption.
6	13,000,000	Mixed moneys for daily use.
7	250,000,000	Bonds held as security for N. B. circulation, &c.
8	393,700,863	Held as reserve to replace worn and mutilated notes unfit for circulation.
Total	817,221,763	Total weight of coin about 4,500 tons

AMOUNT OF MONEY IN CIRCULATION.

	GENERAL STOCK, COINED OR ISSUED.	IN TREASURY.	AMOUNT IN CIRCULATION JANUARY 1, 1895.
Gold Coin	$577,380,396 00	$91,879,020 00	$485,501,376 00
Standard Silver Dollars	422,426,749 00	364,537,659 00	57,889,090 00
Subsidiary Silver	77,155,722 00	14,483,636 00	62,672,086 00
Gold Certificates	53,420,869 00	58,960 00	53,361,909 00
Silver Certificates	336,924,504 00	5,846,720 00	331,077,784 00
Treas'y Notes, Act July 14, 1890	150,823,731 00	28,369,950 00	122,453,781 00
United States Notes	346,681,016 00	81,919,158 00	264,761,858 00
Cur'y Cert'f's, Act June 8, 1872	48,965,000 00	1,960,000 00	47,005,000 00
National Bank Notes	206,605,710 00	4,759,972 00	201,845,738 00
TOTALS	2,220,383,697 00	593,815,075 00	1,626,568,622 00

Population of the United States January 1, 1895, estimated at 69,134,000; circulation per capita, $23.52.

SUPERVISING ARCHITECT OF THE TREASURY.

METHODS IN THE ERECTION OF A PUBLIC BUILDING: When Congress authorizes the erection of a Federal building at any place, in most cases the limit of the cost of the site, building, heating apparatus, elevators, and approaches is fixed in the law, either separately or jointly, and a portion thereof is usually appropriated for purchase of site and commencing the erection of the building. When an appropriation has thus been made, the Secretary, except in cases where the act of Congress otherwise specially directs, advertises in the local papers for proposals for the sale of the necessary land, as required by section 355, Revised Statutes, United States, and designates an officer of the Treasury Department to examine the property offered and recommend the selection of a site therefrom most advantageous to the interests of the Government and convenient to the citizens of the place in which the building is to be erected. Upon the selection of the site of proposal of the owner of the land chosen is transmitted to the Attorney-General of the United States, with request that he cause the title to the same to be examined, and if found valid, to secure deeds of conveyance to the United States, and cession of jurisdiction over the site selected is then secured from the State in which the same is located. The sketch plans for the building, specifications, and detail estimates are next prepared and approved by the Secretary of the Treasury, Secretary of the Interior, and Postmaster-General; work is commenced on the working drawings and specifications for each branch of work on the building, which form the immediate basis upon which to invite by public advertisement, proposals and the execution of contracts; and when such drawings and specifications are completed action is promptly taken to place the work on the market and to secure the early commencement and rapid prosecution of the same. When the working drawings and definite specifications are sufficiently advanced to warrant the commencement of active building operations and securing uninterrupted prosecution of the same, a superintendent, technically qualified and a resident (when a competent person can be

secured in the locality of the building, is appointed by the Secretary
of the Treasury to represent the Department in superintending the
construction and securing the satisfactory prosecution of all work on
the building to the best interests of the Government and in full compliance with specifications, drawings, and terms of contract. To assist
the superintendent in the performance of his duties the Department
authorizes the employment of a clerk, and, at buildings of considerable
magnitude, an assistant superintendent, a general foreman, and watch-

G. C. HIXON.
FIRST PREST. LA CROSSE NATIONAL BANK, LA CROSSE, WIS.

man. Funds on account of the appropriation for the building are
from time to time remitted to the disbursing agent, (who is duly appointed, in accordance with section 8, R. S., U. S., by the Secretary of
the Treasury, under a bond, at a maximum rate of three-eighths of one
per cent. commission),with which to pay certificates issued by the superintendent on account of the work, authorized by the Supervising
Architect and approved by the Secretary of the Treasury, and of which
authority he has been duly advised.

Proposals to supply labor and material are, except in cases here-
inafter stated, invited by publishing advertisements in local news-

papers and certain technical or trades journals which are printed for the benefit and information of parties engaged in building pursuits throughout the United States. After the proposals are secured, in response to such advertisements, they are opened at the designated time, in the presense of such bidders as choose to be present, and forwarded to the Department (in accordance with section 3710 R. S., U. S.), and are submitted by the Supervising Architect, with a specific recommendation, to the Secretary of the Treasury, and upon his approval the most economical proposal is accepted and the bidder required to execute a bond or formal contract for the faithful compliance therewith. The cases which are exceptional to this practice are those in which the superintendent, in view of public exigency demanding the immediate performance of the work or delivery of material (as provided for by section 3709 R. S., U. S.), recommends the employment of the labor by the day or the purchase of the material in open market and such recommendations are approved by the Supervising Architect and by the Secretary of the Treasury.

CONTINENTAL CURRENCY.

REASONS WHY IT IS NOT REDEEMABLE: "The mass of debt which devolved upon the United States, as an inheritance from the Continental Congress and the several colonies, engaged the attention of the national legislature soon after the adoption of the Constitution. The debt was very large and depreciated, and was still depreciating in value; but it was the price of liberty, and the payment of that portion of it contracted by national authority was made obligatory by the new Constitution." (Bayley's History of the National Loans.)

All debts contracted and engagements entered into, before the adoption of this Constitution, shall be as valid against the United States under this Constitution, as under the Confederation. (Constitution, Article VI.)

"It was necessary, therefore, to provide for it in some way, although the payment of even the interest seemed impossible in the exhausted condition of the country at that time." (Bayley's History of the National Loans.)

On September 21, 1789, the House of Representatives adopted the following resolutions:

Resolved, That this House consider an adequate provision for the support of the public credit as a matter of high importance to the national honor and prosperity.

Resolved, That the Secretary of the Treasury be directed to prepare a plan for that purpose, and to report the same to this House at its next meeting.

"There were two kinds of debt in the adjustment of which there seems to have been no difficulty: One was the unadjusted foreign debt, where the lenders had paid for their bonds in gold, on the faith of the Continental Congress: *the other was the paper money issued by Congress and the several States.*"

"Authorities vary as to the amount of paper money issued during the struggle for independence. Possibly Mr. Jefferson's statement in his writings may be taken as approximate to the truth, and it affords, at the same time, a striking exhibit of the effects of the inflation of our paper currency: (Bayley's History of the National Loans.)

The total issue was estimated by Jefferson at about $200,000,000. He states that this "paper money continued for a twelvemonth equal to gold and silver;" it then began to de-

S. S. BURTON
FIRST CASHIER, LA CROSSE NATIONAL BANK, LA CROSSE, WIS.

preciate. "In two years it had fallen to two dollars of paper money for one of silver; in three years to four for one; in nine months it fell to ten for one; and in the six months following, that is to say, by September, 1779, it had fallen twenty for one." * * *

"It continued to circulate and to depreciate till the end of 1780, when it had fallen to seventy-five for one; and the money circulated from the French army being, by that time, sensible in all the States north of the Potomac, the paper ceased its circulation altogether in those States. In Virginia and North Carolina it continued a year longer, within which time it fell to one thousand for one, and then expired, as it had done in the other States, without a single groan. *Not a murmur was heard on this occasion among the people.* On the contrary, universal congratulations took place on their seeing this gigantic mass, whose dissolution had threatened convulsions which should shake their infant Confederacy to its center quietly interred in its grave." (Jefferson's Works, Vol. IX, p. 248, quoted in Bayley's History of the National Loans.)

Jefferson estimates the value of the two hundred millions of Continental currency at the time of its emission at $36,367,719.83 in specie, and says:

"If we estimate at the same value the like sum of $200,000,000 supposed to have been emitted by the States, and reckon the federal debt, foreign and domestic, at about $43,000,000, and the State debts at $25,000,000, it will form an amount of $140,000,000, the total sum which the war cost the United States. It continued eight years from the Battle of Lexington to the cessation of hostilities in America. The annual expense was, therefore, equal to about $17,500,000 in specie." (Ibid. p. 260.)

COUNTERFEITING. The Continental bills would have rapidly sunk by reason of the enormous quantity issued, even if they had not been weighed in any other manner; but not long after the appearance of the first issue, the country was inundated with counterfeits which found their way among the people, and hastened the depreciation and fall of paper money. Counterfeiting was not confined solely to individuals. The British Government also embarked in the business. (Bolles' Financial History of the United States.)

"On the 9th of January, 1790, Hamilton made his report to the House of Representatives, in obedience to the resolution of September 21, 1789, before referred to, in which he gave many reasons for assuming the debts of the old government and of the several States, and furnished a plan for supporting the public credit. His recommendation was finally adopted, and embodied in the act making provision for the payment of the debt of the United States, approved August 4, 1790, (1 Statutes, 138.) (Bayley's History of the National Loans.)

By the act above cited a loan to the full value of the domestic debt was authorized, the subscription to be payable in certificates issued for the said debt. The terms of subscription as to Continental currency were as follows:

"And in the bills of credit issued by the authority of the United States in Congress assembled, *at the rate of one hundred dollars in the said bills, for one dollar in specie.*"

By the Act of March 3, 1797, (1 Stautes, 516), it was declared that said money should be receivable as above until December 31, 1797, and no longer.

By the Act of July 9, 1798, (Ibd. p. 580) it was provided that "all credits on books of the Treasury of the United States, for transactions during the late war, which, according to the course of the Treasury, have hitherto been discharged by issuing certificates of registered debt, shall be forever barred and precluded from settlement or allowance, unless claimed by the proper creditors, or their legal representatives on or before the first day of March, in the year of one thousand seven hundred and ninety-nine."

CHAS. BEST.
VICE-PREST. WISCONSIN NATIONAL BANK, MILWAUKEE, WIS.

DECISION OF THE FIRST COMPTROLLER. In a claim submitted by the Register of the Treasury under date of June 5, 1886, asking for an opinion as to the legal authority for payment, the First Comptroller, under date of August 2, 1886, decided that:

"Owing to the loss of papers and documents in the Treasury Department, first by fire which occurred January 20, 1801, second by the incrusion of the British, August 24, 1814, and third by the fire of March 31, 1833, it is now impossible to tell what was the basis of said claim, or the evidence of its payment, if it was ever paid. If it was never paid, it may be barred by the act of July 9, 1798, * * * and is so barred if issued to pay a claim embraced by that act. Whether that is so or not, I am of the opinion that the claim should not now be paid, on account of the long lapse of time before its presentation for payment.

LEGAL TENDER QUALITIES. "The question has been raised and disputed as to whether what was called the "Continental currency," issued during the War of the Revolution by the old Government, was or was not legal tender. The facts appear to be that while the Continental Congress did not by any ordinance attempt to give it that character, they asked the States to do so, and all seem to have complied except Rhode Island. The Continental Congress only enacted that the man who refused to take the money should be deemed an enemy of his country. George Washington complained, in one of his letters, that he had been obliged to receive the currency at par, in payment of a debt, when it had so depreciated that its value was almost nominal." (Bayley's History of the National Loans.)

FESSENDEN ON "FINANCE."

The bill for the issue of Legal Tender notes was approved February 25, 1862, (12 Stat., p. 345.) Mr. Fessenden, in his speech in the Senate on the bill, referring to the legal tender clause, said:

"Nobody knows much upon the question of finance, not even those who are most familiar with it; for, sir, I declare today that, in the whole number of learned financial men that I have consulted, I never have found any two of them who agree, and therefore it is hardly worth while for us to plead any very remarkable degree of ignorance when nobody is competent to instruct us; and yet such is the fact. I can state to you, Mr. President, that on one day I was advised very strongly by a leading financial man, at all events to oppose this legal-tender clause; he exclaimed against it with all the bitterness in the world. On the very same day I received a note from a friend of his, telling me that we could not get along without it. I showed it to him, and he expressed his utter surprise. He went home, and the next day telegraphed to me that he had changed his mind and now thought it was absolutely necessary; and his friend who wrote to me again that he had changed his, and they were two of the most eminent financial men in the country." (Congressional Globe, 2d Session 37th Congress, p. 766, quoted in Bayley's "History of the National Loans," p. 80.)

THE WILES OF "GREEN GOODS" MEN.

The following description of the methods of a very numerous class of swindlers, known by the title of "Green Goods Men," or "Boodlers," is taken from a circular letter (Form 20) of the Secret Service Division of the Treasury Department. Parties offering to sell counterfeit money "never deal in it, but make a pretense of doing so on purpose to inveigle dishonest persons—who would buy counterfeit money if they could—into parting with their good money in the hope of getting counterfeit. These swindlers are usually located in large cities, but New York contains by far the greater number.

They send circulars in imitation of letters by thousands all over the country, inviting their correspondents to visit New York, naming the hotel at which they should stop, and offering them great inducements to purchase. Those who go after such bargains never obtain counterfeit money, and seldom return home without leaving all of their good money in the hands of these plausible but dangerous men.

PRESIDENT PRO TEMPORE FIRST NATIONAL BANK, DETROIT, MICH

In August, 1885, James T. Holland, of Abilene, Tex., allured to the City of New York by a circular * * * * * met Tom Davis and Theodore, his brother. These men, while pretending to sell Holland ten thousand dollars of so-called counterfeit money, but which were genuine notes, cheated him of his good money. Holland, at once discovering the cheat, shot Tom Davis, killing him instantly. A jury subsequently acquitted Holland.

Another practice is to toll on their victims by sending a *genuine* one or two dollar note, or parts of the same, and representing them to be specimens of the counterfeit notes they have for sale.

Under the various names of "Green Articles," "Green Cigars," "Green Leaves," etc., they offer for sale counterfeit money which they aver is printed on plates stolen from the Bureau of Engraving and Printing of the Government. *Not a plate of any kind has ever been stolen from that establishment.*

Those who have counterfeit money for sale do not write letters requesting strangers to buy it. Even after the introduction of a new man by one counterfeiter to another, it takes a long time to establish such friendly relations as would induce a counterfeiter to trust a new-comer.

L. A. GODDARD,
CASHIER FORT DEARBORN NATIONAL BANK, CHICAGO, ILL.

Yet thousands of criminally foolish people believe they can purchase counterfeit money as they would butter or cheese, and in their attempts to obtain it, are robbed, and an honest public sentiment says, "Serves them right."

The crime of which the "Boodler" is guilty is covered by Section No. 5480, United States Revised Statutes, as amended and approved March 2, 1889, and the offender, upon conviction, is liabel to a fine of $500 and imprisonment for eighteen months. It is next to impossible to obtain legal evidence against these swindlers; and were one of them arrested and brought to trial, the testimony of the main witness (he who lost the money) would be weakened by the fact that he *would have been* a criminal if he *could*.

PREMIUM ON COINS.

(Circular letter of Treasurer U. S.)

(1) The Department makes no distinction between the various issues of coin and currency of the United States, *neither receiving nor paying a premium in any case.*

N. W. HARRIS.
SENIOR PARTNER OF N. W. HARRIS & CO., CHICAGO, ILL.

NOTE: None of the coins of the United States have been "called in." All statements to the contrary are erroneous, and their origin and purport unknown.

(2) Applications for list of, and correspondence in relation to, premium coins, should be addressed to some of the COIN DEALERS to be found in all large cities.

CONFEDERATE AND STATE BANK NOTES.

(Circular letter of Treasurer U. S.)

Notes issued by the late so-called CONFEDERATE States of America, and by the various STATE BANKS, are not redeemable by the United States.

GOLD COINS MINTED BY PRIVATE PARTIES.

The only denominations of gold coins whose issue was authorized by law are the $20, $10, $5, $3, $2½ and $1 pieces. Of these the coinage of the $3 and $1 pieces was discontinued by the Act of September 26, 1890. There have been a great many gold coins, of denominations varying from 25 cents up to $50, which were minted by private parties. In the year 1851 there were fifteen minting establishments in the United States, only one of which was authorized by law. Many of the coins were in imitation of the United States coins, but the greater portion were stamped with the names and bore the devices and legends of the persons by whom issued.

The Director of the Mint in his report for the year 1840 observed: "It seems strange that the privilege of coining copper should be carefully confined by law to the general government, while that of coining gold and silver, though withheld from the States, is freely permitted to individuals, with the single restriction, that they must not imitate the coinage established by law."

This private coinage appears to have been confined to the far Western States, especially California, and the State of North Carolina. The Mint of the Bechtlers in the State last named seems to have done an extensive business—basing the assumption upon the number of coins formerly in circulation.

The $50 piece, commonly known by the name of "gold slug" was octagonal in shape, and was regarded as a novelty on account of its shape and general design, as well as its extraordinary size. The 50 cent and 25 cent pieces were coined in California and Colorado. They are extremely rare, and, on this account, are frequently counterfeited. There was also coined a piece known as the "Twenty-five dollar piece of Templeton Reid."

The majority of the coins issued by private parties were of the same denomination as the coins of the United States. As these private coins were not authorized (although permitted) by law, they are not redeemable by Government, and, as a matter of course, none of them are in the Treasury. Applications for any of the coins referred to, or any correspondence on the subject, should be addressed to some of the numerous dealers in rare coins to be found in all large cities. (Compiled principally from Eckfeldt & Du Bois' "Manual of Coins," 1851.)

ORIGIN OF THE DOLLAR MARK ($)

The dollar unit, as a money of account, was established by Act of Congress of April 2, 1792, and the same Act provides for the coinage of a silver dollar of the value of a Spanish milled dollar as the same is

OFFICERS OF
THE PREFERRED BANKERS' LIFE ASSURANCE COMPANY,
OF MICHIGAN.

now current. It was the Spanish pillar dollar (called also the milled dollar from its milled edge) that was taken as the basis of the United States coinage and money of account.

Spanish dollars were chiefly coined in the Spanish-American colonies. The best known variety was the pillar dollar, so-called from the two pillars on its reverse, representing the "Pillars of Hercules," the ancient name of the opposite promontories at the Straits of Gibraltar. The rude imitations of these pillars in writing, connecting them with a scroll, is said to have been the origin of the dollar mark ($). Another explanation is that, as the dollar consists of 8 reals (8 R being stamped upon it), the mark was designed to stand for the "piece of eight," as the dollar was commonly called, the two vertical lines being employed to distinguish it from the figure 8. (Compiled from Appleton's Cyclopaedia, title "Dollar.")

"One writer says it comes from the letters U. S. (United States), which, after the adoption of the Federal Constitution, were prefixed to the Federal currency, and which afterwards, in the hurry of writing, were run into one another; the U being made first and the S over it. Another, that it is derived from the contraction of the Spanish word *pesos*, dollars, or *pesos fuertes*, hard dollars. A third, that it is a contraction for the Spanish *fuertes*, hard, to distinguish silver or hard dollars from paper money. The more probable explanation is that it is a modification of the figures 8 formerly used to denote a piece of eight reals, or, as a dollar was then called, a *piece of eight*." ("Bartlett's Dictionary of Americanisms.")

"As to my boat it was a very good one, and that he saw, and told me he would buy it of me for the ship's use; and asked me what I would have for it. I told him that I could not offer to make any price of the boat, but left it entirely to him; upon which he told me he would give me a note of hand to pay me eighty *pieces of eight* for it in Brazil." (Robinson Crusoe, quoted in "Bartlett's Dictionary of Americanisms.")

Of the many theories advanced, several of which are plausible, it is difficult to determine to which the most weight should be given, but inasmuch as the Spanish pillar dollar has on its reverse two pillars, from each of which floats a scroll similar in shape to an S, and in view of the fact that the Spanish pillar dollar was taken as the basis of American coinage, the theory that the dollar mark was derived from the pillar and scroll ($) is surely entitled to much consideration; but a great deal may be said in favor of the "piece of eight" (8), with the two pillars II, written thus: ($), which would result, when rapidly written, in the eight bearing a similarity to the letter S. The theory as to the letters U. S. (United States), written one over the other, appears to be based merely upon sentiment.

"PILLARS OF HERCULES." Among the ancient peoples of the East there were many versions of miraculous deeds performed by such wonderful beings as Hercules, or Herakles. The researches of modern scholars, however, have showed these tales to be nothing more or less than Sun-myths. The Phœnicians regarded the opposite promontories at the Straits of Gibraltar as the Western limits of the land—all beyond was a vast, unknown extent of water, apparently "world without end." When Herakles (the Sun) had run his brilliant course through the heavens, and slowly retired at the close of day into the "dark unfathomed caves," the glorious picture as seen between these two noble promontories might well suggest the designation:—"The Pillars of Hercules."

WILLARD FORESTER WARNER,
WASHINGTON, D. C.

MUNICIPAL BONDS

(Not Subject to Federal Taxation)

> Pledging the faith and credit and the real and personal property of the corporation are second only to U. S. Government Bonds in point of security, while yielding a much higher rate of interest.

W. J. HAYES & SONS
BANKERS

7 EXCHANGE PLACE
BOSTON, MASS.

311-313 SUPERIOR ST.
CLEVELAND, OHIO, U.S.A.

WE BUY AND SELL

CABLE ADDRESS "KENNETH"

FIRST NATIONAL BANK

ESTABLISHED 1863

(191)

KALAMAZOO, MICH.

CAPITAL - - - - $100,000.00
SURPLUS AND PROFITS - $150,000.00
Loans 190,000   Deposits 450,000

Collections a Specialty

L. M. GATES, Pres   F. N. ROWLEY, Cashier
J. W. OSBORN, Vice-President

Mercantile National Bank, N. Y.
National Bank Illinois, Chicago

Jas. W. English, President
Jas. R. Gray, Vice President
Jno. K. Ottley, Cashier
Chas. I. Ryan, Assistant Cashier

American Trust & Banking Co.

ATLANTA, GEORGIA

CAPITAL, - - - - $500,000.00
SURPLUS AND PROFITS, - - - $40,000.00

LARGEST CAPITAL OF ANY BANK IN ATLANTA

Liability same as National Banks
Transacts a General Banking Business

COLLECTIONS

We make a specialty of COLLECTIONS and have Superior Facilities for handling business throughout the State

Any information cheerfully furnished. Write us for terms

CORRESPONDENTS

American Exchange National Bank, New York
Independence National Bank, Philadelphia

THE PEOPLE'S BANK
OF BUFFALO, NEW YORK

CAPITAL - - $300,000   SURPLUS - - $100,000

President, DANIEL O'DAY.   Vice President, ARTHUR D. BISSELL
Cashier, C. W. HAMMOND

BOARD OF DIRECTORS

DANIEL O'DAY, ... Standard Oil Company
CHAS. F. BISHOP, Mayor of City of Buffalo, . Wholesale Teas, Coffees and Spices
P. H. GRIFFIN, ... New York Car Wheel Works
GEO. H. LEWIS, of Bell & Lewis, ... Miners and Wholesale Coal
E. G. S. MILLER, ... Brewer
W. H. GRANGER, ... Wholesale Grocer
JOHN HUGHES, of Swope, Hughes, Waltz & Benstead . . Live Stock Dealers
CLARENCE W. HAMMOND, ... Cashier
W. RICHARDSON . . . . Capitalist
WILLIAM W. SLOAN . . . . Malster
JOHN M. BRINKER, of Brinker & Jones . . . . . Miners and Wholesale Coal
JOHN T. STEWART, of Stewart Bros. . . . . Wholesale Lumber
ARTHUR D. BISSELL . . . . Vice President

THE PEOPLE'S BANK can handle COLLECTIONS to advantage in Buffalo and vicinity, also all points East and West, and will be pleased to have your patronage. Send your Collections to THE PEOPLE'S BANK.

THE
Central National Bank

(PERRY-PAYNE BUILDING)

CLEVELAND, OHIO

COMMENCED BUSINESS MAY 26TH, 1890

CAPITAL - - $800,000.00

OFFICERS

THOMAS WILSON, President   JOSEPH BLACK, Vice President
J. J. SULLIVAN, Cashier   C. A. PAINE, Ass't Cashier

DIRECTORS

JOSEPH BLACK, of the D. Black Cloak Company
N. C. BREWER, President Cleveland Rubber Paint Company
WILLIAM CHISHOLM, Sr., Iron Manufacturer and owner of Chisholm Steel Shovel Works
JOHN H. FARLEY, Brass Founder, and Ex-Mayor of Cleveland
H. P. McINTOSH, Counselor and Agent of Hon. H. P. Payne and Col. Oliver H. Payne
C. MORRIS, President Morris Coal Company
E. W. OGLEBAY, Iron Ore Merchant and President Nat. Bank of West Va., Wheeling
CHARLES L. PACK, Pack, Gray and Company, Wholesale Lumber
B. L. PENNINGTON, of The Lockwood-Taylor Hardware Company
J. J. SULLIVAN, Cashier
THOMAS WILSON, Vessel Owner and President Wilson Transit Company

The record and business standing of the gentlemen comprising the Board of Directors will be a guarantee of careful, conservative management.

We invite correspondence, or a personal interview with a view to business.

First National ..Bank..

PAID-UP CAPITAL, -   -   -   - $500,000
SURPLUS -   -   -   -   - $35,000

WACO, TEXAS

E. ROTAN, President
WM. CAMERON } Vice Presidents
TOM PADGITT
J. K. ROSE, Cashier
R F. GRIBBLE, Ass't Cashier

D. V. RIEGER, President   HENRY C. KUMPF, Vice-President
R. D. COVINGTON, Cashier

MISSOURI NATIONAL BANK
NEW YORK LIFE BUILDING
KANSAS CITY, MO.

DIRECTORS

F. H. KUMP   D. A. McKIBBEN   D. V. RIEGER   S. S. SERAT   H. C. KUMPF
H. J. HUCKE   R. D. COVINGTON

Des Moines Savings Bank

DES MOINES, IOWA

CAPITAL · · · · $300,000

TRANSACTS ANY BUSINESS
CONNECTED WITH
BANKING

...COLLECTIONS...

Carefully made and proceeds promptly accounted for
on moderate terms

AVERAGE DEPOSITS · $1,000,000

P. M CASADY, President
G. M. HIPPEE, Vice President
SIMON CASADY, Cashier

MEDFORD B. WILSON, PRESIDENT WM. F. CHURCHMAN, CASHIER

The Capital National Bank
INDIANAPOLIS, IND.

CAPITAL STOCK, - $300,000 SURPLUS AND EARNINGS, - $50,000

ESPECIAL FACILITIES FOR MAKING COLLECTIONS ON ALL POINTS IN INDIANA

ESTABLISHED 1865

...THE

FIRST NATIONAL BANK

OF

EAST SAGINAW — — MICHIGAN

CAPITAL · · $100,000
SURPLUS · · $100,000

SPECIAL ATTENTION GIVEN TO COLLECTIONS

E. T. JUDD, President   CLARENCE L. JUDD, Cashier

ORRIN BUMP, PRES. D. C. SMALLEY, VICE PRES. M. M. ANDREWS, CASHIER C. M. BUMP, Ass't CASHIER

THE OLD SECOND NATIONAL BANK, AT BAY CITY, MICH.

CAPITAL AND SURPLUS, $450,000

DIRECTORS—Wm. Westover, Selwyn Eddy, L. E. Hayes, Jas. Davidson, D. C. Smalley, J. W. M'Graw, A. J. Cooke, Orrin Bump, Frank P. Chesbrough

L. C. NELSON, President   H. M. NOEL, Vice Pres.   C. W. ISAACS, Cashier

No. 1112

—THE—

ST. LOUIS NATIONAL BANK

ST. LOUIS, MO.

(ESTABLISHED 1857)

CAPITAL STOCK,	- -	$1,000,000.00
SURPLUS	- - -	$150,000.00

DIRECTORS

I. C. NELSON	H. M. NOEL
W. T. ANDERSON	J. B. M. KEHLOR
G. PADDOCK	F. MITCHELL
JNO S. CULLIN	F. H. MCKITTRICK
A. K. ROOT	JAS. M. NELSON
CALVIN F. BURNES	

ALL THE ADVANTAGES OF SAFETY
AND CONSERVATIVE
BANKING OFFERED....

NO. 4939

First National Bank of Buchanan County

ST. JOSEPH, MISSOURI

CAPITAL - - - $500,000.00

Accounts of banks, bankers, corporations
and individuals respectfully solicited

----------------COLLECTION DEPARTMENT A SPECIALTY

OFFICERS

J. M. FORD
S. C. WOODSON, President   B. B. FRAZER   Vice Presidents   J. W. McALISTER, Cashier
A. KIRKPATRICK
E. A. HARTWIG, Ass't Cashier   JULIUS ROSENBLATT, 2nd Ass't Cashier

DIRECTORS

JOHN P. HAX .... of HAX B's Capitalist   J. M. FORD .... Capitalist
A. KIRKPATRICK .... Capitalist   R. L. McDONALD ...... of R. L. McDonald & Co.
LOUIS HAX ...... Pres. Louis Hax Furniture Co.   W. S. HENDRICK
C. A. CONNETT, Pres. St. Joseph Pressed Brick Co.   Treas. Geo. A. Kennard Grocery Co.
EDWARD C. SMITH ...... Pres. C. D. Smith Drug Co.   DR. C. R. WOODSON
W. C. BROWN .... Supt. State Lunatic Asylum No. 2
    Gen'l Mgr. Burlington Route in Missouri   G. W. WILLIAMS ...... Banker, Senece, Kansas
B. B. FRAZER .... President Park Bank   S. C. WOODSON .... President
C. A. HUPACHER .... Capitalist   J. W. McALISTER .... Cashier

DISCOUNT COMMITTEE

J. M. FORD   LOUIS HAX   EDW. C. SMITH   J. W. McALISTER   S. C. WOODSON

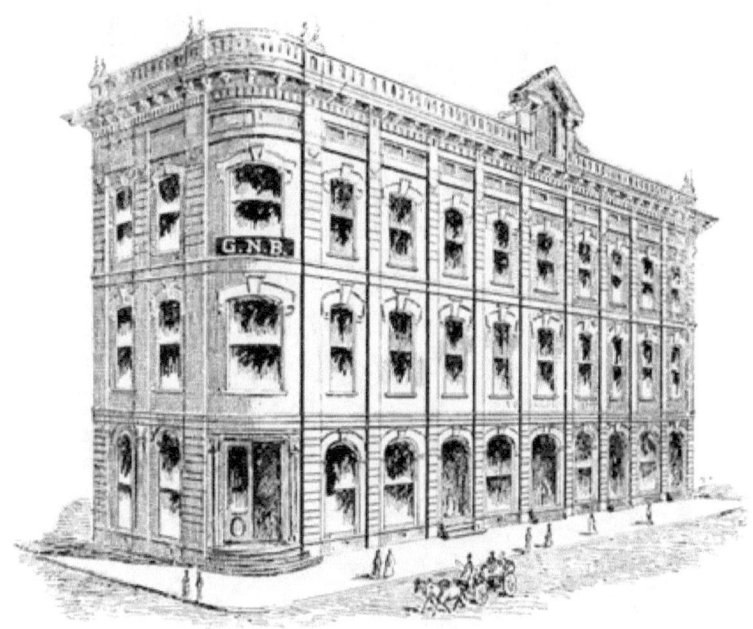

THE
GALVESTON NATIONAL BANK
GALVESTON, TEXAS

CAPITAL - - $500,000

T. J. GROCE, President   H. A. LANDES, Vice President
A. J. COMPTON, Cashier

SEND US ALL OF YOUR TEXAS COLLECTIONS

THE HOME NATIONAL BANK - - - OF ARKANSAS CITY, KANSAS
Paid capital One Quarter of a Million Dollars. Surplus and Profits $50,000
F. M. STRONG, President. HOWARD ROSS, Cashier   THE LARGEST BANK IN SOUTHERN KANSAS.   THE ONLY CHEMICAL SAFETY DEPOSIT BOXES.
A FEW OF OUR MOST PROMINENT STOCKHOLDERS
F. D. Armour, Esq. Packer, Chicago, Ill. SIDNEY A. KENT, Esq. Packer, Chicago, Ill. G. B. SHAW, Esq. Pres. American Trust & Savings Bank, Chicago, Ill. J. T. HURD, Esq. Pres. National Bank of North America, Boston, Mass. W. H. STRONG, Esq. Ex-Pres. A. T. & S. F. Ry, Beloit, Wis. Hon. DARWIN R. JAMES, New York, N.Y. JOHN R. MULVANE, Esq. Pres. Bank of Topeka, Topeka, Kan.
C. K. HOLLIDAY, Esq., Director of A. T. & S. F. Ry, Topeka, Kan.

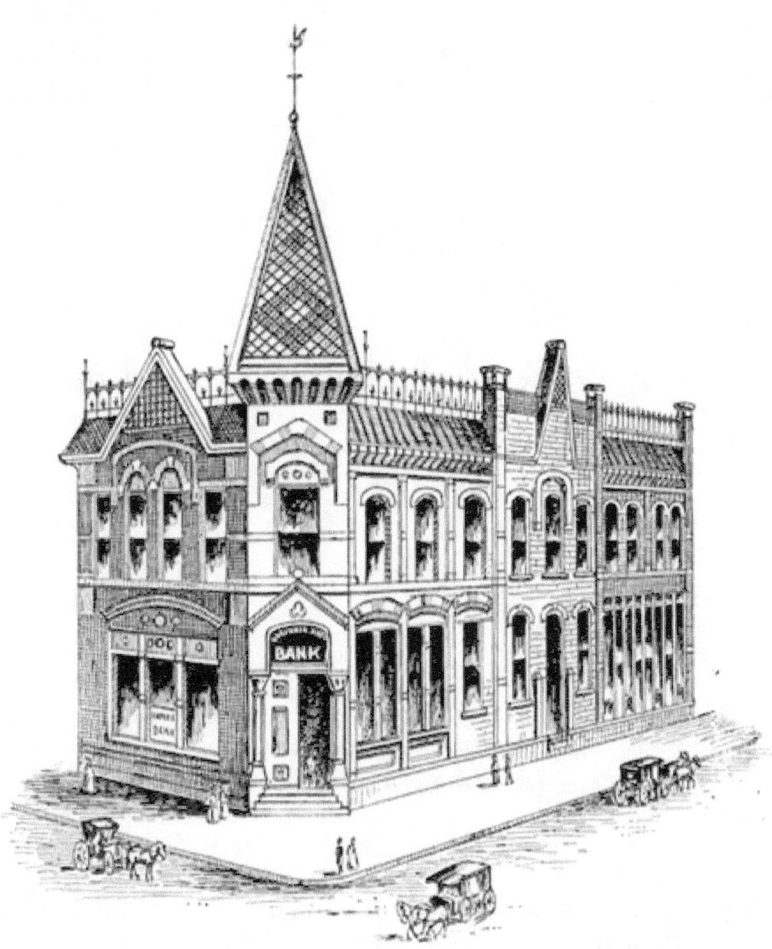

CALVIN HOOD, President
W. T. SODEN, Vice President
L. T. HERITAGE, Cashier
J. M. STEELE, Assistant Cashier

Capital $100,000.   Surplus $100,000

Emporia National Bank

EMPORIA, KANSAS

PROMPT ATTENTION PAID TO COLLECTIONS

Rudolph Kleybolte & Company

...INVESTMENT BANKERS...

STATE, COUNTY, MUNICIPAL AND SCHOOL

...BONDS...

SPECIALLY ADAPTED FOR

SAVINGS BANKS
TRUST COMPANIES..
AND **INVESTORS**

MUNICIPAL OFFICERS HAVING LOANS TO NEGOTIATE
ARE SOLICITED TO CORRESPOND WITH US

INVESTMENT LISTS MAILED ON APPLICATION

MASONIC TEMPLE. ∴ ∴ CINCINNATI, OHIO

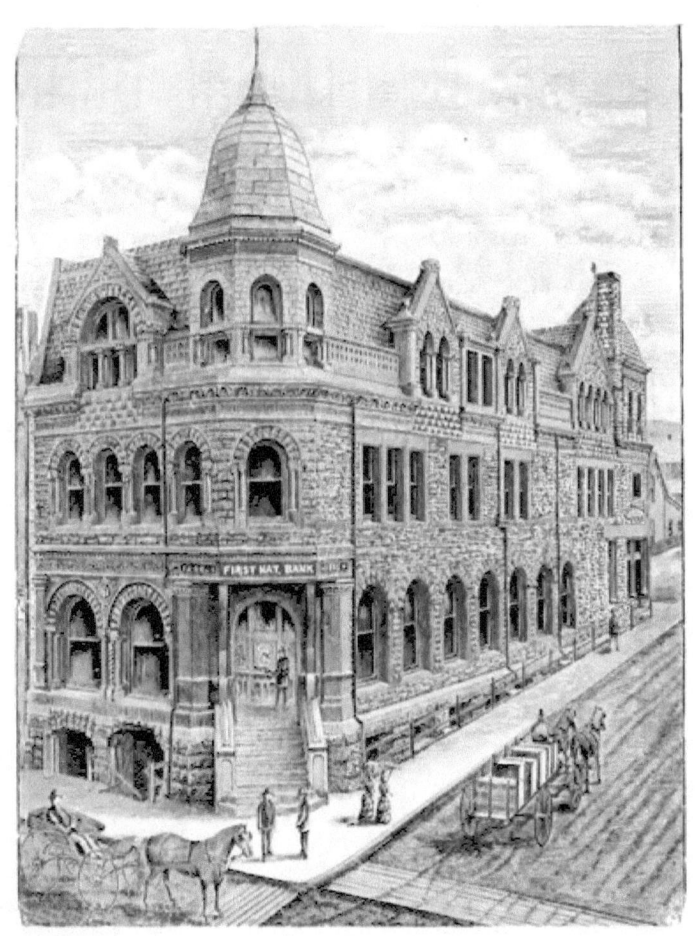

FIRST NATIONAL BANK
HELENA, MONTANA

Capital and Profits, $1,000,000
Average Deposits, $3,000,000

S. T. HAUSER, President   E. D. EDGERTON, Vice-President
GEO. F. COPE, Cashier   GEO. H. HILL, Asst. Cashier

Do a general banking business
Collect on all western points

THE FIRST NATIONAL BANK

DENVER, COLORADO

THE OLDEST NATIONAL BANK IN COLORADO

CAPITAL AND SURPLUS   -   -   - $1,000,000.00

A GENERAL BANKING BUSINESS TRANSACTED

D. H. MOFFAT, President
W. S. CHEESMAN, Vice President

G. E. ROSS-LEWIN, Cashier
THOMAS KEELY, Asst. Cashier
J. A. VICKERS, 2d Asst. Cashier

ACCOUNTS OF BANKS AND BANKERS INVITED

Special Attention Given to Western Collections, and Remittance Made on day of Receipt at Most Favorable Rates

STATEMENT

Of the condition of the FIRST NATIONAL BANK, DENVER, COL., at the close of business, December 22, 1876:

ASSETS.		LIABILITIES.	
Loans and Discounts	$ 648,105 86	Capital and Profits	$ 319,798 10
U. S. Bonds	100,000 00	Circulating Notes	44,900 00
Other Stocks and Bonds	3,267 45	Total Deposits	705,830 85
Cash on Hand and Sight Ex.	269,042 01		
Real Estate, Furn. & Fix.	33,404 30		
Current Expenses and Taxes paid	6,709 13		
Premiums Paid	10,000 00		
	$1,070,528 95		$1,070,528 95

STATEMENT

of the condition of the FIRST NATIONAL BANK OF DENVER, COL., at close of business, March 5, 1895.

RESOURCES.		LIABILITIES.	
Loans and Discounts	$3,998,715 43	Capital Stock	$ 500,000 00
U. S. Bonds, Circulation	200,000 00	Surplus	530,298 52
Premiums	37,114 98	Circulation	180,000 00
Local Securities	189,821 96	Deposits	6,539,311 69
Real Estate	19,395 00		
U. S. Bonds, Deposits	150,000 00		
Due from Banks	1,510,061 95		
Cash on Hand	1,664,500 89		
	$7,769,610 21		$7,769,610 21

NEW YORK CORRESPONDENTS—First National Bank.   Fourth National Bank.
American Exchange National Bank.   National Park and Mechanics National Bank.
CHICAGO CORRESPONDENT—Chicago National Bank
LONDON AGENTS—Brown, Shipley & Co.

Hoge, Brownlee & Co.

BANKERS

Butte City - - - - - Montana

TRANSACT A
GENERAL BANKING
BUSINESS....

COLLECTIONS A SPECIALTY

HOGE, DALY & CO.

ANACONDA

xx

H. G. THOMAS, President E. W. DOWDEN, Vice-President F. L. DOBBIN, Cashier

─THE─
OKLAHOMA NATIONAL BANK

CAPITAL, $50,000

OKLAHOMA CITY, O. T.

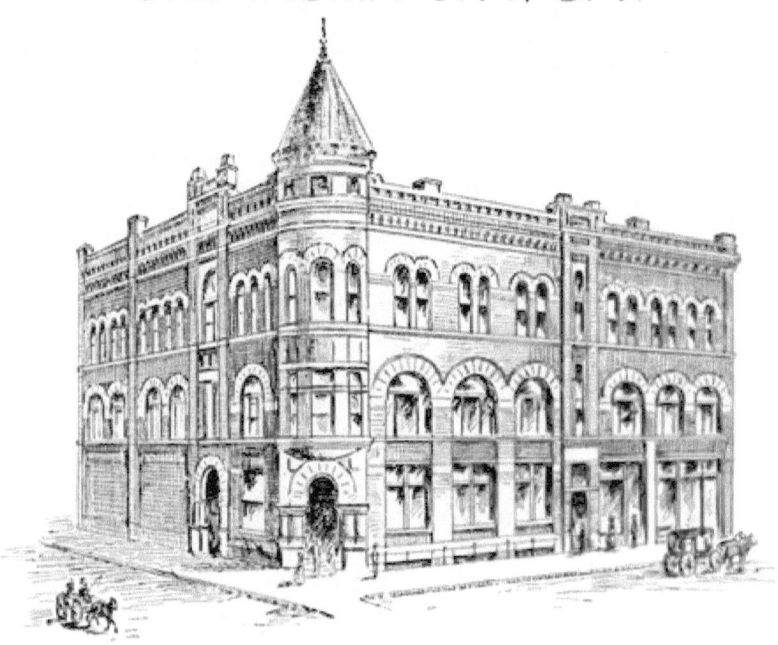

COLLECTIONS
Made in Indian Territory and Oklahoma Territory

INQUIRY IN REGARD TO INVESTMENTS IN OKLAHOMA
PROMPTLY ANSWERED

C. W. GIBSON, President
B. G. CONNOR, Vice-President
R. G. PHILLIPS, Cashier
H. H. DUNN, 2d Vice-President

FIRST NATIONAL BANK

CAPITAL - - $100,000
SURPLUS - - - $20,000

WAXAHACHIE, TEXAS

Collections · Promply · Made

ON ALL ACCESSIBLE POINTS

J. J. SQUIER, President WM. C. HENRICI, Cashier
S. B. ARMOUR, Vice-President C. N. PROUTY, Asst. Cashier

— NO. 4381 —

Inter-State National Bank

THE ONLY BANK LOCATED AT THE STOCK YARDS

KANSAS CITY

POST OFFICE ADDRESS - - STATION A, KANSAS CITY, MO.

Member of the Kansas City, Mo., Clearing House

PAID UP CAPITAL - $1,000,000.00

COLLECTIONS A SPECIALTY

Made on all Points in the United States and Canada

ACCOUNTS OF BANKS, BANKERS, CORPORATIONS AND INDIVIDUALS RECEIVED

ALL BUSINESS INTRUSTED TO US WILL HAVE PROMPT AND CAREFUL ATTENTION

DIRECTORS

GEO. W. WILLIAMS, Seneca, Kan.
THOMAS KIRBY, Abilene, Kan.
J. C. ROGERS, Wamego, Kan.
LEE CLARK, Parsons, Kan.
C. HOOD, Emporia, Kan.
J. V. ANDREWS, Kansas City, Kan.
S. B. ARMOUR, Kansas City, Mo.
G. W. MCKNIGHT, Junction City, Kan.
J. J. SQUIER, Kansas City, Mo.

L. V. MCKEE, Frankfort, Kan.
E. N. MORRILL, Hiawatha, Kan.
J. D. ROBERTSON, Jewell City, Kan.
J. R. MULVANE, Topeka, Kan.
JOHN R. FOSTER, Garnett, Kan.
FORD F. HARVEY, Kansas City, Mo.
C. F. MORSE, Kansas City, Mo.
M. R. PLATT, Kansas City, Mo.

The First National Bank
OF
ALBUQUERQUE

UNITED STATES DEPOSITORY   *NEW MEXICO*

CAPITAL	$100,000
SURPLUS	50,000
TOTAL	$150,000

JOSHUA S. RAYNOLDS, President   A. A. KEEN, Cashier
M. W. FLOURNOY, Vice President   FRANK McKEE, Asst. Cashier

DEPOSITS, $900,000

CORRESPONDENTS—Chemical National Bank, N. Y.
First National Bank, Chicago

BUSINESS ESTABLISHED 1873

JORALMON & CO.

BANKERS

Financial Agents and Attorneys

229 TO 235 EQUITABLE BUILDING
DENVER, COL.

INVESTMENTS IN
BONDS, MORTGAGES
AND REAL ESTATE

COLLECTIONS ON COLORADO POINTS

Investigate, appraise and report impartially upon Real Estate, Industrial and Mining Properties.

Act as Attorneys in the foreclosure and reconstruction of defaulted mortgages and other securities.

Represent non-residents in the general management of their interests.

Complete facilities and extended experience guarantee prompt and efficient service.

NO. 1833.

The First National Bank of Pueblo,
COLORADO.

United States Depository.

Capital - - - $ 300,000.
Surplus and Profits - 200,000.
Average Deposits - 2,000,000.

ESTABLISHED 1871

The Largest and Oldest Banking Institution in Southern Colorado. Transacts a General Banking Business.

Special Attention Given to Collections.

M. D. THATCHER, President.   JOHN A. THATCHER, Vice-President.
R. F. LYTLE, Cashier.

— NO. 2300 —

THE FIRST NATIONAL BANK
OF TRINIDAD, COL.

CAPITAL - - $100,000   SURPLUS - - $100,000

A General Banking Business Transacted.
Prompt Attention Given to Collections.

M. D. THATCHER, President   H. J. ALEXANDER, Cashier
D. A. CHAPPELL, Vice President   J. C. HUDELSON, Asst. Cashier

The Fifth National Bank of Cincinnati.

Capital - - - - - $500,000.00.
Surplus and Profits - - - 40,000.00.

OFFICERS:

ROBERT M. NIXON, President,
Ex-Deputy Comptroller of the Currency.
CHAS. A. HINSCH, Cashier.
T. J. DAVIS, Assistant Cashier.

Your Collections Solicited.   Prompt Returns.   Lowest Rates.

J. FURTH, President.   E. C. NEUFELDER, Vice-President.
R. V. ANKENY, Cashier.

The Puget Sound National Bank of Seattle,
SEATTLE, WASH.

Capital - - - - - $600,000.00.
Surplus - - - - - 120,000.00.

The First National Bank
OF
EL PASO, TEXAS

CAPITAL	- - -	$100,000
SURPLUS	- - -	25,000
TOTAL	- -	$125,000

JOSHUA S. RAYNOLDS, President   ULYSSES S. STEWART, Cashier
M. W. FLOURNOY, Vice President   JOSEPH F. WILLIAMS, Asst. Cashier

WE BUY AND SELL
MEXICAN SILVER AND MEXICAN EXCHANGE
xxx

M. D. BALLARD, President. H. C. HENRY, Vice-President. R. R. SPENCER, Cashier. O. A. SPENCER, Ass't Cashier.

THE NATIONAL BANK OF COMMERCE,
OF SEATTLE, WASHINGTON.

Capital Stock, $300,000. Special attention paid to Collections.

T. B. WALLACE, Pres.　　　JNO. S. BAKER, Vice Pres.　　　P. C. KAUFFMAN, Cash.

FIDELITY TRUST CO.

TACOMA, WASHINGTON

PAID UP CAPITAL　-　-　-　-　-　-　$500,000

TRANSACTS A GENERAL BANKING BUSINESS

ACTS AS TRUSTEE, EXECUTOR, OR
IN ANY FIDUCIARY CAPACITY

TRUSTEES

T. B. WALLACE　　　JOHN S. BAKER　　　L. D. CAMPBELL
　CHESTER THORNE　　GEORGE BROWNE　　C. W. GRIGGS

The First National Bank
OF CHICAGO.

Paid in Capital   -   - $3,000,000.
Surplus   -   -   -   3,000,000.

OFFICERS:

LYMAN J. GAGE, President.
JAS. B. FORGAN, Vice-President.
RICHARD J. STREET, Cashier.
HOLMES HOGE, Ass't Cashier.
FRANK E. BROWN, 2d Ass't Cashier.

THE BANKERS NATIONAL BANK·
CHICAGO, ILLINOIS.

Capital - - - $1,000,000.

OFFICERS:

E. S. LACEY, President.   D. B. DEWEY, Vice President.
GEORGE S. LORD, 2nd Vice President.   JOHN C. CRAFT, Cashier.
J. C. McNAUGHTON, Asst. Cashier.   FRANK P. JUDSON, 2nd Asst. Cashier.

WE SOLICIT YOUR BUSINESS.

C. H. HACKLEY, President.
THOS. MUNROE, 2nd Vice President.
C. T. HILLS, Vice President.
GEO. A. ABBOTT, Cashier.

HACKLEY NATIONAL BANK,

MUSKEGON, MICH.

Capital — — — — $100,000.
Surplus — — — — — 50,000.

DIRECTORS:

C. H. HACKLEY.
   L. G. MASON.
      C. T. HILLS.
         LUTHER WHITNEY.
           THOS. HUME.
              THOS. MUNROE.
                 GEO. A. ABBOTT.

PRESTON NATIONAL BANK,

DETROIT, MICHIGAN.

CAPITAL, - - - $1,000,000.

F. W. HAYES, President,   A. E. F. WHITE, Vice-President.
H. L. O'BRIEN, Cashier.   J. P. GILMORE, Auditor.

DIRECTORS.

F. W. HAYES.   C. A. BLACK.   WM. H. ELLIOTT.   JAS. E. DAVIS.
JAS. D. STANDISH.   JOHN CANFIELD.   A. E. F. WHITE.
A. L. STEPHENS.   JEROME CROUL.   J. B. BOOK.   H. K. WHITE.

The business of this Bank was established by David Preston in 1852. The present organization dates from July, 1887.

The Bank does a large business with individuals, firms, corporations, banks and bankers, and solicits business from all such, tendering the attention and courtesies given by banks conducted in a safe, conservative and prompt manner.

THE FIRST NATIONAL BANK
OF DULUTH

Capital - - - - - $1,000,000.
Surplus - - - - - - 200,000.

THE AMERICAN EXCHANGE BANK
OF DULUTH.

Capital - - - - - $500,000.
Surplus - - - - - - 385,000.

THE MARINE NATIONAL BANK
OF DULUTH.

Capital - - - - - $200,000.
Surplus - - - - - - 33,000.

THE NATIONAL BANK OF COMMERCE
OF DULUTH.

Capital - - - - - $200,000.
Surplus - - - - - - 27,000.

THE STATE BANK
OF DULUTH.

Capital - - - - - $100,000.
Surplus - - - - - - 40,000.

THE SECURITY BANK
OF DULUTH.

Capital - - - - - $100,000.
Surplus - - - - - - 40,000.

THE IRON EXCHANGE BANK
OF DULUTH.

Capital - - - - - $100,000.
Surplus - - - - - - 5,500.

Duluth Clearing House Association.

The Preferred Bankers Life Assurance Company
OF MICHIGAN

This assurance company was organized by one hundred prominent Michigan bankers and business men, nearly every city of importance in the state being represented by one or more of its leading citizens, as incorporators.

A GUARANTEE FUND

This fund is accumulated by the payment of fifty cents for every year of a member's age on each certificate of $1,000, and may be secured by four notes on two years' time drawing six per cent, payable in quarterly installments. A man at the age of forty puts $20 into the guarantee fund on each $1,000 of insurance. This fund is held as security or collateral to the payment of premiums and is returned to the beneficiary at the death of a member, but on failure to pay is forfeited to this company, and is at once transferred to the surplus fund to pay death losses when the deaths shall amount to more than one per cent of the membership, or 10 to each 1,000. Each member's guarantee fund, being in amount proportionate with his age, his calls to pay death losses being a percentage on that amount, makes his premium in proportion to the balance of the members, equal to his expectancy of life, so each member is paying always the just and proper amount. This amount makes up the

BENEFIT FUND

This fund is exclusively for the purpose of paying to the designated beneficiaries the amount belonging to them on the death of a member, and is only called for that purpose, and is only sufficient in amount to meet said death losses, and provide for the maximum amount at risk on any three members in advance.

SURPLUS FUND

This fund is to pay death losses when the death rate shall exceed one per cent in any one year, or 10 deaths to the 1,000. This fund is made up of all guarantee deposits that are forfeited to this company, and from all interest on the funds of said company.

THE CONTINGENT FUND

This fund is composed of the membership fee, which is 2 per cent of the guarantee amount paid by each member. A man at the age of 40 years puts $20 into this fund for every $1,000 of insurance, at the same time he puts $20 into the guarantee fund.

MEMBERSHIP

We will write only men, and between the ages of 21 and 55 years, always reckoning from his nearest birthday, and he must be sober, industrious and of good moral character, and must not be engaged in any hazardous occupation, or in the sale of intoxicating liquors, and must be in all respects what is meant by the word a "preferred risk," which is the watch tower of this assurance company.

AMOUNT OF INSURANCE LIMITED.

Age.	Highest Am't.
21 to 35	$5,000
35 to 45	4,000
45 to 50	3,000
50 to 55	2,000

OFFICERS

President, ARTHUR O. BEMENT,
   Ex-Mayor of Lansing, Mich., and President of E. Bement & Sons, Lansing, Mich.
1st Vice President, ROBERT SMITH,
   State Printer, Lansing, Mich.
2d Vice President, EUGENE A. SUNDERLIN,
   Deputy State Bank Commissioner, Lansing, Mich.
Secretary and Manager, IRA E. RANDALL,
   Lansing, Mich.
Treasurer, J. EDWARD ROE,
   Cashier Lansing State Savings Bank, Lansing, Mich.
Medical Director, HENRY B. BAKER, M. D.,
   Secretary State Board of Health, Lansing, Mich.
Legal Director, EDWARD CAHILL,
   Ex-Justice of Supreme Court, Lansing, Mich.

ANNUAL COST ON $1,000

25	$5.00	40	$8.00	50	$10.00
30	6.00	45	9.00	55	11.00
35	7.00				

Actual results on six deaths per 1,000.

THE PREFERRED BANKERS' LIFE ASSURANCE CO.,
HOME OFFICE, LANSING, MICHIGAN.

BOARD OF TRADE BUILDING,
FORT WORTH, TEXAS,
CONTAINING THE OFFICES OF

LAND MORTGAGE BANK OF TEXAS, LIMITED,

Subscribed Capital, . £750,000.
Surplus, . . £60,000.

HOME OFFICE:
LONDON, ENGLAND.

C. H. SILLIMAN, AMERICAN MANAGER.
FORT WORTH, TEXAS.

Negotiates Loans Upon Improved Real Estate Anywhere in Texas.

OFFICERS AND DIRECTORS.

JEFFERSON RAYNOLDS, President.   ALFRED B. SMITH, Cashier.

JOHN W. ZOLLARS, Vice-President.

JOSHUA S. RAYNOLDS.   A. A. JONES.

...THE...
First National Bank,

LAS VEGAS, NEW MEXICO.

CAPITAL AND SURPLUS, - $125,000.

New Mexico and Southwestern Collections a Specialty.

CORRESPONDENCE INVITED.

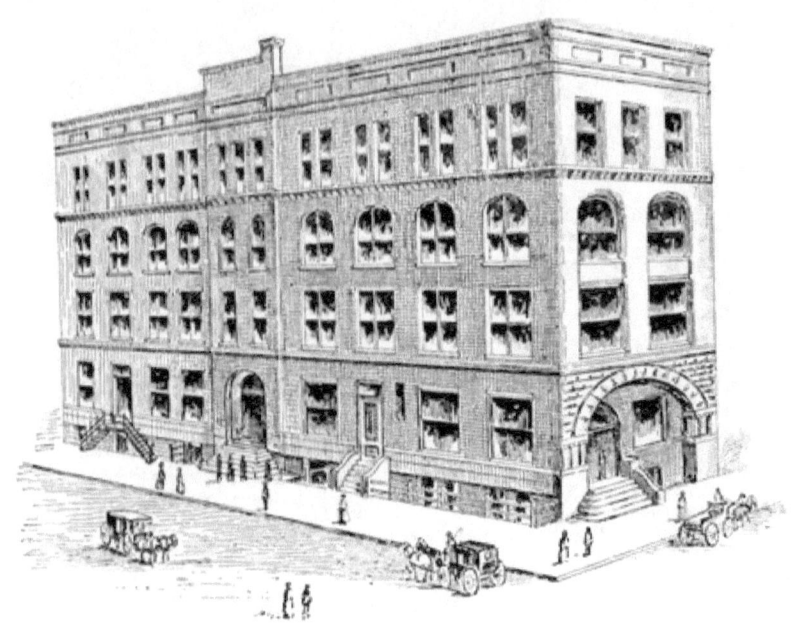

P. I. BONEBRAKE, President.   A. S. JOHNSON, Vice-President.
EDWIN KNOWLES, Cashier.   F. M. BONEBRAKE, Asst. Cashier.

THE CENTRAL NATIONAL BANK

... OF ...

Topeka, Kansas.

CAPITAL, - - $250,000

DEALS IN

UNITED STATES AND MUNICIPAL BONDS

DOES A GENERAL BANKING BUSINESS.

THE NATIONAL EXCHANGE BANK
―――― OF ――――
DALLAS.

PAID UP CAPITAL,   - $300,000.

DALLAS, TEXAS

JOHN N. SIMPSON, President.
W. H. GASTON, Vice-President.
W. H. GETZENDANER, 2nd Vice-President.
ROYAL A. FERRIS, Cashier.
R. C. AYRES, Asst. Cashier.

Accounts of Banks, Corporations and Individuals Solicited.

Collections Made on all Texas Points and Remitted at Lowest Rates of Exchange.

The St. Paul National Bank
ST. PAUL, MINN.

Capital . . $600,000.

OFFICERS:

F. W. ANDERSON, President. A. C. ANDERSON, Cashier.
PHILIP REILLY, Vice President. W. B. GEERY, Assistant Cashier.

The Nicollet National Bank of Minneapolis,
MINNESOTA.

Capital $500,000.   Surplus and Profits, $100,000.

Transacts any business consistent with legitimate banking.

DIRECTORS.

H. W. BROWN,   C. E. WALES,   H. ALDEN SMITH,   A. T. RAND,   T. B. CASEY.
J. A. BOHN,   R. R. RAND,   J. F. R. FOSS.

CORRESPONDENTS.

NEW YORK: Merchants' Exchange National Bank.
CHICAGO: Continental National Bank.   Bank of Nova Scotia.
BOSTON: National Bank of the Commonwealth.
PHILADELPHIA: First National Bank.

No interest paid on any form of deposits with the exception of accounts from Banks and Bankers. No time certificates of deposit issued.

SEND US YOUR COLLECTIONS ON

Minneapolis, St. Paul and other Points of the Northwest.

H. W. BROWN,   J. F. R. FOSS,
President.   Vice-President and Cashier.

American National Bank,
LOUISVILLE, KY.

Capital - - - $800,000 00

J. H. LINDENBERGER, President.   CHAS. WARREN, Cashier.
LOGAN C. MURRAY, Vice President.   H. C. TRUMAN, Asst. Cashier.

Accounts of Banks and Bankers received on favorable terms.
Collections on all points a specialty.

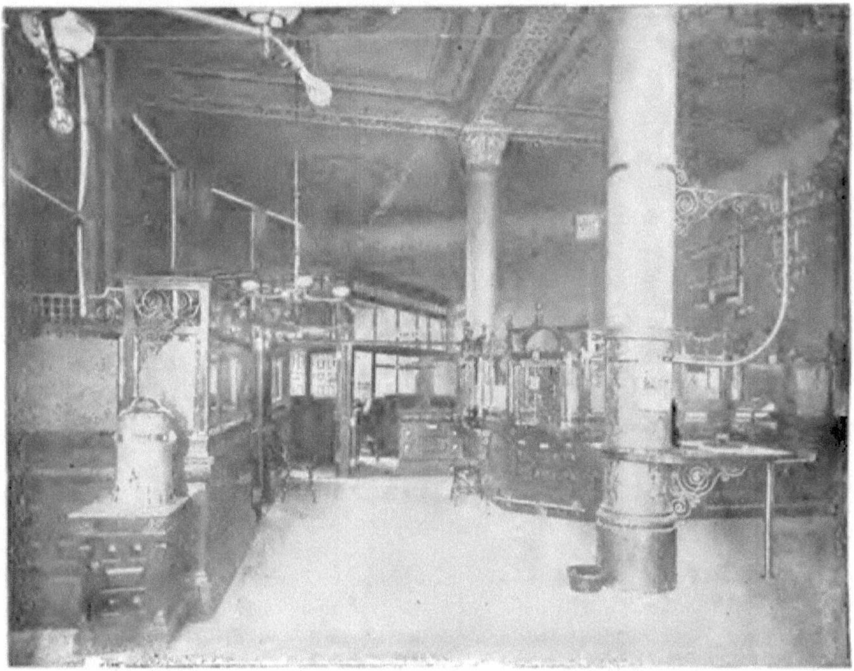

| GEO. H. RUSSEL, President | M S SMITH, Vice-President | R S. MASON, Cashier | A E. WING, Auditor |

STATE
Savings Bank

CAPITAL $ 200,000.
SURPLUS $ 150,000.

HAMMOND BUILDING,
Cor Fort and
Griswold Streets

DIRECTORS

R A ALGER   H M CAMPBELL
W C COLBURN   W H ELLIOTT
C L FREER   F J HECKER
H B LEDYARD   HUGH McMILLAN
WM McMILLAN   M S MASON
H W GILLETT   HENRY RUSSEL
GEO H RUSSEL   M S SMITH
        CHAS STINCHFIELD

COMMERCIAL & SAVINGS DEPARTMENTS

THE UNION NATIONAL BANK OF CHICAGO

Was organized in December, 1864, succeeding the well-established business of W. F. Coolbaugh & Co. It immediately took the front rank among the banks of Chicago and the Northwest, the high standing attained by its first president, Mr. W. F. Coolbaugh, being at once reflected in the business of the bank. It was one of the earliest organizations in the national banking system, and was organized with a paid up capital of $500,000, and embraced in its board of directors some of the leading citizens of Chicago and New York. David Dows, of New York, was one of its organizers and directors, and continued in the directory during the remainder of his lifetime. Mr. Coolbaugh died in 1877, and was succeeded by Mr. C. T. Wheeler, who was subsequently succeeded by Mr. W. C. D. Grannis, who was afterwards followed by Mr. C. R. Cummings. In 1890 Mr. J. J. P. Odell succeeded to the presidency, after having served as cashier and vice-president successively from 1880 until that period, and he still occupies the presidency and managership of the bank. The capital of the bank was increased from time to time, until in 1886 it was raised to $2,000,000. It now has a reserve of $500,000, in addition to its capital, and has paid continuous dividends to its stockholders. It has extended its field of usefulness so as to embrace all parts of the commercial world, its connections reaching the far east and the distant west. Its board of directors now consist of the following gentlemen:

DAVID KELLEY	O. C. BARBER	J. W. ELLSWORTH
J. H. BARKER	D. B. DEWEY	RICHARD C. LAKE
S. K. MARTIN	H. H. GETTY	J. J. P. ODELL
H. N. MAY	W. T. BAKER	

THE WISCONSIN NATIONAL BANK
OF MILWAUKEE.

CAPITAL, - - $1,000,000
SURPLUS, - - - $100,000

FREDK. PABST,   CHARLES BEST,   FREDK. KASTEN,
President.   Vice-President.   Cashier.

DIRECTORS.

FREDK. PABST.   A. A. L. SMITH.   CHARLES BEST.   EDWARD BRADLEY.
CHARLES SCHRIBER.   E. P. MATTHEWS.   PHILETUS SAWYER.
WM. W. ALLIS.   ROBERT HILL.   DAVID ADLER.   FREDK. KASTEN.

Wisconsin Marine and Fire Insurance Company Bank,
MILWAUKEE, WISCONSIN.
ESTABLISHED 1839.

PAID UP CAPITAL, - $500,000

GENERAL BANKING BUSINESS DONE,
INTEREST PAID ON TIME DEPOSITS

We solicit accounts of Banks, corporations, firms and individuals, and promise to give them the best terms and most careful attention.

DIRECTORS.
WASHINGTON BECKER. ANGUS SMITH. EDWARD P. BACON. GEORGE HILES.
ALFRED JAMES. JOHN L. MITCHELL. SAM'L McCORD.
WM. H. BRADLEY. JOHN JOHNSTON.

OFFICERS.
WASHINGTON BECKER, JOHN L. MITCHELL, JOHN JOHNSTON,
President. Vice-President. Cashier.

THE NATIONAL BANK OF COMMERCE
TACOMA, WASH.

Capital - - $200,000

CHESTER THORNE, President EDWARD HUGGINS, 2d Vice-President
L. W. ROYS, Vice-President J. W. WALLACE, Cashier

Transacts a General Banking Business, and will cheerfully answer all inquiries concerning Tacoma, Seattle or the State of Washington. Have unsurpassed facilities for making collections.

Manufacturers National Bank
OF RACINE, WISCONSIN.

Capital and Undivided Earnings, $400,000.

Savings Department. Affords all the advantages of the best Savings Banks in the country. Interest 3 per cent. per annum on deposits left three months, according to the rules.
Investment Securities. The bank keeps on hand a choice supply of Bonds, which will be sold to customers who desire to realize a larger interest than Banks allow.
Foreign Exchange and Letters of Credit. Furnished at lowest New York rates and available in all parts of the world.
Passports. Procured from the State Department at Washington for those going abroad.
Ocean Steamship Tickets. By Cunard, White Star, Anchor and principal steamship lines for sale at lowest New York rates.
Domestic Exchange. Drafts available throughout the United States and Canada, in small or large amounts.
Collections. Special care and attention given to collections at home and abroad.

Your banking business respectfully solicited,

STEPHEN BULL, President.
JOHN S. CLEMENT, Ass't Cashier.   E. J. HUEFFNER, Vice-President.
EDWARD B. KILBOURN, Paying Teller.   B. B. NORTHROP, Cashier.
EDWARD W. RAPPS, Receiving Teller.

Report Made to the Comptroller of the Currency, upon his first call for 1895, showing condition of the bank at the close of business.

MARCH 5, 1895.

RESOURCES

Loans and Bills Discounted	$978,633 58
Overdrafts	1,360 94
United States Bonds at Washington to secure Circulation	50,000 00
Railway, City and County Bonds	99,849 59
Banking House, 440 Main Street	15,000 00
Due from United States Treasurer, 5 per cent. Redemption Fund	2,250 00
Due from United States Treasurer, other than above	$5,000 00
Due from National and State Banks	162,552 92
Cash on hand in Vault	146,004 58
	313,557 50
	$1,460,651 61

LIABILITIES

Capital Stock	$250,000 00
Surplus Fund, 40 per cent. of Capital	100,000 00
Undivided Profits, less Expenses and Taxes paid	77,692 62
Circulating Notes outstanding	45,000 00
Individual Deposits	$524,536 71
Demand Certificates of Deposit	454,459 04
Due Banks and Bankers	8,963 24
	987,958 99
	$1,460,651 61

STATE OF WISCONSIN, } ss.
COUNTY OF RACINE,

I, B. B. Northrop, Cashier of the above named bank, do solemnly swear that the above statement is true to the best of my knowledge and belief.   B. B. NORTHROP, Cashier.

Subscribed and sworn to before me this 9th day of March, 1895.
EDWARD B. KILBOURN, Notary Public, Racine County.

Correct Attest:
   JOSEPH MILLER,
   O. W. JOHNSON, } Directors.
   E. J. HUEFFNER,

DIRECTORS 1895.

STEPHEN BULL, President, Manufacturers National Bank of Racine. President, J. I. Case Threshing Machine Co. President, Milwaukee Harvester Co.
JACKSON I. CASE, President, Bank of Burlington, Wis. President, J. I. Case Plow Works. President, Belle City Street Railway Company. Mayor of the City of Racine.
CHARLES E. ERSKINE, Capitalist.
AUGUST C. FRANK, Capitalist.
WILLIAM HORLICK, President, Horlick's Food Co. President, Malted Milk Co. President Horlick's Investment Co.
ERNST J. HUEFFNER, Dealer in Hides and Leather. Vice-President, Manufacturers National Bank of Racine.
OTIS W. JOHNSON, President, First National Bank of St. Ignace, Mich. Vice-President, Fish Bros. Wagon Company.
JOSEPH MILLER, President, J. Miller Company, Manufacturers of Boots and Shoes. President, Racine Nail & Tack Co. President, Chicago Rubber Clothing Co. of Racine.
BYRON B. NORTHROP, Cashier, Manufacturers National Bank of Racine, Wis.

UNITED STATES DEPOSITARY.

... THE ...

FIRST NATIONAL BANK

.... OF ....

DETROIT, MICHIGAN.

D. M. FERRY, President.   EMORY WENDELL, Pres. Pro Tempore.
L. E. CLARK, Vice-President.   JOHN T. SHAW, Cashier.

DIRECTORS.

HON. GEO. V. N. LOTHROP, Lawyer.
EMORY WENDELL, President Pro Tempore.
HON. DON M. DICKINSON,
    of Dickinson, Thatcher & Stevenson,
    Attorneys.
WILLIAM J. CHITTENDEN,
    of Chittenden & McCreary, Proprietors of
    the "Russell House."

EDWIN S. BARBOUR,
    President Detroit Stove Works.
LORENZO E. CLARK, Vice-President.
WM. C. McMILLAN,
    Managing Director Michigan-Peninsular
    Car Co.
HON. JAMES McMILLAN,
    United States Senator.

D. M. FERRY, President.

This Bank will receive the accounts and collections of Banks, Bankers, Corporations, Firms and Individuals, and will give prompt and careful attention to any business entrusted to us. Correspondence solicited.

DENVER NATIONAL BANK,
DENVER, COL.

Capital - - - - - - - $500,000
Surplus - - - - - - - 150,000

J. A. THATCHER, President   G. B. BERGER, Cashier
J. B. GRANT, Vice President   E. S. IRISH, Assistant Cashier.
J. W. HUDSTON, 2d Assistant Cashier.

THE MERCHANTS NATIONAL BANK,
HELENA, MONT.
UNITED STATES DEPOSITORY.

Paid in Capital	$350,000
Surplus and Undivided Profits	170,000

L. H. HERSHFIELD, President   A. J. DAVIDSON, Vice President
T. P. BOWMAN, Assistant Cashier

Exchange sold on the principal cities of the United States and Europe. Prompt attention given to collections. Issues letters of credit. Transfers of money made by telegraph. Accounts of banks, firms and individuals solicited.

FIRST NATIONAL BANK.

J. H. McGRAW.   MAURICE McMICKEN.   LESTER TURNER.
President   Vice-President.   Cashier.

FIRST NATIONAL BANK,
OF SEATTLE, WASHINGTON.

Capital   - - - - - $150,000
Surplus   - - - -   150,000
Undivided Profits   - - -   50,000

Inquiries regarding Seattle and Washington Investments answered with pleasure.

SECURITY NATIONAL BANK,
SIOUX CITY, IOWA.

Capital — $250,000.
Surplus — 50,000.

W. P. MANLEY, President
C. L. WRIGHT, Vice President
F. M. CASE, Cashier
F. C. SWAN, Assistant Cashier

CORRESPONDENCE INVITED

Midland National Bank,
KANSAS CITY, MO.

CAPITAL - - - $500,000

OFFICERS

S. B. ARMOUR, President.   W. H. WINANTS, Vice-President.
L. E. PRINDLE, Cashier.

DIRECTORS

S. B. ARMOUR,
  President Armour Packing Co.
GEO. H. NETTLETON,
  Prest. Kansas City, Ft. Scott & Memphis Ry.
W. W. KENDALL,
  Prest. W. W. Kendall Boot & Shoe Co.
JOHN R. MULVANE,
  Prest. Bank of Topeka, Kas.
GEO. W. FULLER,
  Secy. and Treas. John Deere Plow Co.
RICHARD H. KEITH,
  Prest. Central Coal & Coke Co.

A. R. MEYER,
  Prest. Kansas City Smelting & Refining Co.
K. B. ARMOUR,
  Vice-Prest. Armour Packing Co.
A. F. SAWYER,
  Pt. Chrisman-Sawyer Bkg. Co., Independence, Mo.
GARDINER LATHROP,
  Of Lathrop, Morrow, Fox & Moore, Attys.
F. W. SCHULTE,
  Probst Construction Co., Chicago, Ill.
CHARLES A. MURDOCK,
  Prest. C. A. Murdock Mfg. Co.

W. H. WINANTS, Vice-President.

CONDENSED STATEMENT

Of the condition of the Midland National Bank, of Kansas City, Mo., at the close of business, March 6, 1895.

Resources		Liabilities	
Loans		Capital Stock	
Overdrafts		Surplus and Undivided Profits, less	
U. S. Bonds and Premiums		Expenses and Taxes Paid	
Redemption Fund		Circulation	
Other Stocks and Bonds		Deposits Individual	
Real Estate, Furniture and Fixtures		Banks	
Cash and Sight Exchange			

I certify that the above is correct.

L. E. PRINDLE, Cashier.

JOHN A. KING, President.   L. A. GODDARD, Cashier.
JOHN H. WITBECK, Vice-President.   WM. COX, Ass't Cashier.

Fort Dearborn National Bank.

UNITED STATES DEPOSITORY.

CAPITAL   - - $500,000
SURPLUS   - -   100,000

S. W. CORNER MONROE AND CLARK STREETS,

CHICAGO.

The Old National Bank

—— OF ——

GRAND RAPIDS, MICHIGAN.

Capital	$800,000
Surplus	160,000
Undivided Profits	77,000

JAMES M. BARNETT,
PRESIDENT

W. BARNHART,
VICE-PRESIDENT.

HARVEY J. HOLLISTER,
CASHIER

CLAY H. HOLLISTER,
ASST. CASHIER.

JOHN PAUL, President. GEO. W. BURTON, Cashier.
W. W. CARGILL, Vice-President. F. H. HANKERSON, Asst. Cashier.

The La Crosse National Bank,

LA CROSSE, WISCONSIN.

Capital - - $200,000
Surplus and Profits - 100,000

DIRECTORS

JOHN PAUL.   B. B. HEALY.   L. H. MOULTON.   CHAS. MICHEL.
G. R. MONTAGUE.   F. P. HIXON.   W. W. CARGILL.
JOHN PAMPERIN.   GEO. W. BURTON.

GEORGE BAUMAN, Prest.   J. H. JENKINS, Vice Prest.
R. B. EVANS, Cashier.

The
German National Bank
OSHKOSH, WISCONSIN.

CAPITAL   -   - $100,000
SURPLUS   -   -   100,000

DIRECTORS:

G. W. WASHBURN	B. C. GUDDEN	F. J. BARBER
J. H. JENKINS	R. B. EVANS	R. C. RUSSELL
GEO. BAUMAN	J. V. HULL	G. H. GILE
F. H. JOSSLYN	D. C. BUCKSTAFF	JULIUS MARTIN

The Farmers and Mechanics National Bank,
FORT WORTH, TEXAS.

Capital - - - $400.000
Surplus - - - 40.000

J. W. SPENCER, President.   H. W. WILLIAMS, Vice-President.
BEN O. SMITH, Cashier.

FIRST NATIONAL BANK,
OMAHA, NEBRASKA.

Capital	$500,000
Surplus	100,000

HERMAN KOUNTZE, President.   F. H. DAVIS, Cashier.
J. A. CREIGHTON, Vice-President.   W. H. MEGQUIER, Asst. Cashier.

O. T. CRA?, President
N. O. NELSON, Vice-President

T. A. STODDART, Cashier
J. R. COOKE, Asst. Cashier

THIRD NATIONAL BANK,
ST. LOUIS, MO.

Capital, $1,000,000.   Surplus and Profits, 300,000.

Omaha Safe and Iron Works,

G. ANDREEN, Proprietor,

MANUFACTURER OF

FIRE PROOF SHUTTERS, WIRE WORK.

Anchors and Wrought Iron Work for Buildings,

FIRE ESCAPES.

AGENT FOR

Diebold Safe and Lock Co.

BANK WORK A SPECIALTY.   CORRESPONDENCE SOLICITED

Opening and Repairing Safes and General Job Work Promptly Done.

OMAHA, NEB.

STATE OF ILLINOIS

WESTERN BANK NOTE COMPANY

FIRE PROOF BUILDING
Madison St. and
Michigan Ave.

CHICAGO

Steel Plate and Lithographic
Engraving and Printing

BONDS

FOR RAILWAYS, TOWNS AND CITIES, REAL ESTATE BONDS, STREET RAILWAYS, WATER-WORKS, GAS COMPANIES

Certificates of Stock, Drafts, Checks, Letter and Bill Headings, Etc., for

Railways, Banks, Merchants and Corporations

Bonds and other Securities Engraved by this Company Accepted on the New York Stock Exchange

C. C. CHENEY, President
   C. A. CHAPMAN, Vice-President
      C. HEINEMAN, Secretary

N·W·Harris & Company

BANKERS

204 DEARBORN ST., CHICAGO

NEW YORK
BOSTON

FOR INVESTMENT We
Offer MUNICIPAL BONDS
AND SECURITIES BASED ON
MUNICIPAL FRANCHISES

Well Selected Securities of
this kind rank next to
GOVERNMENTS
in point of Safety

GOVERNMENT BONDS
BOUGHT AND SOLD

All bonds offered our clients for investment have been purchased outright with our own funds, after a searching investigation into their security and legality. No investment is offered a client which has not first been accepted for ourselves, a point, in view of the countless offerings of securities on the market, which the discriminating investor will appreciate.

EDWARDS WHITAKER   CHARLES HODGMAN

WHITAKER & HODGMAN,
BOND AND STOCK BROKERS

300 N. FOURTH ST.,

ST. LOUIS, MO.,

DEAL IN FIRST-CLASS INVESTMENT SECURITIES AND HIGH GRADE COMMERCIAL PAPER.

MONTHLY CIRCULAR QUOTING LOCAL SECURITIES MAILED ON APPLICATION.

COMMERCIAL NATIONAL BANK,
PORTLAND, OREGON.

Capital $500,000

Surplus $100,000

Jno. J. Valentine, President
R. L. Durham, Vice-President
E. Cookingham, Cashier
R. M. Dooly, Ass't Cashier

ESTABLISHED 1852

Wells, Fargo & Co.'s Bank

San Francisco, Cal.

JOHN J. VALENTINE, President. H. WADSWORTH, Cashier.
HOMER S. KING, Manager. F. L. Lipman, Asst Cashier.

BRANCHES: NEW YORK — H. B. PARSONS, Cashier.
SALT LAKE — J. E. Dooly, Cashier.

A General Banking Business Transacted
Domestic and Foreign Exchange Bought and Sold.
Travelers' and Commercial Credits Issued, available in all parts of the World;
Bullion and Mexican Dollars Bought and Sold.
Collections Made promptly and economically
Accounts Received on Favorable Terms.
Correspondence Invited.

Correspondents in all the principal cities of the world.

STATEMENT OF CONDITION
DECEMBER ...

ASSETS		LIABILITIES	
Real Estate	...	Capital paid in	...
Bonds, Stocks and Warrants	...	Surplus	...
Furniture and Fixtures	...	Undivided Profits	...
Loans	...	Deposits Banks and Bankers	...
Due from Banks and Bankers	...	Deposits Individual	...
Cash on hand	...		

INDEX TO PORTRAITS

PART ONE

	PAGE		PAGE
Bull, Stephen	29	McGraw, J. H.	45
Cannon, H. W.	21	Moffat, D. H.	48
Carlisle, John G	7	Murray, Logan C.	32
Casady, P. M.	16	Nelson, L. C.	20
Chick, J. S.	36	Nixon, Robert M.	17
Cope, George F	57	Odell, J. J. P.	10
Durham, R. I.	37	Ottley, John K.	65
Flournoy, M. W	40	Rotan, E	28
Furth, Jacob	44	Raynolds, Joshua S.	49
Gage, Lyman J.	9	Raynolds, Jeffer on	52
Groce, T. J.	33	Silliman, C. H.	68
Hershfield, L. H.	56	Simpson, J. N.	41
Hood, C.	24	Thatcher, M. D.	60
Joralmon, H. M.	61	Valentine, John J.	8
Kountze, Herman	13	Wilson, Medford R.	64
Lacey, E. S.	12	Zollars, John W	53
Lindenberger, J. H.	25		

PART TWO

	PAGE		PAGE
Abbott, George A	70	Hollister, H. J.	64
Baker, Henry B.	96	Jobes, A. C.	23
Bement, Arthur O	96	Judd, E. T.	98
Best, Chas.	96	Kasten, Frederick	49
Bissel, Arthur D.	35	King, John A	82
Bump, Orrin	31	O'Brien, Herbert I.	61
Burton, S. S.	88	Pabst, Fred'k	58
Cahill, Edward	96	Randall, Ira E.	96
English, Jas. W.	25	Roe, J. Edward	96
Evans, R. B.	78	Rowley, F. N.	46
Gates, L. M.	43	Russel, Geo. H.	21
Goddard, L. A.	93	Smith, Robert	96
Hackley, C. H.	73	Sullivan, J. J.	27
Hammond, Clarence W	39	Sunderlin, Eugene A.	96
Harris, N. W.	94	Thatcher, J. A	52
Hayes, F. W.	55	Warner, Willard Forester	7
Hayes, W. J.	29	Warren, Charles	19
Hills, C. T.	76	Wendell, Emory	92
Hixon, G. C.	86	White, A. E. F.	67

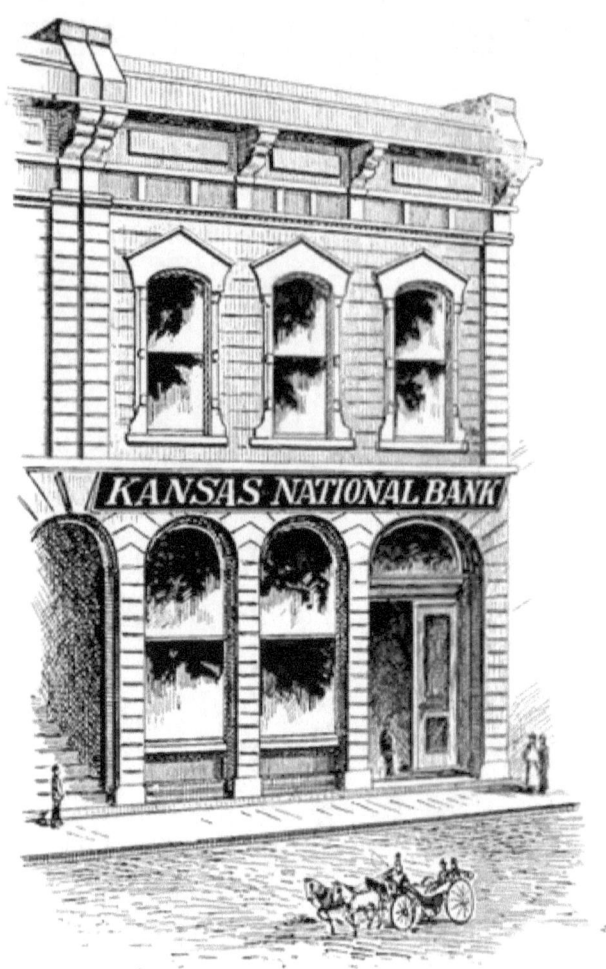

J. N. ROACH, President
C. W. BROWN, Vice-President
A. C. JOBES, Cashier
J. A. DAVISON, Asst. Cashier

✻ KANSAS NATIONAL BANK ✻

Capital, $100,000.

WICHITA, KANS.

We solicit the accounts of individuals, firms, corporations, banks and bankers on terms as liberal as would be consistent with safe and conservative banking. We transact an exclusive commercial banking business, and are always in the market for high grade commercial and cattle feeders' paper. Personal interviews and correspondence with a view to forming business relations requested. All letters promptly answered. Special and careful attention given to collections.

Respectfully,

A. C. JOBES, Cashier.

INDEX TO ADVERTISEMENTS

American National Bank	Louisville, Ky.	xlv
American Trust & Banking Co.	Atlanta, Ga.	iii
Andrews, A. H. & Co.	Chicago, Ill.	lxvi
Bankers' National Bank	Chicago, Ill.	xxxiv
Capital National Bank	Indianapolis, Ind.	ix
Central National Bank	Cleveland, O.	v
Central National Bank of Topeka, Kansas		xli
Commercial National Bank	Portland, Ore.	lxx
Denver National Bank	Denver, Colo.	liv
Des Moines Savings Bank	Des Moines, Iowa.	viii
Duluth Clearing House Association	Duluth, Minn.	xxxvii
Emporia National Bank	Emporia, Kan.	xvi
Fidelity Trust Co.	Tacoma, Wash.	xxxii
First National Bank	Albuquerque, N. M.	xxiv
First National Bank	Butte, Mont.	xlix
First National Bank of Chicago, Ill.		xxxiii
First National Bank	Denver, Colo.	xix
First National Bank of Detroit, Mich.		liii
First National Bank	East Saginaw, Mich.	x
First National Bank of El Paso, Texas		xxx
First National Bank	Helena, Mont	xviii
First National Bank	Kalamazoo, Mich.	ii
First National Bank	Las Vegas, N. M.	xl
First National Bank	Omaha, Neb.	lxiv
First National Bank of Pueblo, Colo.		xxvi
First National Bank	Seattle, Wash.	lvi
First National Bank of Buchanan Co.	St. Joseph, Mo	xiii
First National Bank	Trinidad, Col.	xxvii
First National Bank	Waxahachie, Texas	xxii
First National Bank	Waco, Texas.	vi
Fifth National Bank of Cincinnati, Ohio.		xxviii
Farmers' & Mechanics National Bank	Fort Worth, Texas	lxiii
Fort Dearborn National Bank	Chicago, Ill	lix
Galveston National Bank	Galveston, Texas.	xiv
German National Bank	Oshkosh, Wis.	lxii
Hackley National Bank	Muskegon, Mich.	xxxv
Harris, N. W. & Co., Bankers.	Chicago, Ill.	lxviii
Hayes, W. J. & Sons	Cleveland and Boston	i
Hoge, Brownlee & Co.	Butte City, Mont.	xx
Home National Bank of Arkansas City, Kansas.		xv
Inter State National Bank	Kansas City, Mo.	xxiii
Joralmon & Co.	Denver, Col.	xxv
Kansas National Bank	Wichita, Kansas.	lxxiii
Kleybolte, Rudolph & Co.	Cincinnati, O	xvii
Land Mortgage Bank of Texas, Ltd.	Fort Worth, Tex	xxxix
La Crosse National Bank	La Crosse, Wis.	lxi
Manufacturers' National Bank of Racine, Wis.		lii
Merchant's National Bank of Helena, Mont		lv
Midland National Bank	Kansas City, Mo.	lviii
Missouri National Bank	Kansas City, Mo	vii
National Bank of Commerce	Tacoma, Wash.	li
National Bank of Commerce	Seattle, Wash.	xxxi
National Exchange Bank of Dallas, Texas.		xlii
Nicollet National Bank of Minneapolis, Minn.		xliv
Old National Bank of Grand Rapids, Mich		lx
Old Second National Bank at Bay City, Mich		xi
Omaha Safe & Iron Works		lxvi
Oklahoma National Bank	Oklahoma City, O. T.	xxi
People's Bank of Buffalo, N. Y.		iv
Preferred Bankers' Life Assurance Co.	Lansing, Mich.	xxxviii
Preston National Bank	Detroit, Mich.	xxxvi
Puget Sound National Bank	Seattle, Wash.	xxix
Security National Bank	Sioux City, Ia.	lvii
St. Louis National Bank	St. Louis, Mo.	xii
St. Paul National Bank	St. Paul, Minn.	xliii
State Savings Bank	Detroit, Mich	xlvi
Third National Bank	St. Louis, Mo	lxv
Union National Bank of Chicago, Ill		xlvii
Wells, Fargo & Co.'s Bank	San Francisco, Cal.	lxxi
Western Bank Note Co. of Chicago, Ill		lxvii
Whitaker & Hodgman	St. Louis, Mo	lxix
Wisconsin Marine & Fire Ins. Co.'s Bank, Milwaukee, Wis.		l
Wisconsin National Bank of Milwaukee, Wis		xlviii

www.ingramcontent.com/pod-product-compliance
Lightning Source LLC
Chambersburg PA
CBHW020759230426
43666CB00007B/774